Families and other systems

THE GUILFORD FAMILY THERAPY SERIES
Alan S. Gurman, *Editor*

Families and other systems

The macrosystemic context of family therapy

edited by
JOHN SCHWARTZMAN
Center for Family Studies/The Family Institute of Chicago
Institute of Psychiatry
Northwestern Memorial Hospital and Northwestern University Medical School

Foreword by Carlos E. Sluzki

THE GUILFORD PRESS
New York   London

© 1985 The Guilford Press
A Division of Guilford Publications, Inc.
200 Park Avenue South, New York, N.Y. 10003

Printed in the United States of America

Library of Congress Cataloging in Publication Data

Main entry under title:

Families and other systems.

  (The Guilford family therapy series)
  Bibliography: p.
  Includes index.
   1. Family psychotherapy.   2. Family social work.
3. Family psychotherapy—Case studies.   I. Schwartzman,
John.   II. Series.
RC488.5.F295   1985   616.89'156 .   84-4626
ISBN 0-89862-057-0

Contributors

Peter J. Bokos, PhD, Director, Interventions, Chicago, Illinois

John R. Farella, PhD, Family Practice Residency Program, MacNeal Memorial Hospital, Berwyn, Illinois, and Department of Family Practice, University of Illinois Medical School, Chicago, Illinois

George S. Greenberg, DSW, Family Therapy Institute of Greater New Orleans, Inc., and Department of Psychiatry, Louisiana State University Medical School, New Orleans, Louisiana

Henry T. Harbin, MD, Institute of Psychiatry and Human Behavior, University of Maryland Medical School, and Maryland Mental Hygiene Administration, Baltimore, Maryland

Anita W. Kneifel, BA, Chicago, Illinois

Howard A. Liddle, EdD, Division of Family and Community Medicine, University of California, San Francisco, California, and Faculty, Mental Research Institute, Palo Alto, California

Robert J. Restivo, BA, Former Chief Probation Officer, Du Page County, Illinois

George W. Saba, PhD, Division of Family and Community Medicine, University of California, San Francisco, California, and Faculty, Mental Research Institute, Palo Alto, California

Helen B. Schwartzman, PhD, Department of Anthropology, Northwestern University, Evanston, Illinois

John Schwartzman, PhD, Center for Family Studies/The Family Institute of Chicago, Institute of Psychiatry, Northwestern Memorial Hospital, and Northwestern University Medical School, Chicago, Illinois

Ross V. Speck, MD, Department of Psychiatry and Human Behavior, Jefferson Medical College, Philadelphia, Pennsylvania

Howard F. Stein, PhD, Department of Family Medicine, University of Oklahoma Health Sciences Center, Oklahoma City, Oklahoma

Froma Walsh, PhD, School of Social Service Administration, University of Chicago, and Faculty, Center for Family Studies/The Family Institute of Chicago, Department of Psychiatry and Behavioral Sciences, Northwestern University Medical School, Chicago, Illinois

Foreword

Kindly open the eyes of your imagination and accompany me in a space–time excursion. We are inside an ultramicroscopic vehicle that is going to increase in size at great speed and increase in distance from its target each time it increases in size. We look through the porthole. Our visual field is filled with particles that are moving in what appear to be random trajectories. As our size increases and, correspondingly, the objects we observe decrease in relative size, and as our visual field widens with our expansion, we notice suddenly a harmonious relationship between all the particles: They are, in fact, subatomic elements, electrons, neutrons, and protons that configurate together the magic gestalt of the atomic orbital structure. As we continue growing, the atom, which at that distance reminds us of a star with its constellation of planets, reduces itself to a dot, and our visual field is progressively occupied by many dots, in what appears to be a random aggregate. We gain further distance and disorder is followed by order: Randomness is followed by the pattern of a molecular structure configurated by all those atomic dots. With greater distance and a larger focus, a new period of randomness reigns. The collection of molecules that occupy our field of vision seems now thrown together by chance. And, again, as distance increases, a new pattern emerges in our focus: the harmonious order of the constituents of a cell. As size and focus enlarge further, we witness a progression of images of disorder and order, of randomness and pattern, that indicates the successive passage from one level of the organization of the living system to the next. Cell, tissue, and organism intersperse with disordered aggregations. The focus of our ever-expanding vehicle now abandons the boundaries of the skin and catapults itself to broader magnitudes. The organism in question—be it an insect, a whale, or a human being—appears as a finite structure/system, interacting with a random environment. However, a still broader view shows that what we have labeled as "environment of the subject" is in turn a collection of equally finite structure/systems, and each of these organisms interacts harmoniously, according to regularities, following patterns, with other organisms of similar and of different nature: The ecological niche dances its own dance. Within that niche certain shapes relate with a tighter, more predictable, patterning: Maybe it is just a symbiotic interspecies association, maybe a meaningful relationship of kinship, maybe an equally meaningful one of predator–prey. But our relentless travel continues and, as we abandon the dimension of these beings already turned microscopic, we observe first the eco-regions and then the whole spaceship Earth in its luminescence, isolated in space— isolated, that is, until we gain enough perspective to allow us to see an aggregate of celestial bodies tumbling through space. And then, again, at the appropriate distance, suddenly, this collection becomes a whole and that aggregate becomes our stellar system, the sun and its planets in harmonious orbits. Still increasing distance until only the dot of the sun remains in our porthole, our field of vision becomes progressively covered with a mantle of stars that do not show any particular pattern, beyond that of disorder. Another small jump of a million light-years' distance and we discover a new level of patterning, our galaxy, the Milky Way. We keep on gaining distance, and the Milky Way itself becomes a nebula, and we witness other nebulas suddenly appearing in our visual field. There, at the very edge of our field of ignorance, we stop. And if witnessing the overinclusive cosmos sitting on its edge make us feel dizzy, we may reverse the trip and, shifting through alternating layers of chaos and pattern, return to a more familiar size and surrounding; and eventually, opening the door of our marvelous vehicle, we greet each other welcome at the end of the journey. And what a journey it was! A journey through the multiple layers of order and disorder, of pattern and chaos, of systems included in systems included in systems included in systems. (My own first journey through the multidimensional layers of systems had as its tour-guide Edgar Morin, the French logician and philosopher, in the course of a conference on "Order and Disorder" at Stanford University in 1980. He, in turn, followed the blueprint proposed in the award-winning short film entitled *Cosmic Zoom*, produced by the National Film Board of Canada, which carries the viewer from ultra micro-cosmos to mega-cosmos and back in some 8 minutes.)

Patterns or regularities or order (and, complementarily, irregularity or disorder) are the traits that define a system, any system, systems at any level, and of any magnitude. The selection and specification of the boundaries of a system are determined by our encompassing abilities— or by an operational definition of what we choose to consider a *meaningful* system. In fact, in any naturalistic observation, from the micro- to the mega-cosmic, in order to be able to "think systems" in a feasible way, we *have to* make a choice of relative and operational meaningfulness, and by that device impoverish our sets of observables *almost* to the level of meaninglessness. The margin between the level at which the information is overwhelming (and therefore unmanageable) and that at which the information is impoverished beyond meaning or use is irritatingly narrow. However, we have to acknowledge and inhabit precisely this margin in order to expand our thinking tools, our models.

The systemic nature of any aggregate is determined by (consists of) the patterned nature of the relationship between its components. The abstract, unspecific nature of this description is, I am sure, patent to the reader. But, how to specify its components, to pinpoint their attributes, to determine their relationships, to draw the boundaries of these aggregates? Or, perhaps more appropriately, *who* does these operations, who specifies, pinpoints, determines, and draws? The choice of the unit of analysis and all these operations *is the prerogative of the observer*. On the basis of defining a *meaningful* set of relationships and of attributes, the observer can eventually define what constitutes a meaningful membership, and in that way establish the boundaries of a system of which a given observable is a part. The active process of impoverishment mentioned above must be carefully selective, but is necessary and, what is more, unavoidable. In fact, in the long run, it allows subsequent enrichment through a more complex analysis of multidimensional systems, such as those explored in this book.

It is amazing to realize that no more than 30 years have passed since some unusual thinkers began to observe the family from the vantage point of the rudimentary sets of paradigms of the new and evolving field of general systems theory and cybernetics. Since then, passing through unavoidable bouts of reification, and emerging from them with renewed determination, losing focus and struggling to regain it again, the field of family therapy has evolved, defining the components, attributes, relationships, and boundaries of its domain of observation with a reasonable degree of consensus. In these 30 years, thousands of articles, chapters, and books provide a sound testimony of its conceptual growth. *Families and Other Systems* is a solid contribution to this unfolding.

This collection belongs clearly to the third generation of products in the field of family therapy. We may consider that the first generation corresponds to those papers that established the focus, the second generation is characterized by writings that charted the territory, and the third is in charge of challenging that territory and opening up new frontiers, establishing new bridges. During the first period there was probably no other way but to observe the family in isolation: Its focus had to be narrow and its boundaries needed to be defined with tight exclusionary rules; its vicissitudes needed to be isolated from the larger social, political, and economic vicissitudes. In fact, the number of variables was so gigantic that unless that isolation was arbitrarily established, no clarity would have been drawn from the observations, no models would have been developed. However, that isolationist, rarified view of the family, useful as it may have been for the purpose of establishing a language and a model for the field, was in and by itself cutting one subsystem from larger, equally meaningful processes and structures: The family, part and parcel of the individual, is also part and parcel of larger systems. The time has come to recuperate other dimensions of family, to underscore the arbitrary nature of the definition of what is unit of analysis and what is context, so as to increase the permeability of boundaries and grant credit to the multidimensional influences that affect and are affected by family processes.

This collection, wisely edited and framed by John Schwartzman, is devoted to mapping some of these influences. It conceives of the family as part of larger frames, from social and cultural to institutional contexts. This book explores cogent ways of thinking "family in context," of thinking about training, of organizing a militant delivery of services with a family-centered perspective. But, what I find most attractive, this book is stimulating in its conceptual implications: The boundaries of a system lie wherever we choose to draw them and that decision defines not only the reach of our practice but that of our social responsibility.

Carlos E. Sluzki, MD
*University of Massachusetts Medical School
and Berkshire Medical Center*

Contents

PART II. FAMILY AND HUMAN SERVICE ORGANIZATIONS

PART III. FAMILY AND CULTURE

Chapter 9. Values and Family Therapy   201
HOWARD F. STEIN

Chapter 10. Social Change, Disequilibrium, and Adaptation in Developing Countries: A Moroccan Example   244
FROMA WALSH

Chapter 11. Culture as Intervention   260
JOHN R. FARELLA

Families and other systems

1

Macrosystemic approaches to family therapy: An overview

JOHN SCHWARTZMAN
Center for Family Studies/The Family Institute of Chicago
Institute of Psychiatry
Northwestern Memorial Hospital and
Northwestern University Medical School

Introduction

This volume provides clinicians and researchers with an outline of a macrosystemic perspective for assessment and intervention in dysfunctional family systems. The authors of this book expand some of the basic ideas developed over the past 20 years in family therapy: (1) family systems are always part of more inclusive systems and (2) these systems should be considered in any family assessment and often must be utilized for successful family treatment. This text's authors all hold this perspective.

A number of works in family therapy and related fields have influenced the orientations of these writers and researchers. Perhaps the most important of these is Jackson's (1957) classic "The Question of Family Homeostasis," in which he first links cybernetic self-regulation with family process in families with a schizophrenic member. In *Strategies of Psychotherapy*, Haley (1963) articulated this concept more clearly with his notion of the self-regulatory function of symptomatic behavior for the family. This step provided the theoretical basis for the "wholeness" of the family as a system, rather than merely a collection of individual members. Initially described in work on the contextual nature of those most bizarre symptoms characteristic of schizophrenia, the symptoms were reinterpreted by the Bateson group and in work of the closely related Mental Research Institute (MRI) as meaningful multileveled communications. It has been argued that this reinterpretation changed the understanding of psychopathology and the dysfunctional family by redefining it as an aspect of social process. Bateson's group and the MRI researchers asserted that the homeostatic function of symptomatic behavior was a crucial aspect of family adaptation. Somewhat later Weakland's (1960) article "The Double-Bind Hypothesis and Three-Party Interaction" identified a basic characteristic of families with seriously disturbed members: that is, covert coalitions within which the symptomatic member's behavior is regulated and regulates the behavior of his or her parents. Thus, a self-correcting system is created. Haley (1967) generalized this idea in his article "Toward a Theory of Pathogenic Systems," in which he deduced that cross-generational coalitions between two family members against another member are characteristic of families with dysfunctional members. In this article he mentions Stanton and Schwartz's (1954) book, *The Mental Hospital*, in which the authors described an analogous process on hospital wards among two staff members and a patient to that which Haley (1967) found in dysfunctional families. This concern with generational and hierarchical levels and the dysfunction caused by their confusion or ambiguity has become the theoretical basis for a structural approach to family therapy. In fact, clear hierarchy is found to be basic to all adaptive biosocial systems (Simon, 1969).

In this book the reinterpretation of psychopathology as an aspect of family dysfunction is expanded to include the more inclusive system of which the family is a part. Consideration of this macrosystem is a crucial aspect of both the problem and its treatment. This perspective includes social systems created by dysfunctional families and those attempting to treat them and also the interaction by these families with other social and cultural contexts. This volume fills a need for a more inclusive perspective in conceptualizing the self-maintaining character of dysfunctional families in terms of more inclusive levels of organization (social) and abstraction (cultural) of which they are a part. Many would argue that the developmental process of family theory was clearly defined by the "epistemological jump" made when problems "in" individuals began to be seen as aspects of family process. Collectively, the authors presented in this volume take the next logical step in this process.

The context of noncybernetic science at least partially explains the tardy beginnings of family therapy as a mode of psychotherapy and, as has been suggested, a new epistemology (Bateson, 1972; Haley, 1963; Hoffman, 1981). This scientific context is generally described as positivistic (Kolakowski, 1968) and characterized by the almost universal transformation of process into measurable atomistic entities. Therefore, atomistic least particulars were assumed to be the basic elements of reality. This made the patterns of interaction—the most obvious manifestation of family structure—difficult to perceive. One result was the difficulty in making the jump from classifying the behavior of individuals, for example, personality, to the patterned interaction of the family and their relationships (Bateson, Jackson, Haley, & Weakland, 1956; Jackson, 1957; Haley, 1963; and others). As suggested above, this must be expanded to include perceiving the family and its problems in terms of the nested contexts of which it becomes a part in attempts to solve problems. Specifically, the most serious and chronic problems that therapists encounter (e.g., schizophrenia, alcoholism, heroin addiction) seem to require the adoption of a macrosystemic perspective because families with members having these symptoms are often involved concurrently or serially with several therapists, other mental health personnel, and other social institutions. In addition, these and other natural systems (e.g., neighbors and churches) may be the best resources for effective family interventions, as suggested by Speck (Chapter 4).

This book will be an important addition to the theory and practice of family therapy because the macrosystemic perspective has often only been addressed as a peripheral issue by clinicians, leaving a gap in the field, especially in terms of the most serious, chronic mental health problems. In the systems created by those who treat severely disturbed individuals, what is especially clear in their structure is basic dissonance at some level in the macrosystem, which is often a crucial aspect of the problem. Changes in the system at a more inclusive level than most clinicians consider are often a necessary aspect of resolving the problems being treated. In fact, if clinicians ignore this more inclusive level of organization, the problem can be maintained by the structure created but unperceived by those treating it.

Because the macrosystemic perspective remains largely unexplored but intuitively important, this book will be useful for family therapists and researchers. Directive family therapists may plan strategies for intervention from this perspective, while researchers may apply the macrosystemic approach to conceptualizing problems for investigation.

Structural Analogues

Since Stanton and Schwartz's classic mental hospital study, there have been a large number of studies of internal functioning in mental hospitals. Of special interest for the concerns of this book are those studies since Szurek (1951) and Stanton and Schwartz (1954) such as Caudill (1958), Rapoport and Rapoport (1960), Kellam and Chassan (1962), Williams, Marr, Lewis, Tucker, and Copeland (1977), and Levonson and Crabtree (1979) that have described their structure and function and their relationship to their patient's dysfunction.

Main (1957) addressed these issues and notes:

> Our findings agree with those of Stanton and Schwartz, that certain patients by having unusual but not generally accepted, needs cause splits in attitudes of the staff, and that these splits, if covert and unresolved, cause the greatest distress to the patients who could be described as "torn apart" by them. (p. 139)

Amini, Burke, and Edgerton (1978), Greenwood (1955), Miller (1961), and McGlashan and Levy (1977) have all described how hospitalized adolescents actually manipulate dissonances and intrastaff conflicts, which is analogous to descriptions of internal family functioning of families of acting-out adolescents. Steinfeld (1970) has found many similarities in communication in both families with a schizophrenic member and mental hospitals, especially the pervasive incongruent and paradoxical communications. Sacks and Carpenter (1974) have described what they term a pseudotherapeutic community: wards that overtly reinforce patient autonomy and competence while covertly undercutting it, creating contradictory expectations about responsibility, again analogous to the process of many families with dysfunctional members (Sluzki & Veron, 1971; Haley, 1963). These studies and several others describe at different levels of abstraction (e.g., structure, communication, etc.) obvious similarities in characteristics of dysfunctional systems, especially between families and those institutions that are treating family members.

Hirschorn and Gilmore (1980) have outlined an attempt to use structural orientation in order to intervene in a dysfunctional social agency. Their goal was to identify the covert coalitions that maintained its dysfunction and then to restructure the organization, to correct the confused hierarchies and cross-generational coalitions. Interventions were to be designed that would force these structural changes. Consequently, a number of studies have not only compared the analogous processes created by staff and patients to those in dysfunctional families but have in at least one study attempted analogous interventions.

At another level of organization, Dell, Sheehy, Pulliam and Goolishian (1977) describe the structural similarities between a family therapy seminar and family therapy. They describe the difficulty in getting group members to alter their basic premises about therapy.

Sluzki (1974) is one of the few theorists (prior to Liddle & Saba, Chapter 2, this volume) to have considered structure as an essential aspect of teaching content in his family practice and community medicine residency program. He warns against the problems inherent in training by contradictions at various levels of organization and abstraction, especially between content and structure. He states that organizing courses on specific topics disqualifies at the level of structure a systemic world view that is being taught as content. Sluzki attempted to remove the dissonance between an atomistic context characterized by separate subjects and courses and a systems orientation to health care, suggesting instead the mutual interaction of many systems. The major problem he encountered, as in family therapy, was an epistemological one, to change the basic premises of those who had traditional medical training based on another paradigm in order to understand the systemic perspective that was the basis of his training. As Sluzki states:

> Epistemologies are conveyed by the manner in which reality and concepts are organized and conveyed throughout the training of the specific subject matter . . . the operational relativistic epistemology implied by the systems-oriented interactional perspective clashes with the positivist rationalism conveyed by the more traditional, atomistic approach to the medical sciences. (1974, p. 483)

In their review of the literature on training and supervision Liddle and Halpin (1978) found that the goals of both are dependent on the theoretical orientation of the program. For example, the psychodynamic programs emphasize personal growth; the structural, a number of cognitive competences; and so forth. They note the influence that teaching and learning family therapy exerts on the context where this takes place both for teachers and students.

This is only a small part of the literature that addresses structural issues. Specifically, these researchers and others continue to find that the structures of mental hospitals, human service organizations, and training programs are at times analogous to the structures of dysfunctional families treated in these institutions. All suggest that the structure of the context is a crucial aspect of what is communicated as content in that context.

More Inclusive Systems

Until recently only scattered attention has been paid to more inclusive levels of organization than the family, suggested in a cybernetic perspective in which the family is itself viewed as an element of a more inclusive social system (Crawley, 1982). Blackwell and Wilkins (1981) state that

> the next logical step is to suggest that the family and its behavior might be better viewed not merely as a function of the particular family and its internal relations, but as a constituent of other wider systems, for example, the community, the economy, the society. (p. 79)

At these more inclusive levels, the family interacting with other individuals, organizations, and ideologies exhibits just as much order as internal family functioning revealed in 25 years of research on family interaction. The pattern is maintained at these more inclusive levels by the structure of the interacting systems including the family and ideology about the family's problems and their treatment.

The Family and the Hospital

Fleck, Cornelison, Norton, and Lidz (1957) and Lidz (1963) were among the first to be aware of the importance of the relationships between the family of a schizophrenic and the hospital. They described the family dynamics that make it difficult for these organizations to cooperate in treatment.

Bell and Zucker (1968) described the relationship created when a family member is hospitalized, frequently characterized by "distance, dissatisfaction, and mutual misunderstanding." The hospital staff wants the family to be involved but to accept the hospital's authority. Often the family refused to accept this and would seek allies on the staff, thus creating confused hierarchies in the treatment system composed of both organizations.

The crisis of hospitalization, at times, causes the family to attempt to self-correct and maintain itself by changing hospital functioning, by splitting the treatment team (Harbin, 1978). Harbin has found that differences in the ideology of staff members makes them more vulnerable to splitting by the family.

The factors in a medical setting that prevent the family and the hospital from functioning together in treatment have been described by Shapiro (1980). She believes that the differences in expectations are especially important. The hospital personnel are interested in the restoration of the patient's illness-determined losses rather than his or her more inclusive biosocial context. As a result, the staff often assume an adversary relationship with the family, and the patient may become dependent and passive.

Polak and Jones (1973) believe that psychiatric hospitals function on the basis of staff values and social needs while ignoring those of the patient. They argue for changes to make hospital functioning more responsive to the needs of individuals in their communities. Polak (1970) found that often the basic dissonance between hospital and the patient was ideological in the locus of the problem, which the patient thought was in his or her social context while the staff thought it was in the patient (see also Burch, 1971). Polak discovered that generally, social disturbances, rather than the patient's symptoms, resulted in admission to the hospital. At the same time, he notes that "present psychiatric hospitals are basically irrelevant to the real world from which the patient comes and to which he must return" (1970, p. 783).

Polak and Kirby (1976) have described a model to replace traditional psychiatric hospitals in which they consider the family's social context. They developed community-based therapeutic environments using crisis intervention, home treatment, social system intervention and rapid tranquilization as their primary techniques. Follow-up evaluation indicated that this provided the most effective treatment. Similarly, Fish (1971) described a crisis unit at a mental health center that "focuses on the naturally occurring systems of people, such as family, friends, or co-workers, surrounding any given patient" (p. 40). He believes that symptoms appear when the social system is disrupted. It is dysfunctional if the agency becomes a buffer for the patient and his or her social system instead of attempting to change the functioning of the patient as part of that system. He argues for open communication within the patient's social system as the best general strategy. Brief hospitalization seems to be the most effective in allowing patients to reenter their social system in their prehospitalization roles (Herz, Endicott, & Spitzer, 1975). Moreover, Gould and Glick (1971) among others have identified the most important aspect of family involvement in inpatient treatment: the intake process.

Bell (1977) described the life cycle of the relationship between the family and the hospital. His program for the treatment of the severely disturbed emphasizes maintaining the relationship between the family and the hospital staff during the patient's hospitalization and planning for the patient's discharge and reintegration into the community. Reiss (1980) and his associates developed a method of classifying families according to their adaptive styles. Using this method, these researchers were able to predict success or failure of a family's engagement in a family-oriented inpatient ward. Stewart (1981), in his review of the literature, states that an alliance between the family and the hospital is clearly related to effective outcome. Harbin, in Chapter 6 of this volume, describes his techniques for establishing this alliance.

Another crucial aspect of hospital function is the context it creates for the therapist. For example, Lansky warns, "It is crucial to preserve the boundaries of the ward and it is vital to see that conflicts in large systems in the organization are not played out using ward personnel" (1977, p. 73). An increase in conflict with and among hospital wards is noted by Deikman and Whitaker (1979), which they describe as the result of a change in treatment ideology from primarily pharmacological to psychological, suggesting that the more inclusive aspects of the whole treatment system must be included in any assessment. As Adams states, "The clinic has a place in the social system. It matters what coalitions it makes, whose agent it is, and how it socially defines problems. That they are appearing in a defining professional world is part of the family's problem" (1979, p. 2). Framo (1976) has made an analogous point when he says, "Unhappily, the relation of agency to therapist rarely merits a footnote." Adams (1979) believes that the creation of an informal network among individuals within agencies is the primary means to change them into a more systems-oriented perspective.

Auerswald (1968) was one of the first to seriously consider the

family as an element in a more inclusive system, using an ecological
systems approach. His primary focus was in following the "communications within and between systems" and thus the more inclusive systems,
including culture and the institutions in which symptomatic individuals
are intimately involved (e.g., school, extended family, medical personnel,
and human service agencies). In the introduction to a paper (Hoffman &
Long, 1969) describing a system that includes a family, the state housing
authority, and a social work agency, Auerswald states:

> Neither individual nor family diagnosis, nor the contributions of the larger
> system (in this case a housing system and a system of medical care) will, if
> viewed separately, explain the state of the man in question. Only when the
> contributions of all of these systems are more clear, and their interrela-
> tionships explained, do the origins of the phenomena described begin to
> emerge. (p. 212)

In this example, if the individual in question continued working, he
would lose his low-income apartment; but if he quit, he could not pay
for his children's education. This situation suggests that the family
must be understood in "a context of other wider systems" (Blackwell &
Wilkins, 1981, p. 79). In a later paper, Hoffman (1971) notes that the
nested, hierarchical contexts that compose the social system of every
individual are often trying to function simultaneously in both deviation-
amplifying and self-regulating systems at different levels of organization.

Roberts (1979) has noted the importance of clear communication
among agencies because of the frequency of family members' involvement with more than one agency. If they do not communicate clearly,
the family may find itself trapped between them. If this continues, the
family will probably manipulate them in order to maintain itself. Concurrently, the family may become trapped in a system being maintained
by the agencies for their own interests. In practice, the discovery of
other interests and involved agencies is frequently delayed until a crisis
occurs. Rivalries may then become evident—between individual workers
and/or between agencies.

> Sometimes rivalries mirror those within the family so that unless they are
> recognized and worked with, the family is in danger of becoming trapped in
> the agency system. There is evidence to suggest that some families un-
> consciously re-create the pattern of the extended families in which lie the
> roots of the current dilemma. (Roberts, 1979, p. 206)

Miller (1958) has noted that one of the major impediments in the
prevention of juvenile delinquency results from conflict over goals and
methods between concerned institutional systems and subunits of these
systems. Kaplan (1952) has described a more inclusive system and its

accompanying problems created between a referring agency and a child guidance clinic. He found triangles in the structure created among the two organizations and the child analogous to those described by Haley (1967) except at a more inclusive level in which covert differences between the two agencies were expressed through the client. Piliavin (1970) also found covert conflict and triangling of the patients between cottage parents and caseworkers at a correctional institution for boys as did Montalvo and Pavlin (1966) in a residential treatment center between child-care workers, their supervisors, and clinicians. Aponte (1970) includes both school and family as essential parts of the social system of a child with school problems. He diagnoses the structural confusions of this more inclusive system as the locus of the problem.

As they will describe more fully in Chapter 8 of this volume, Schwartzman and Bokos (1980) identify aspects of a state methadone treatment system that are analogous to the families of the opiate addicts who are clients of this system. As they describe treatment, the interaction of staff and clients of the present clinic, of former clinics, and of the client's family of origin creates and maintains systems similar to the clients' families at a more inclusive level of organization of structure and basic premises.

Mannino and Shore (1972) have noted that more inclusive systems have generally been seen as more important for economically disadvantaged families and ignored for the more affluent ones. They believe that a good deal of all family dysfunction is ecological, and a consequence of discordant patterns of relationships between families and the larger ecological context of which both the individual and the family are components. They make the important point that the therapist must be prepared to assume a role beyond that of traditional therapist because the job "embraces the broad context of a family's functioning within its culture and society" (Mannino & Shore, 1982). Similarly Hoffman and Long (1969) note that "it will be increasingly harder to separate the specialist in emotional problems from the specialist in community problems" (1969, p. 5).

Selig (1980) suggests that the fragmentation of services may do more to create the multiproblem family than treat it. In fact, he defines multiproblem families as those involved with a variety of agencies. He states, "The multi-problem family is really a multi-problem delivery system" (Selig, 1976, p. 527). Aponte (1978) also describes poor families as oppressed by the social agencies which "help" them.

Selig blames individualistically oriented training for overlooking systemic aspects of treatment. An important initial step is to change the locus of the problem from the individual to the system. In Selig's experience this is often the most difficult aspect of therapy. He believes that the most effective approach proposes systematic linkages between agencies and services to provide comprehensive, accessible interventions. Once a systematic orientation is accepted, the next step is to make contact with others providing service and to reach an agreement on problems and objectives, including assigning one person the role as a "primary therapist," responsible for the integration of services, helping with assessment, goals, intervention, and evaluation. Selig strongly suggests a "social network approach emphasizing the interpersonal nature of emotional difficulties and therefore interpersonal strategies and treatment techniques to alleviate them" (1976, p. 529) in which the primary thrust involves the client's natural social network as a core aspect of treatment.

Bell states that the system's oriented therapist by necessity must be able to work with more inclusive systems including the therapist's own agency. He describes himself as a "family context therapist," whose function is "mobilizing the community, its institutions, and their resources to center attention and effort on family change . . . by providing settings for family problem-solving and attainment of well-being" (1978, p. 113).

Similarly, Garrison (1974) describes what he has termed "The Screen–Linking–Planning Conference Method," which is a technique for social network intervention. In this process Garrison convenes all those in the social network of the individual in crisis. If the identified patient is hospitalized, contact is actively maintained with his or her social network. Links are created between the patient and helping organizations in the community as part of the treatment plan. Garrison (1974) describes setting up intersystem meetings between the agencies involved with the family, bringing together representatives of different agencies, assigning different functions to each, and attempting to make contracts among them. As this brief review suggests, it is difficult to utilize any type of systems orientation without considering the more inclusive treatment system.

Natural Contexts

Even more basic to the family's functioning is the "natural" social context of which all families are a part and which affects their functioning in a number of ways. Killilea (1982) states:

> Review by Cobb (1976), Kaplan, Cassel, and Gore (1977), Dean and Lin (1977), the President's Commission on Mental Health (1978), and Hamburg and Killilea (1979) of research findings conclude that social support may play a major role in modifying the deleterious effects of stress on health, influencing the use of health services and affecting other aspects of health behavior such as adherence to medical regimens. (p. 177)

Anderson (1982) has reviewed the literature in family social networks and has found unsurprisingly that the social contexts of the
healthier or more successfully functioning individuals are "thicker" and
"deeper" in that they often contain more individuals with more intimate
contact than those of individuals with medical and psychiatric symptoms.
She concludes that "networks appear to supply a number of vital provisions for the family and its members" (p. 437). She also found in her
review that homogeneity in the network was generally inversely pro-
portional to the frequency of symptoms. She believes the relevant
variables of the social context include size, congruence, density, and
proportion of kin. At the same time, she quotes Walker, MacBride, and
Vachon (1977) in stating that the crucial aspects of the network are
contingent on the nature and time of the crisis and the internal and
external resources of the individual. She believes that a network assessment that reveals the potential stresses and disruptions, along with
resources and supports, is an essential aspect of family diagnoses.

Speck (1967) was one of the first to actively utilize the family's
natural social context as a means of altering family functioning. He does
this by increasing the intimacy among the identified patient's relationships that compose his or her social network to maximize group support
and a sense of belonging. Similarly Attneave (1969), in her work on
networks, conceives of what she terms network therapy as "mobilizing
the family, relatives and friends into a social force that counteracts the
depersonalizing trend in contemporary life patterns" (p. 192). She notes
that a crucial aspect of network therapy is creating the link between the
network and the resources of the community. She believes that in most
urban areas there are at least vestiges of functioning networks that
ought to be utilized.

Kingston (1979) describes some aspects of families' contexts that
have been almost completely overlooked by family therapists, especially
the social-control function of family therapy. She states that what has
been almost universally ignored is the power and authority of the
therapist in regard to other institutions, for example, the courts, professional organizations, and so forth. In addition, she comments on the
law's individualistic biases for personal diagnoses and responsibility.
Intervention at this level of organization has not been described in the
family therapy literature.

Cultural Context

At a more abstract level, the concept of *culture* has been considered in
various ways by a number of family therapists. For example, Selvini-
Palazzoli, Cecchin, Prata, and Boscolo (1978) have considered the cultural

context of families in their construction of therapeutic rituals. Bell, Trieschman, and Vogel (1961), in an early paper, note the necessity of including the sociocultural context of fathers to understand their resistance to becoming involved in family therapy.

A number of researchers (Minuchin, 1969; Schwartzman & Kroll, 1977; Stannard-Friel, 1981; Andrade & Burstein, 1973; Rich, 1975) have dealt with culture or ideology at a more concrete level, that is, differences between professionals and paraprofessionals providing treatment. Minuchin describes the paradox of introducing paraprofessionals into the mental health field and concurrently attempting to maintain the traditional belief systems about mental illness needing professionals to treat it. Rich (1975) notes the conflict for black mental health personnel in relating to the community that is often poor and black and concurrently pleasing their white superiors at work. Often, the solution is withdrawal from the community or from the organization. Schwartzman and Kroll (1977) note an analogous problem in methadone clinics between the professionals and paraprofessionals. Often ex-addicts and friends of the clients, paraprofessionals ally with the clients against the professionals, who are generally middle-class and not ex-addicts. The paraprofessionals believe treatment is helping addicts "get off the street," even if this means that treatment results only in substituting legal methadone for illegal heroin. The professionals believe treatment should include "insight" on the part of the client, eventually leading to abstinence from all opiates. Each undercuts the other's attempts at change. The professionals act out their beliefs that the paraprofessionals are untrained, and the paraprofessionals act out their beliefs that the professionals do not "understand drugs." This process validates for the clients that they are "out of control" in a context without constraints, where this is appropriate behavior, thus maintaining their problem—the inability to control drug use.

More abstractly, Ebner (1979) describes a basic dichotomy in the treatment of children and adolescents between behavior-modifying "hard-hats" and insight-oriented "soft-hearts." Obviously, this provides potential for creating splits and triangles when both groups are involved in the treatment of the same patient or family.

A yet higher level of abstraction, but an omnipresent system, that of "culture" and values, has generally been ignored by family therapists (see Vogel & Bell, 1968; and Jackson, 1965, for exceptions). Another exception to this is the work of Kluckhohn (1958) and Spiegel (1971), who have developed a number of ways to analyze the "value orientations" of people, which unconsciously order their patterns of behavior and thought in all areas. These provide the solution to five universal, abstract problems: Kluckhohn and Spiegel define these five problems as crucial for all human groups: the character of innate human nature; the relationship of humanity to nature; the temporal focus of human life; the modality of human activity; and the modality of humans' relationship to other humans. These universal problems, and the value orientations that each society adapts to solve them, are perhaps useful comparatively as a "grid" because cultures, subcultures, and families can be categorized in terms of solutions to these core problems, providing for attempted interventions at this level.

The "new ethnicity" (McGoldrick, Pearce, & Giardano, 1982) is perhaps the most inclusive cultural context that is currently being widely considered in family studies. This literature views ethnicity, the belief in a common tradition and ancestry, as a crucial aspect of family functioning. Those therapists and researchers interested in ethnicity are especially concerned with recognizing differences in normality, personal styles, symptoms, and the family's therapeutic behavior. They note the problems that can result from negative feelings about one's own culture or from basic cultural premises that conflict with those of the more inclusive culture. This is obviously a higher level of abstraction than most therapists consider in their attempts to intervene in family functioning. McGoldrick notes that prior to the publication of *Ethnicity and Family Therapy* (McGoldrick *et al.*, 1982), there were few articles in the field that directly dealt with ethnic and cultural differences and their effects in therapy. Boyd (1980) and Foley (1975) on Afro-American families; Zuk (1978) on Jewish-American families; Stein (1978) on Slovak-American families; and McGoldrick and Pearce (1981) on Irish-American families were some of the very few previous works on this huge topic.

McGoldrick suggests that therapists must come to understand their ethnic identities in a differentiated way by becoming aware of the "cultural variability and . . . the relativity of their own values" (McGoldrick, 1982, p. 27). In other words, they must be self-reflexive enough to consider their own cultural context as if they were outside it.

Family therapists generally ignore the more basic issues of what is "culture" and what is its relationship to social organization and family and individual functioning. Stein, in Chapter 9, attempts to understand culture at a yet higher level of abstraction and so to illustrate this relationship.

Summary

There exist several areas of research on systems more inclusive than the family that family theorists and therapists are beginning to investigate. This volume is an attempt to expand on that literature and look at these more inclusive systems in terms of levels of organization and abstraction and the implications these have for treatment. As a number of chapters in this volume suggest, the cybernetic perspective that provides the basis for that which is most novel in family therapy must include multiple levels of abstraction and organization. In terms of levels of abstraction, therapy must consider "culture" used in the traditional anthropological sense. In terms of levels of organization, it must include the social organizations and institutions with which the families with symptomatic individuals form more inclusive systems. This consideration must include those who train therapists to work with families and the organizations and ideology within which these therapists work and families function.

Organization of the Book

Taking these multiple levels into account, this volume is divided into three sections. The first, *Macrosystemic Models*, contains three chapters. The first two describe an isomorph that is generally ignored in the field—the structure of both training and therapy. Successful training, consultation, and therapy can all be seen as needing the same basic structure in essential ways, though at different levels of abstraction. If present, this structure ideally promotes growth and learning for the therapist and the family. Each context should reveal something about the other, for example, successful training should have similarities with successful treatment at the level of both structure and content.

In Chapter 2, Liddle and Saba, using a structural–strategic paradigm, have described, at a higher level of abstraction than most the epistemological foundations of their training model. In addition, they have revealed the isomorphic structure that characterizes both their training and therapy within this structural paradigm. By linking these two contexts, the authors create a more inclusive and abstract system. They describe the similarities in structure and process that lead to successful change in clinical teaching and structural family therapy. They argue that an increase in complexity is a goal both for training therapists and for family members. In both contexts, enactment, experiential learning by doing, is a necessary aspect of change. Both contexts are characterized by the interplay between parts and wholes, making hierarchy and boundaries crucial and, therefore, aspects of structure to which supervisors and trainees must be extremely sensitive. Both supervisor and therapist are parts of (and "meta" to) the systems with which they are involved, making their relationships paradoxical. The authors describe the analogous stages of engagement/joining, challenging, creating new realities, and consolidation of change, especially changing the trainees and family members' worldviews by the intensity of their mutual novel experiences in supervision and therapy respectively. The authors indirectly make another crucial point, ignored by many clinicians: Theories of change always have an epistemological context, composed of their implicit assumptions and basic premises. One's techniques should be in "sync" with one's basic assumptions, or attempts at change are senseless.

In Chapter 3, Greenberg, utilizing an interactional paradigm, describes in detail the techniques of prescribing the symptom and communicating in the client's language at the level of the consultant-consultee interface. He describes the basic attributes of the structure of consultation. An especially important aspect is the paradigm adopted by the consultant to assess the problem and suggest interventions. His chapter describes consultation from a systemic interactional perspective and demonstrates how the paradigm organizes the data. He utilizes the cybernetic model of the brief interactional therapists (Weakland, 1960; Watzlawick, Weakland, & Fisch, 1974) and describes the context of consultation. He then gives a number of examples of the process, emphasizing its analogue to brief interactional therapy.

In Chapter 4, Speck looks at a macrosystem at another level of organization: the family in its sociocultural context. The therapeutic techniques he describes illustrate the means by which the family's natural context—friends, neighbors, and advocates—can be utilized as powerful agents for change. He characterizes his orientation as similar to that of shamans or healers, except in Western society instead of traditional ones. He describes a number of rituals he utilizes by which the family is "retribalized" and rejoined to its natural supportive environment. In a practical fashion, this approach provides support for the family to change, using the family's own traditional resources in the neighborhood and community.

In the second section, *Family and Human Service Organizations*, the contributors describe the ways in which the more inclusive system of which the providers of direct treatment are but a part, inevitably create more inclusive systems when an individual becomes a client in one of these organizations. In Chapter 5, Schwartzman and Kneifel describe a longitudinal approach in which the children are observed being treated in the state mental health system during several years of the life cycle. They note that as a result of the "familization" of human service organizations, bureaucratic qualities are modified to fit the clients and their families, so that they become more similar. They have attempted to determine the relationship between treatment decisions and the structure of the system of all those involved with patients, including the relationship among the organizations treating them. They found that helpers and helping institutions frequently replicate dysfunctional family patterns in their interactions with one another, with the children and families whom they serve, and at the level of the state system. Three types of family patterns are identified. Schwartzman describes the linking of various clinics creating these macrosystems as too richly joined, too poorly joined (Hoffman, 1981), and normal systems. The former two can maintain the problems they are created to change by creating analogues to the family structure.

"Enmeshed" staff keep the child in the system, whereas "disengaged" staff exclude their patients. Treatment by those in the system is contingent more on staff interaction than intrapsychic or interpersonal dynamics of the patient. This chapter suggests the analogy between normal and abnormal family systems and normal and abnormal social service systems and makes suggestions about how treatment decisions involving the entire system can be made more therapeutic.

In Chapter 6, on the family and the hospital, Harbin, describes how family dysfunction can be exacerbated by one member's hospitalization, especially if this is ignored as an essential aspect of family treatment. He describes a number of pragmatic techniques by which the hospital staff can join with the family and utilize it as an essential aspect of the patient's treatment.

He notes the relatively small literature on the interface between family and hospitalized inpatient and hospital staff. He states that this literature is not explicit on "what to do" in treatment. He describes his method for the engagement and treatment for families in his family-oriented inpatient ward and the special problems of chronic hospitalized patients who are currently generally severely disturbed. He notes how confused hierarchies in hospital staffs can interfere with the therapy. He involves both staff and family from the time of admission. To engage them, the family is given extensive attention. At the same time, counter to much family theory, the focus is kept on the patient rather than defocusing to the family. The explicit goal is to change the way family members interact with the patient while overtly attempting to reduce their guilt about causing the patient's problems. The problem necessitating hospitalization is the focus of treatment. Family members are told what they might expect and put in charge of the patient's management. They are encouraged to support as much autonomy as possible in the patient and to help him or her become reestablished in the social system or create a new one. At times this includes a referral to an active, behavior-oriented family therapist. Home leaves are planned for the patient to "practice" living in the real world. Harbin believes that most family therapists are too ambitious, encourage too much interaction, and move too fast on sensitive issues for hospitalized patients and their families.

He also discusses the processes that take place between hospitals and families and the families' means of influencing the hospital's functioning. At the same time, he realizes the essential dissonance in the more inclusive system between the family as an ascribed organization and the hospital as a bureaucratic one.

In Chapter 7, Schwartzman and Restivo have studied a county juvenile probation department of about 40 members and the more inclusive system of which it is a part, the county legal system. In their chapter they describe the structure and basic premises of those providing treatment and those treated in this system, the acting-out adolescents. The "fit" of the functioning of the probation department and the family structure and basic premises of the acting-out adolescents who become part of the systems, also creates—at a more inclusive level—an analogue to these adolescents' families of origin that make behavioral change improbable. The authors make some suggestions on the minimum changes necessary for the system to function in a more therapeutic, change-oriented fashion at the county level using a structural orientation and a number of possibilities for reframing.

Bokos and Schwartzman, in Chapter 8, have described a recurring analogous process in the families of heroin addicts treated in the state methadone system. They describe how beliefs about addiction create and are created by the family's structure and how the state methadone system that attempts to treat them often re-creates an analogous structure at this more inclusive level. In this system the label "addict" and definition of addiction and attempts to stop the behavior by those in the system, both family members and mental health personnel, create a self-regulating process maintained by nonabstinent chronic clients. At the same time, conflict in the relationship between professionals and paraprofessionals, varying ideologies in treatment, personality differences, and other dissonances within each clinic are such that an analogous structure to that of the family is created at a more inclusive level. In this system also, behavior defined as addictive is reinforced at a more inclusive level of organization by the client's manipulation of dissonances at some level of organization between those treating them and/or their families. This covert conflict reinforces the lack of consequences for addictive behaviors that is intimately involved in maintaining the problem of being "out of control" and experiencing oneself this way, and defined as addiction. In addition, the lack of success in treatment reinforces for both staff and clients the ineffectiveness of treatment and the hopelessness of the client's abstinence. The relationship among the clinics also creates the structure of the family at a yet more inclusive level. Bokos and Schwartzman describe changes suggested by state officials to alter this type of functioning so that an analogue to the addict's family and the reinforcement of his or her irresponsible behavior is not created but rather replaced by a clear structural hierarchy with negative consequences for drug use and other irresponsible behavior.

The third section of the book, *Family and Culture*, consists of three chapters that consider those basic premises and patterns of recurring beliefs and behaviors that order and give meaning to individuals in a social system.

In Chapter 9, Stein, adopting a much more elegant approach than most in the family field, demonstrates how culture can be utilized for change in family therapy in a family practice/community medicine setting where the patients were midwestern American families from varying subcultures and socioeconomic statuses. His chapter on values and family therapy utilizes psychoanalytic theory coupled with aspects of culture derived from anthropology. He examines in detail how family values link individuals, their intrafamilial context, social institutions, and society itself, and the means by which they can and must be incorporated into strategies for change in psychotherapy. He makes the interesting argument that "old" symptoms are incorporated as part of culture and only newer symptoms are labeled "symptomatic." As he states, "Normative familial–cultural patterns . . . are symptoms that have stabilized over long periods." In addition, he argues that dominant values are defenses against subordinate ones. He believes that culture is the external re-creation of the family which in turn stabilizes the family dynamics that constitute its source. He makes a radical argument about the role of ethnicity in therapy when he states; "What appear on the surface as conflicts *between* American and traditional ethnic values are in fact conflicts *within* the ethnic and American value systems alike." Stein makes the somewhat revolutionary point that the thrust of family therapy should be intervening to prevent the projection of various conflicts and dissonances onto the sociocultural context. The conflicts should instead be resolved in the family. He believes successful therapy is restructuring and setting boundaries at the level of culture, resulting in differentiation, separation, and resolution. Stein illustrates how family problems are profoundly embedded in the culture of which they are a part, which must be utilized for successful therapeutic change. He also argues that values do not affect people apart from how they are actually used.

Walsh, in Chapter 10, describes her attempt to utilize the values of Moroccan culture in helping to create a social service system, virtually from nothing, in which the prime agent of change is modernism in general, with all its socioeconomic implications. Walsh argues that the pull of the cities on the young makes the kinship and neighborhood market system, the traditional social group in Moroccan culture, irrelevant as a support system for these urban immigrants. At the same time, this social system that they leave to immigrate to the cities cannot successfully withstand the loss of so many members and still function. She suggests that a number of traditional values be utilized in attempts to resolve problems for these same individuals so they can be "modern" by utilizing their social networks, a traditional part of the Moroccan culture, in a different way. She notes the possibility of creative restructuring during periods of transition, when it is especially important to consider the more inclusive social context, both as possible support that must be utilized and as possible hindrance to change that must be neutralized. Walsh suggests the utility of reframing by normalizing the distress of those undergoing radical social change, by defining it as to be expected in a context of change, but also as temporary. She states that the most useful general strategy for adapting to a modernizing society is to find means of continuing the traditional in the modern world. Specifically, she describes how this can be accomplished in the case of the seemingly conflictual values of "modern" female equality and family stability in which women were subordinate. She notes the special importance of the extended family in Moroccan culture, which must be utilized for successful change, both to maintain itself in some form and to help its members function in the extrafamilial context, which they must.

In Chapter 11, a very creative cross-cultural study, Farella describes the basic premises of the Navajo Indians, their social structure, and the dissonances produced by both, within the more inclusive Anglo-American culture. He also describes an intervention at the level of the whole society, the founding of the Native American Church, which by using peyote in their rituals, resolves these dissonances and solves a problem endemic to Native Americans, alcoholism.

Farella argues, like Stein, that when considering psychotherapeutic intervention, all levels of abstraction, including the cultural, can be considered. He states that these are inherently part of the structure of the intervention anyway but are generally implicit and should be made explicit at least by the therapist. The cultural level is crucial because he believes therapy to be primarily resocialization, changing basic premises.

Farella describes Navajo culture as ultimately divided into a basic dichotomy of maleness and femaleness. Everything and everybody has aspects of both. Maleness as a quality is wild and spontaneous, whereas femaleness is stable and conservative. In Navajo culture, the basic social unit is the mother–son dyad. For males the contradictory pulls between family of origin and family of procreation are intense. Men have practically no status between adolescence and old age; and they live with their wives' kinship group, so they also have no support system for much of their lives. Farella argues that alcohol functions as a solution and homeostat for Navajo males, in this case the maintenance of traditional values and a social system of males as peripheral until they reach late middle age. He then describes how the Native American Church provides a cultural solution to the dissonances in the contemporary Navajo culture within its Anglo context. Farella further describes how alcohol, abused by younger males, can be understood as an attempt to maintain traditional Navajo culture by means of symptomatic males legitimating their "one-down" status. The church resolves this dilemma by using peyote, which does not allow the concurrent use of alcohol, allowing the maintenance of traditional culture and also solving the problem of alcoholism by including the correct cultural level of abstraction.

Conclusion

This book develops the perspective that seriously considers the family as a part of more inclusive systems at different levels of abstraction and organization that constrain it in different ways. The contributors to this volume suggest the importance of these levels for effective family therapy. The book's chapters dealing with training, psychotherapy, the "natural" social context, and the cultural context describe the omnipresence of context in family diagnosis and intervention in which the family's functioning must always be at least partially explained as an aspect or element of a more inclusive system. Whatever "wholeness" families possess, they are always part of an ecology whose process and structure must be considered to understand their functioning and to alter it. Consequently, therapy must always be a multileveled phenomenon. The therapist must perceive family functioning, the family as a whole, and the family as a part of its context. Context is not something that exists "out there," but is an inevitable aspect of whatever part of that context is being examined. The paradoxical nature of human communication spreads throughout this context, so that culture and social organization, each of which is a part of the other, includes the other, and the locus of each resides in the individual. What makes this an even more formidable task of translation for the therapist is that diagnosis is made by someone who is part of another more inclusive system.

Clinicians will have to be more aware of their own basic premises and values and those of their clients' sociocultural systems. These are clues to the most successful means by which families accomplish change.

REFERENCES

Adams, R. Agency and family therapy. *Journal of Family Therapy*, 1979, *1*, 211–219.
Amini, F., Burke, E. L., & Edgerton, R. Social structure of a psychiatric ward for adolescents and the therapeutic implications of patient–staff and intra-staff conflicts. *Adolescence*, 1978, *8*, 411–415.

Anderson, C. The community connection: The impact of social networks on family and individual functioning. In F. Walsh (Ed.), *Normal family processes*. New York: Guilford Press, 1982.

Andrade, S. A., & Burstein, A. G. Social congruence and empathy in paraprofessional and professional mental health wards. *Community Mental Health Journal*, 1973, 9,(4), 388–392.

Aponte, H. J. The family–school interview: An eco-structural approach. *Family Process*, 1970, 15(3), 303–311.

Aponte, H. J. Under-organization in the poor family. In P. J. Guerin (Ed.), *Family therapy*. New York: Gardner Press, 1978.

Attneave, C. L. Therapy in tribal settings and urban network intervention. *Family Process*, 1969, 8(2), 192–210.

Auerswald, E. H. Interdisciplinary versus ecological approach. *Family Process*, 1968, 7(2), 202–215.

Auerswald, E. H. Introduction to Hoffman and Long, A systems dilemma. *Family Process*, 1969, 8(2), 211–234.

Bateson, G. *Steps to an ecology of mind*. New York: Ballantine Books, 1972.

Bateson, G., Jackson, D. D., Haley, J., & Weakland, J. Toward a theory of schizophrenia. *Behavioral Science*, 1956, 1, 251–264.

Bell, J. E. The future of family therapy. *Family Process*, 1970, 9, 127–142.

Bell, J. E. Family in medical and psychiatric treatment—selected clinical approaches. *Journal of Operational Psychiatry*, 1977, 8(1), 57–65.

Bell, J. E. Family context therapy: A model for family change. *Journal of Marital and Family Counseling*, 1978, 4(1), 111–126.

Bell, N., Trieschman, A., Vogel, E. A sociocultural analysis of the resistances of working class fathers treated in a child psychiatric clinic. *American Journal of Orthopsychiatry*, 1961, 21(2), 388–405.

Bell, N., & Zucker, R. Family–hospital relationships in a state hospital setting. *International Journal of Social Psychology*, 1968, 14, 73–82.

Blackwell, R. D., & Wilkins, M. P. Beyond the family system. *Journal of Family Therapy*, 1981, 3, 79–90.

Boyd, N. Family therapy with black families. In S. Corchin & E. Jones (Eds.), *Minority mental health*. New York: Holt, Rinehart & Winston, 1980.

Burch, C. A study of families' expectations and experiences of a child guidance clinic. *British Journal of Social Work*, 1971, 8, 145–158.

Caudill, W. *The psychiatric hospital as a small society*. Cambridge: Harvard University Press, 1958.

Cobb, S. Social support as a moderator of life stress. *Psychosmatic Medicine*, 1976, 38, 300–314.

Crawley, J. The ecological perspective revisited. *Australian Journal of Family Therapy*, 1982, 3, 104–116.

Dean, A., & Lin, N. The stress buffering role of social support: Problems and prospects for systematic investigation. *Journal of Nervous and Mental Disease*, 1977, 165, 403–417.

Deikman, A., & Whitaker, L. Humanizing a psychiatric ward: Changing from drugs to psychotherapy. *Psychotherapy: Theory, Research, and Practice*, 1979, 16, 204–214.

Dell, P. F., Sheehy, M. D., Pulliam, G. P., & Goolishian, H. A. Family therapy process in a family therapy seminar. *Journal of Marriage and Family Counseling*, 1977, 3(2), 43–44.

Ebner, M. J. Hard hats vs. soft hearts: The conflict between principles and reality in child and adolescent care and treatment programs. *Child Care Quarterly*, 1979, 8, 36–45.

Fish, L. Using social systems techniques in a crisis unit. *Hospital and Community Psychiatry*, 1971, 22(8), 40–43.

Fleck, S., Cornelison, A., Norton, N., & Lidz, T. Interaction between hospital staff and families. *Psychiatry*, 1957, 20(4), 343–350.

Foley, V. C. Family therapy with black disadvantaged families: Some observations on roles, communication, and techniques. *Journal of Marriage and Family Counseling*, 1975, 1, 157–165.

Framo, J. L. Chronicle of a struggle to establish a family unit within a community health center. In P. L. Guerin (Ed.), *Family therapy.* New York: Gardner Press, 1976.

Garrison, J. Network techniques: Case studies in the screening–linking planning conference method. *Family Process,* 1974, *13*(3), 337–353.

Gould, E., & Glick, I. D. The effects of family presence and brief family intervention in global outcome for hospitalized schizophrenic patients. *Family Process,* 1977, 503–517.

Greenwood, E. D. The role of psychotherapy in residential treatment. *American Journal of Orthopsychiatry,* 1955, *25,* 692–698.

Haley, J. *Strategies of psychotherapy.* New York: Grune & Stratton, 1963.

Haley, J. Toward a theory of pathogenic systems. In G. Zuk & I. Boszormenyi-Nagy (Eds.), *Family therapy and disturbed families.* Palo Alto, Calif.: Science & Behavior Books, 1967.

Hamburg, B. A., & Killilea, M. Relation of social support, stress, illness, and use of health services. In the Surgeon General's Report on Health Promotion and Disease Prevention, *Healthy people: Background papers* (Vol. 2). Washington, D.C.: U.S. Government Printing Office, 1979.

Harbin, H. Families and hospitals: Collision or cooperation. *American Journal of Psychiatry,* 1978, *135,* 1496–1499.

Hirschorn, L., & Gilmore, T. The application of family therapy concepts to influencing organizational behavior. *Administrative Science Quarterly,* 1980, *25,* 18–37.

Herz, M., Endicott, J., & Spitzer, R. Brief hospitalization of patients with families: Initial results. *American Journal of Psychiatry,* 1975, *132*(4), 413–418.

Hoffman, L. Deviation-amplifying processes in natural groups. In J. Haley (Ed.), *Changing families.* New York: Grune & Stratton, 1971.

Hoffman, L. *The foundations of family therapy.* New York: Basic Books, 1981.

Hoffman, L., & Long, L. A systems dilemma. *Family Process,* 1969, *8*(2), 211–234.

Jackson, D. The question of family homeostasis. *Psychiatric Quarterly Supplement,* 1957, *31*(1), 79–90.

Jackson, D. The study of the family. *Family Process,* 1965, 4(1), 1–20.

Kaplan, B., Cassel, J., & Gore, S. Social support and health. *Medical Care,* 1977, *15* (Supplement), 47–58.

Kaplan, M. Problems between a referring service and a child guidance clinic. *Quarterly Journal of Child Behavior* 1952, *4,* 80–96.

Kellam, S. G., & Chassan, J. B. Social context and symptom fluctuation. *Psychiatry,* 1962, *25,* 370–381.

Killilea, M. Interaction of crisis theory, coping strategies and social support systems. In H. C. Schulberg & M. Killilea (Eds.), *The modern practice of community mental health.* San Francisco: Jossey-Bass, 1982.

Kingston, P. The social context of the family. In S. Walrond-Skinner (Ed.), *Family and marital psychotherapy* London. Routledge & Kegan Paul, 1979.

Kluckhohn, F. R. Variations in the basic values of family systems. *Social Casework,* 1958, *39,* 63–72.

Kolakowski, L. *The alienation of reason.* New York: Doubleday, 1968.

Lansky, M. Establishing a family-oriented inpatient unit. *Journal of Operational Psychiatry,* 1977, *8,* 66–74.

Levonson, D., & Crabtree, L. Ward tension and staff leadership in a therapeutic community for hospitalized adolescents. *Psychiatry,* 1979, *42,* 220–239.

Liddle, H. A., & Halpin, R. J. Family therapy training and supervision literature: A comparison review. *Journal of Marriage and Family Counseling,* 1978, *4,* 77–98.

Lidz, T. *The family and human adaptation,* New York: International Universities Press, 1963.

Main, T. F. The ailment. *British Journal of Medical Psychology,* 1957, *30*(3), 129–145.

Mannino, F. V., & Shore, M. F. Ecologically oriented family intervention. *Family Process,* 1972, *14,* 499–505.

Mannino, F. V., & Shore, M. F. The wider context of family intervention. *Family Therapy Networker*, 1982, Jan.–Feb., 13–15.

McGlashan, T. H., & Levy, S. T. Sealing-over in a therapeutic community. *Psychiatry*, 1977, 40, 55–65.

McGoldrick, M. Ethnicity and family therapy: An overview. In M. McGoldrick, J. K. Pearce, & J. Giordano (Eds.), *Ethnicity and family therapy*. New York: Guilford Press, 1982.

McGoldrick, M., & Pearce, J. K. Family therapy with Irish. *Family Process*, 1981, 20(2), 223–241.

McGoldrick, M., Pearce, J. K., & Giordano, J. (Eds.). *Ethnicity and family therapy*. New York: Guilford Press, 1982.

Miller, D. H. Psychosocial factors in the etiology of disturbed behavior. *British Journal of Medical Psychology*, 1961, 34, 43.

Miller, W. B. Inter-institutional conflict as a major impediment to delinquency prevention. *Human Organization*, 1958, 17(3), 20–23.

Minuchin, S. The paraprofessional and the use of confrontation in the mental health field. *American Journal of Orthopsychiatry*, 1969, 39, 722–729.

Montalvo, B., & Pavlin, S. Faulty staff communications in a residential treatment center. *American Journal of Orthopsychiatry*, 1966, 36, 706–711.

Piliavin, I. Conflict between cottage parents and caseworkers. In A. Kadushin (Ed.), *Child welfare services: A source book*. London: Macmillan, 1970.

Polak, P. Patterns of discord. *Archives of General Psychiatry*, 1970, 23, 277–283.

Polak, P., & Kirby, M. A model to replace psychiatric hospitals. *Journal of Nervous and Mental Disease*, 1976, 162(1), 13–21.

Polak, P., & Jones, M. The psychiatric nonhospital: A model for change. *Community Mental Health Journal*, 1973, 9(2), 123–131.

President's Commission on Mental Health. *Task panel report on community support systems* (Vol. 2). Washington, D.C.: U.S. Government Printing Office, 1978.

Rapoport, R. N., & Rapoport, R. *Community as doctor*. London: Tavistock Publications, 1960.

Reiss, D., Costell, R., Jones, C., & Berkman, H. The family meets the hospital. *Archives of General Psychiatry*, 1980, 37, 142–154.

Rich, W. Special role and role expectation of black administrators of neighborhood mental health programs. *Community Mental Health Journal*, 1975, 11(4), 394–400.

Roberts, W. Family or agency network—where to intervene. *Journal of Family Therapy*, 1979, 1, 203–209.

Sacks, M., & Carpenter, W. The pseudotherapeutic community: An examination of antitherapeutic forces on psychiatric units. *Hospital and Community Psychiatry*, 1974, 21(4), 315–316.

Schwartzman, J., & Bokos, P. Methadone maintenance: The addict's family recreated. *International Journal of Family Therapy*, 1980, 1(4), 338–355.

Schwartzman, J., & Kroll, L. Addict abstinence and methadone maintenance. *International Journal of the Addictions*, 1977, 12(4), 497–507.

Selig, A. The myth of the multiproblem family. *American Journal of Orthopsychiatry*, 1976, 4(3), 526–532.

Selig, A. Changing organizational systems to treat family systems. In D. Freeman (Ed.), *Perspectives on family therapy*. Vancouver: Butterworth, 1980.

Selvini-Palazzoli, M. S., Cecchin, G., Prata, G., & Boscolo, L. *Paradox and counterparadox*, New York: Aronson, 1978.

Shapiro, J. Changing dysfunctional relationships between family and hospital. *Journal of Operational Psychiatry*, 1980, 11(1), 18–26.

Simon, H. *The sciences of the artificial*, Cambridge, Mass.: MIT Press, 1969.

Sluzki, C. On training to "think interactionally." *Social Science and Medicine*, 1974, 8, 483–485.

Sluzki, C., & Veron, E. The double bind as a universal pathogenic situation. *Family Process,* 1971, *10* (4), 397–410.

Speck, R. Psychotherapy of the social network of a schizophrenic family. *Family Process,* 1967, *6,* 208–214.

Spiegel, J. *Transactions: The interplay between individual family and society.* New York: Science House, 1971.

Stannard-Friel, D. Ward 3R revisited. *Psychiatry,* 1981, *44,* 150–160.

Stanton, A., & Schwartz, M. *The mental hospital,* New York: Basic Books, 1954.

Stein, H. F. The Slovak-American swaddling ethos: Homeostat for family dynamics and cultural persistence. *Family Process,* 1978, *17,* 31–46.

Steinfeld, G. J. Parallels between the pathologic family and the mental hospital: A search for a process. *Psychiatry,* 1970, *33*(1), 36–55.

Stewart, R. P. Building an alliance between the families of patients and the hospital: Model and process. *Journal of the National Association of Private Psychiatric Hospitals,* 1981, 63–68.

Szurek, S. A. The family and staff hospital psychiatric therapy of children. *American Journal of Orthopsychiatry,* 1951, *21,* 597–611.

Vogel, E. F., & Bell, N. W. The emotionally disturbed child as the family scapegoat. In N. F. Bell & E. F. Vogel (Eds.), *A modern introduction to the family.* New York: Free Press, 1968.

Walker, K. N., MacBride, A., & Vachon, M. L. Social support and the crisis of bereavement. *Social Science and Medicine,* 1977, *11,* 35–41.

Watzlawick, P., Weakland, J., & Fisch, R. *Change: Principles of problem formation and problem resolution.* New York: Norton, 1974.

Weakland, J. The double-bind hypothesis and three-party interaction. In D. Jackson (Ed.), *The etiology of schizophrenia.* New York: Basic Books, 1960.

Williams, J. C., Marr, J., Lewis, C. P., Tucker, L. S., & Copeland, F. The evolution of a psychotherapy group on a children's inpatient unit. *Smith College Studies in Social Work,* November 1977, 3–8.

Zuk, G. H. A therapist's perspective on Jewish family values. *Journal of Marriage and Family Counseling* 1978, *4,* 110–111.

Macrosystemic models

i

2

The isomorphic nature of training and therapy: Epistemologic foundation for a structural-strategic training paradigm

HOWARD A. LIDDLE
GEORGE W. SABA
University of California, San Francisco, and
Mental Research Institute, Palo Alto

> *The true method of philosophical construction is to frame a scheme of ideas, the best that one can, and unflinchingly to explore the interpretation of experience in terms of that scheme . . . all constructive thought, on the various topics of scientific interest, is dominated by some such scheme, unacknowledged, but no less influential in guiding the imagination. The importance of philosophy lies in its sustained effort to make such schemes explicit, and thereby capable of criticism and improvement.*—Alfred North Whitehead, *Process and Reality*

Through its relatively brief course of evolution, family therapy has been more adequately developed as a body of techniques than as a unified, coherent framework. Recently, however, an epistemologic renewal has taken hold in the family therapy field, a major thrust of which is attending to the presuppositions that underlie our techniques. Although this emphasis on theoretical development can have its calamitous side effects (Coyne, Denner, & Ransom, 1982; Liddle & Saba, 1981), certain aspects of this trend's spirit should nonetheless be encouraged and focused in a productive direction.

The family therapy training and supervision area has been immune to this renewed fervor for epistemological articulation (Liddle, 1982a). The present chapter addresses this conceptual gap. It elaborates a previously recognized but still underdeveloped overarching schema—the principle of the isomorphic, interrelated, and interconnected nature of family therapy and family therapy training. Like other contributions in this text, this chapter examines a topic at a broad macrosystemic level.

We also explore the microsystemic holons[1] of training and therapy that help comprise the larger family therapy field (which itself must also be seen in its wider context[s]). In partnership with other subsystems (e.g., research), training and therapy are viewed as ever-changing, coevolving (Jantsch, 1980) holons, which interact fluidly to constitute the theoretic and pragmatic parameters of the broader field.

This kind of complex, evolving organism, with its multiple, interacting subsystems, requires a schema that permits access to and creative utilization of this complexity. The concept of isomorphism is presented as a blueprint that allows examination of the interconnected macrosystems and the larger macropattern in which these subsystems exist and evolve. More basically, isomorphism is construed as a basic interactional phenomenon spanning the domains of training and therapy. Because these processes operate at this elemental level, the chapter offers a conceptual map for family therapy trainers from any theoretic persuasion.[2] Isomorphisms, particularly those between a structural-strategic training and therapy model, are presented as a foundation for an *epistemologic declaration* (Liddle, 1982) for family therapy trainers.[3] The present contribution should be viewed as foundational to and in the context of our related work on the skills of family therapy training (Liddle & Saba, in press), the skills of live supervision/consultation (Liddle & Schwartz, 1983), teaching family therapy concepts (Liddle & Saba, 1982a), research on supervision (Liddle, Davidson, & Barrett, in press), training supervisors (Liddle, Breunlin, Schwartz & Constantine, 1984), and evaluation of training (Breunlin, Schwartz, Selby, & Krause, 1983).

Isomorphism Defined in Relation to Training and Therapy

In his outstanding analysis of structuralism as a paradigm encompassing both macro- and microperspectives, Levinson (1972) offers a lucid conception of the isomorphism principle.

1. "To get away from the traditional misuse of the words 'whole' and 'part,' one is compelled to operate with such awkward terms as 'sub-whole,' or 'part-whole,' 'substructures' . . . and so forth. To avoid these jarring expressions, I proposed, some years ago, a new term to designate those Janus-faced entities on the intermediate levels of any hierarchy, which can be described either as wholes or parts, depending on the way you look at them from 'below' or from 'above.' The term I proposed was the 'holon,' from the Greek *holos* = whole, with the suffix *on*, which, as in proton or neutron, suggests a particle or part" (Koestler, 1978, p. 33).

2. The isomorphic nature of training and therapy transcends theoretical orientations. The theoretical precepts of the training model are reflections of the model of therapy being taught.

3. Other aspects of an epistemological declaration for family therapy trainers can be found in Liddle and Saba (in press).

Categories which appear widely unrelated in content will reflect the same patterning of form, will be, in a word transformations or isomorphs of each other. It is important to realize that this is not idle analogizing. It is a literal belief that structure, or form, is constant in spite of changing content. (p. 36)[4]

Douglas Hofstadter has imaginatively employed the notions of recursion, self-reference, and endless regress to demonstrate the underlying order which forms the basis of Gödel's Incompleteness Theorem, Escher's perplexing drawings, and Bach's self-regenerating musical structures. In *Gödel, Escher, Bach: An Eternal Golden Braid*, he asserts that there is a grand scheme to things: reality is a web of interconnecting and interrelating "braids" that are isomorphically patterned in relation to each other. This text stands as one of the works available from other fields that can aid our own model and theory-building efforts, especially as these efforts relate to the principle of isomorphs.

For example, in one section Hofstadter details the multilevel nature of Bach's *Musical Offering*, noting how this as well as other compositions of Bach contain complex canons—self-regenerating and self-referencing pieces where a single theme is played against or copies itself.

Notice that every type of "copy" preserves all the information in the original theme, in the sense that the theme is fully recoverable from any of the copies. Such an information preserving transformation is often called an isomorphism. (Hofstadter, 1979, p. 9)

Hofstadter's thoughts on isomorphs can be more explicitly useful, as we strive to more precisely define the parallel nature of training and therapy.

The word isomorphism applies when two complex structures can be mapped onto each other, in such a way that to each part of one structure there is a corresponding part in the other structure, where "corresponding" means that the two parts play similar roles in their respective structures. (1979, p. 49)

This chapter begins this mapping or superimposition process of the training and therapy structures onto one another. Along the way we define the corresponding components in each structure and describe the similar processes inherent in the components' interactions.

Hofstadter's treatment of what he terms copies, sameness, and differentness can further extend our comprehension of isomorphism. In discussing M. C. Escher's ability to portray an object's parts as being "copies" of the object itself, Hofstadter asks:

4. Levinson (1972, p. 34) also points out the contributions made by Piaget (transformations) and Levi-Strauss (deep structures) to the principle of isomorphism.

What is there that is the "same" about all Escher drawings? It would be quite ludicrous to attempt to map them piece by piece onto each other. The amazing thing is that even a tiny section of an Escher drawing or a Bach piece gives it away. Just as a fish's DNA is contained inside every tiny bit of the fish, so a creator's "signature" is contained inside every tiny section of his creations. We don't know what to call it but "style"—a vague and elusive word. (1979, pp. 147–148)

In a parallel way, this chapter asks: What is there that is the "same" about training and therapy?, and How are the elements of each contained in the other? We address how the "sameness-in-differentness" principle applies to the domains of training and therapy.

Isomorphism is also illuminated by Hofstadter's discussion of *recursiveness*, which is viewed as a basic phenomenon in the grammars of languages, in mathematics, in solid state physics, in music and art, and in computer programs.

Now we are going to see yet another way in which the whole world is built out of recursion. This has to do with the structure of elementary particles. . . . We are going to see that particles are in a certain sense . . . nested inside each other in a way which can be described recursively, perhaps even by some sort of "grammar." (1979, p. 142)[5]

When these particles become tangled up together in interaction,

no particle can even be defined without referring to all other particles, whose definitions in turn depend on the first particles, etc. Round and round, in a never-ending loop. (1979, p. 142)

This kind of recursion at even the lowest levels of matter should itself be seen as isomorphic to our discussion of training and therapy. That is, as in the example of the subatomic particles' definitional interrelatedness, training and therapy are also best defined interdependently. The recursiveness of the never-ending loop of protons, neutrons, and so forth, also exists at the training and therapy level. These domains have a correspondence and interpenetration that require further exploration.[6]

5. Hofstadter's use of *"grammar"* is a particularly apt word choice. We are just beginning to comprehend the ways in which our world is interconnected. A more sophisticated appreciation of these *connections* (Bateson's *"patterns which connect"*) will require a corresponding coevolution of a grammar for the isomorphism principle (just as it has been important to devise an *interpersonal language* in order for the interpersonal or interactional view to become more sophisticated).
6. In this regard, "further exploration" includes our accessing other fields that have and are developing ideas related to isomorphic and systemic thinking (e.g., the arts, architecture, evolutionary theory). The family therapy field deals with contexts, yet it also exists within and is interrelated to other contexts and fields, which have much to offer in theory development and application.

Isomorphism in the Psychotherapy Literature

Long regarded as an epistemological mentor in the family therapy field, Gregory Bateson acknowledged and promoted the implementation of isomorphic thinking. The central thesis throughout his work was the concept of a metapattern—a pattern of patterns. Essentially this grand perspective searched for the "patterns which connect" all living things in the universe. In his own words,

> We have been trained to think of patterns, with the exception of those of music, as fixed affairs. It is easier and lazier that way but, of course, all nonsense. In truth, the right way to begin to think about the pattern which connects is to think of it as *primarily* . . . a dance of interacting parts. (1979, p. 13)

Far from being unique to family therapy, the psychotherapy literature contains several treatments of parallel or synchronous processes. Searles (1962) described a reflection phenomenon that occurs in supervision; that is, the interpersonal processes in the therapist–client relationship are often mirrored in the supervisor–therapist dyad. Ekstein and Wallerstein (1972) record a similar process. Doehrman's (1976) research on the process of supervision produced evidence for this reflexive event as well. The previous work by Searles, Ekstein and Wallerstein, and Doehrman was accomplished with a psychoanalytic theoretic orientation. More recently Haley (1976, 1980) and Minuchin and Fishman (1981) have reflected on the isomorphic nature of training and therapy from strategic and structural perspectives. For Haley (1976), "A theory of therapy and a theory of training are often synonymous" because there are clear "parallels between the premises of therapy and the premises of training" (p. 170).

With the intent of the chapter and the broader context and history of isomorphs in mind, let us now turn to the manner in which the isomorphic relationship between therapy and training is realized in an evolving model of structural–strategic family therapy training.

Structural–Strategic Model of Training[7]

Assumptive Level: Theories of Learning and Change[8]

This level addresses the interrelationship between a training model's theory of learning (i.e., how trainees learn and change) and the corresponding therapy models' theory of change. Philosophically, this follows

7. Work has begun in the area of building an integrative model of structural–strategic family therapy (Fraser, 1982; Liddle, in press-a, in press-b; Liddle, Breunlin, Schwartz, & Constantine, 1981; Stanton, 1981). The developing training model proposed in this chapter

Haley's criteria for a useful theory of therapy: The theory leads to successful outcome, is simple enough for the average therapist to comprehend, is reasonably comprehensive, guides the therapist to action, and explains why failure occurs (1980, pp. 9–10). Let us examine some assumptive isomorphs between theories of learning and change from a structural–strategic viewpoint.

GOALS

A central goal in both structural and strategic therapy is the introduction of a greater degree of complexity into families' lives. The generic training objective is synonomous: to generate a wider conceptual and behavioral range with trainees. Therapists enter a training experience with a seemingly narrow range of alternatives. Previous experience, training, current work contexts, and their personalities often create a narrow, stylized way of defining their roles in the therapeutic process. Training in family therapy loosens some of therapists' previous conceptions of people and problems and infuses their conceptual schema with more complexity—a broader, more systemic view of therapy and life (Liddle & Saba, 1982a; Sluzki, 1974).

A critical assumption of the structural–strategic training model concerns the idea of *competence*. Trainers search for, enforce, and build upon the strengths and competencies of their trainees. Thus, the avoidance of a deficit-based, conceptual set in structural–strategic therapy is reflected in the training paradigm. Training develops the theoretical (cognitive amplification) and therapeutic (use of self) *resources* of therapists, extending their repertories in these areas beyond the pretraining limits.

ROLE OF THE TRAINER

The trainer/supervisor holds a highly responsible position in this process. It is a role that emphasizes the organization and shaping of the training context. These are settings where the key ingredients in trainees'

---

rests firmly on the theoretical/therapeutic formulations of those originators of structural therapy (Minuchin, Montalvo, Guerney, Rosman, & Schumer, 1967; Minuchin, 1974; Minuchin & Fishman, 1981) and the strategic therapy of Haley (1963, 1976, 1980), which of course has been strongly influenced by the work of Milton Erickson (Haley, 1973). Our debt and acknowledgment to these pioneering innovators is substantial.

8. The various levels (assumptive, conceptual, etc.) represented in this chapter are arbitrary punctuations of reality. They constitute a kind of "chopping of the ecology" (Hoffman, 1981) with which we disagree, yet these categories exist in this work for purposes of imposing a certain order through the proposed schema and facilitating concept description. Further, we acknowledge that considerable overlap may exist.

learning and change are supplied and fostered. These context characteristics ideally extend beyond the support provided when trainee strengths and competencies are accessed. Central to trainee learning and change is the trainer's skillful oscillation of support and challenge—the capacity to both access strengths *and* extend the trainee's range by pushing for competent behavior.

CHALLENGING REALITIES

In therapy the relational realities and worldviews of family members are challenged, as alternatives and reformulations of their everyday patterns of living are proposed by the therapist. In training, trainees' monadic, nonsystemic worldviews are similarly challenged, as the relationship with the trainer, the training context, and the influx of interactional cognitive constructs takes hold. When a trainer's support or challenge exists in isolation, or exist too abundantly or sparsely, the training context cannot be considered optimal for learning and change.

Minuchin has often utilized the concept of "partial selves" in his therapy and teaching. Essentially, this view acknowledges the influence differential contexts have upon behavior. We are different or "partial selves" in different contexts. Thus, certain ranges of behavior become available in one but not necessarily another context. Along these lines certain training contexts will increase the probability of certain kinds of productive or unproductive behaviors being elicited from the trainers and trainees within that context. Hence the importance of a trainer's cognizance of both the kind of training context he or she wishes to construct and the manner in which it should be constructed. Workable realities are created both at the therapeutic and training levels.

ENACTMENT AS TECHNIQUE AND THEORY OF CHANGE

A key mechanism by which this philosophy is implemented is the technique of enactment (Minuchin & Fishman, 1981). It reflects a view of change that is at once experiential and experimental. Enactment is clearly represented in the live supervision/consultation model of training (Liddle & Schwartz, 1983; Liddle & Saba, in press; Montalvo, 1973). It embodies a learning-by-doing philosophy (experiental aspect), and values a spirit of risk taking in trying new behaviors (experimental aspects). Just as a therapist organizes family members in enactments with one another, the supervisor constructs enactments between the therapist and the family. Enactments create interpersonal contexts where alternatives can be explored and generated and contexts that yield new kinds of data (interpersonal vs. self-report information). Thus, in training and therapy, enactments have assessment and intervention functions. From this perspective the trainer's unit of diagnosis and intervention becomes this context of enactment—the therapeutic system of therapist/trainee and family. Of course, a more complete and more accurate assessment of the trainer's treatment unit would always include him- or herself in the formulation. This level of conceptualization is particularly crucial when relationship difficulties threaten the training context.

IMPORTANCE OF RELATIONSHIPS

Effective trainer–trainee relationships are crucial to success in the training system, especially as they pertain to the live supervision/consultation component of training. More broadly, however, these relationships are important because of the structural–strategic theory of learning and change. Challenging and creating new realities with trainees intentionally creates high degrees of stress. The model's assumption is that people learn and change when they are challenged and concomitantly stressed in a controlled goal-oriented way that offers alternatives. Family members and therapists in training have context-specific tolerance thresholds. The training experience thus stresses and then expands the ways therapists use themselves as instruments of change.

Through the utilization and maximization of the inherent intensity in the training context (along with the aforementioned support or joining), the trainer extends the trainee's acceptable stress and conflict levels, thereby allowing him or her to access a similarly expanded range of competent behaviors from the treatment family.

Conceptual Level

LEVELS OF SYSTEMS

In adapting Koestler's *holon* concept, Minuchin and Fishman (1981) have reminded us to always conceive of families and family members as *both* wholes ("complete" entities) and parts (subsystems of wider, interconnected systems). Training systems should also be construed in this multileveled way. For example, live supervision can be viewed as both a singularly complex, self-contained context (a macromodel) and as an indispensable subsystem existing interdependently within the broader training context (a micromodel). This analysis of course also applies to other aspects of the supervisory and training process (videotape review, case conceptualization, etc.). Training programs as well exist within broader, interrelated contexts, and these programs themselves are subject to several levels of interactive analysis (e.g., administrative, clinical levels). With this in mind, trainers are urged to consider the interdependent and interconnected nature of a training context's multiple layers and components. As we have seen, Koestler's principle of the holon is a useful micro- and macroscopic instrument in guiding these formulations.

CONTEXTUAL CLIMATE

Also addressed under theory of learning/change, this isomorph, contextual climate, refers to the trainer's definition and reproduction of an ideal learning context. Taking into account the contextual constraints of the broader training or clinical context (Liddle, 1978), this principle urges trainers to specify the interactional characteristics of a facilitative learning environment. Training settings, for example, with too little cooperation/collaboration and an oversupply of competitive interactions rarely produce optimal systems of learning and change. Competitive training systems are characterized by a show-business quality— where trainees behave as if the goal of training is to demonstrate a range of *techniques* to their supervisor and trainee colleagues behind the mirror. The contextual-climate domain neatly embodies the relationship necessities so essential for successful trainee–family outcome.

HIERARCHICAL STRUCTURE

This isomorph, hierarchical structure, relates to the inevitability of hierarchically configured organizations in the therapy and training domains. In Koestler's (1978) terms,

> All complex structures and processes of a relatively stable character display hierarchic organization, and this applies regardless of whether we are considering inanimate systems, living organisms, social organizations, or patterns of behavior. (p. 290)

The same author has also, however, acknowledged the relativity of the hierarchy principle. For Koestler, hierarchic structure, "is at the same time a conceptual tool, a way of thinking, an alternative to the linear chaining of events torn from their multidimensionally stratified contexts" (1978, p. 290).

From a therapeutic viewpoint, Haley (1976, 1980) and Minuchin and Fishman (1981) have noted that hierarchies continue to function through cooperative action. When the hierarchical organization of these structures is consistently violated, dysfunction begins in both families and other social organizations, including training systems. Trainers realize the importance of this principle in the organization and facilitation of productive learning contexts. Yet, they must also recall the complimentary nature of these hierarchically structured learning contexts. These structures are reciprocally and not linearly organized systems. Thus, in utilizing this principle in training, a trainer does not need to aggressively impose a rigid hierarchic structure onto a training system. Training systems, like therapeutic systems, will naturally organize themselves in hierarchic fashion. In addition, this should not suggest that a lack of negotiation exists within hierarchic structures. The mutuality and complementarity of the organization does indeed permit such fluidity.

BOUNDARIES

Effective functioning of the training system, as with any other system, occurs when there exists a clarity of boundaries between subsystems. Boundaries are defined as the rules governing participation in subsystems. To quote Koestler once more, "Holons are self-regulating 'open systems' governed by a set of fixed rules which account for the holon's coherence, stability and its specific pattern of structure and function" (1978, p. 293). In any training system, then, it is important to clarify the rules regulating the different kinds and degrees of participation. As we have emphasized previously, the supervisor is responsible for such clarification.

Consistent trainer–trainee coalitions can produce enmeshed subsystems in a training group. Conversely, a supervisor's unavailability to his or her trainees signals a more disengaged structure with rigidly defined boundaries. The point here is that cognizance of boundary issues can preserve differentiation of the system. It is not so much that a supervisor continually engages in boundary-making operations, as that the concept of boundaries is employed as an organizing principle in the formation and maintenance of the training system. Along these lines Montalvo (1973) and Haley (1976, 1980) have previously addressed the rules of participation in training subsystems. These authors underscore the supervisory responsibility in devising an agreed-upon contract with the trainee. The contract issues, negotiable within certain limits, are especially important in live supervision, where relationship concerns are intimately tied to successful training outcome.

ROLE OF TRAINER/SUPERVISOR

As in all other aspects of this model, the trainer's role broadly parallels the therapist's expected behaviors. Supervisors assume considerable responsibility for directly influencing trainee behavior. The structural aspects of the training and therapy model require competence with enactment as a technique and, conceptually, as a theory of change. The strategic aspects necessitate competence in prescribing directives and inducing compliance with trainees and family members. The training is goal focused and emphasizes both the idiosyncratic learning issues of trainees and concerns about treatment of the family. Effective supervisors demonstrate a personal flexibility in the application of their consistent model with trainees. These trainers can creatively adapt a standard procedure to the particular needs of the trainee and context.

Supervisors require an advanced conceptual ability. Their role mandates the simultaneous operation of several observational levels. Simply remaining outside of their unit of analysis and intervention is insufficient (as it is equally insufficient with therapists). Supervision requires the facile capacity to move from one level of analysis and intervention to another. Finally, the crucial nature of the role that relationship skills play in this regard cannot be underestimated. They co-exist in relation to the other complex skills.

GOALS

The training system is a highly goal-oriented one, with several levels of objectives in simultaneous operation (trainee, family, training system, and supervisor goals). The broadest goals seek an expansion of behavioral and conceptual alternatives for trainees (and family members) as well as an interruption of cyclical, unproductive sequences (e.g., between trainees and family members). As the specific goals of the various subsystems develop, the trainer attends to each level through an intentional oscillation between these operational levels of the training context. Trainers do not autocratically set training or trainee goals. At a general level, goals exist *a priori* because of the theoretical orientation of the training and therapy model. At a more content-focused level, goals coevolve with the interactional process between the trainer and the several operative subsystems.

Process Level

CONTEXT REPLICATION/MIRRORING OF SEQUENCES

In living systems patterns have the propensity to repeat or replicate themselves at the various levels of that system (Bateson, 1979; Bronowski, 1977; Dossey, 1982; Hofstadter, 1979; Koestler, 1978; Thomas, 1975). Sequences of interaction and more broadly contexts themselves become replicated at different levels of a system.

Theoretical physicists have used different terminology to describe a similar phenomenon. Their notion, for example, of each part of the universe containing all the information present in the entire cosmos itself might be translated into the axiom: The part contains the whole (or the whole is contained in each part) (Bohm, 1980). Aspects of each subsystem's reality are transformed and/or reflected in distinct but interconnected subsystems.

This principle has tremendous applicability in understanding the interrelatedness of training and therapeutic systems. Just as therapists are inducted into following a family's unproductive rules, supervisors also face similar threats to autonomous[9] functioning. Patterns at the family–therapist level can be reflected in isomorphic sequences between the trainee and supervisor. If a family, for example, is unclear about relationship definitions, the therapist can become quite confused. This vagueness can become a tone of the supervisory system. In this case, the supervisor can intervene before the induction at the therapist or supervisory level becomes too rigidly developed. By focusing the trainee in the direction of obtaining more clarity, the therapist can focus the family in a similar manner. Thus a supervisor's ability to avoid induction into unproductive sequences can creatively enhance the probability of a desired outcome in a session. Mood, affect, energy, content, negativity, talkativeness, inquisitiveness, and avoidance of certain topics or people are all potential domains of context replicability. The mirroring of sequences can assume either a tenor of change or of unproductive repetition. It is a principle that can guide trainers in the construction of effective training contexts.

STAGE-SEQUENTIAL NATURE

Haley (1976) was among the first in the family therapy field to emphasize the stage-specific nature of therapy. Training and the supervisory process can be conceived in like manner. One effort at superimposing the stage-specific model onto the training process uses the stages of a structural–strategic approach (e.g., joining, restructuring through challenging trainee's conceptual realities, and consolidation of change) in teaching a didactic course in family therapy (Liddle & Saba, 1982a). The stage-specific principle has also been applied in a model of live supervision/consultation, similarly from a structural–strategic perspective (Liddle & Schwartz, 1983).

The family life-cycle paradigm assists therapists in making interventions based upon a knowledge of the normative, stage-specific crises and tasks of predictable developmental stages. Trainers can use the same generic formulation in what might be called a *trainee's life cycle*— the stages of a trainee's development.[10] Thus, trainers develop a blueprint allowing for wide idiosyncratic variation and learning styles. A

---

9. Autonomy is used more figuratively than literally here, as its usual connotation underplays the interrelated, complementary aspects of existence.

stage-sequential framework allows trainers to establish and modify their expectation for trainee and family change based upon a realistic assessment of the trainee's developmental level (as well as the developmental level of the context and the trainer).

ASSESSMENT

The supervisor's primary unit of assessment is the interaction in the therapeutic system. Like the therapist, the supervisor includes him- or herself in any diagnosis, as the observer is never separate from the thing observed—they are a unified, interacting, rule-governed unit (Capra, 1982; Jantsch, 1980).

Assessment of the training system is an ongoing rather than single-event endeavor. Data are gathered through experimental and experiential probes, as they are in the therapeutic system. These probes consist of the therapist *plus* the series of supervisory interventions introduced into the therapeutic system. Assessment is never accomplished apart from the context of intervention (Minuchin & Fishman, 1981). From this model, diagnosis is the result of the interventions that are made (hence its experiential quality). Similarly in supervision every aspect of therapist behavior and therapist–family interaction has diagnostic utility. It is the keen observational capacity of the trainer, intertwined with his or her ability to design new interventions (generate alternatives) that allows training to positively change trainee and family behavior. As in other aspects of training, the supervisor assesses and intervenes at different levels concurrently (trainee, family, supervisor-training system in the observation room). Further, the nature of the assessment is shaped according to the kind of training being done. Teaching a family therapy course (Liddle & Saba, 1982a), training therapists (Liddle & Schwartz, 1983), and training supervisors (Liddle *et al.*, 1984) all require different assessment criteria. Along these lines the supervisor needs multilayered conceptual and pragmatic skills. Supervisors and therapists attend to a system's feedback in similar ways. Both calibrate and recalibrate their interventions on the basis of this assessment.

PLANNED INTERVENTIONS

A central component of a structural–strategic model of training is the concept of a trainer's planned interventions. Parallels to other fields exist that support the link between meticulous preparation and a

---

10. The anectdotal reports of trainees (Gershenson & Cohen, 1978; Lowenstein, Reder, & Clark, 1982) and the research of Liddle *et al.* (in press) have begun to illuminate an area in need of further study—the evaluation of training from the trainees' perspective.

polished final product. Filmmaker Steven Spielberg (1982) uses what is termed the "storyboard technique": a sequential series of still sketches that graphically map out the actors moves through complex, action-oriented scenes. This device, which is clearly adaptable at one level to teaching the moves of therapy (Liddle, 1982c), helps the director achieve a more precise execution of a scene (Liddle & Saba, 1982b).

Considering the many variables of the training context (time available, level of training, resources), the supervisor charts a course of action with his or her trainees much as would be done with a family. These planned interventions are tied to the feedback of the ongoing assessment process. A trainer's posture that includes planning will tend to produce trainees more capable of ultimately independent behavior (without supervision), as these trainees will have learned *experientially* the value of careful, sound planning (Liddle, 1981, 1982c).

Two final notes on planned interventions. First, although planning is integral to the structural–strategic model, the ability to modify or abandon ineffectual plans probably represents a higher, more sophisticated class of skill than planning itself. This is the oft-cited need for flexibility within structure. In acting and musical contexts, among others, this quality is known as the art of improvisation. Finally, planned interventions are not a panacea for quality training and therapy. This overall orientation does not connote a rigid adherence to a single plan. Rather, it acknowledges that there is creative exploration and personal expression within the organization any plan provides.

RELATIONSHIP DIMENSIONS

Minuchin and Fishman's (1981) treatise on the skills of structural family therapy explicitly highlights the interrelated nature of a balance between a therapist's techniques and his or her use of self as an instrument of change. A strength of this volume and a contribution to the field is this consistent treatment of technique within the context of the personal translator of any technique—the person of the therapist (Liddle, 1982d). Similarly, the supervisor's interventions are never performed apart from the context of the trainer–trainee relationship. Early research on the family therapy supervisor–supervisee relationship confirms the crucial role relationship variables play in training (Draper, 1982; Gershenson & Cohen, 1978; Liddle *et al.*, in press; Lowenstein *et al.*, 1982).

In therapy the hierarchic nature of the relationship between therapist and family moves toward equalization over time. Similarly, over the course of training, clear changes in the same direction can be charted. Trainees become more capable of confident, independent action, less focused on mistakes, and more able to suggest useful interventions to other trainees. In considering relationship problems in training, the supervisor should be reminded of the aforementioned guiding principle of assessment: to always include oneself in any diagnostic formulation. Thus, it is insufficient to assess a relationship problem in terms of a trainee's resistance or reactance (or in terms of any other monadically based traits). More accurately, there are resistant and reactant supervisory and therapeutic relationships (which themselves exist in context). Trainers can discipline themselves to apply the systemic principles they teach to their own relationships in the training system, all the while acknowledging the difficulty of monitoring the processes in which one is involved.

Intervention Level

The following list and brief discussion of intervention level isomorphs is intended as a suggestive rather than exhaustive list of supervisory skills. The state of the clinical domain of structural–strategic family therapy reflects an increased ability to concretize a comprehensive, yet ever-evolving cluster of expected therapist behaviors or skills (Liddle, in press-a, in press-b). The training and supervision area has not kept pace in this skill specification, yet it currently shows signs of progress (Liddle, 1982b). A comprehensive description of the requisite skills of training and supervision from a structural–strategic viewpoint exceeds the conceptual confines of this paper and have been detailed elsewhere (Liddle & Saba, in press; Liddle & Schwartz, 1983). Nonetheless, a thorough exemplification of the isomorphic nature of training and therapy requires at least a cursory outlining of the supervisory skills of structural–strategic therapy.

For simplification, the skills can be grouped into three categories, corresponding to the stages of training and therapy: (1) engagement/joining; (2) challenging and creating new realities; and (3) consolidation of change.

ENGAGEMENT/JOINING

To assist its formation, the trainer organizes and structures the training context. The personal skills of accommodating to and joining with members of the training system are prerequisite to the stressful challenges that follow. The trainer motivates trainees to become personally involved in the learning process through the commitment and energy he or she brings to the training experience. Trainers must demonstrate respect for trainees' backgrounds and experience and actively confirm their competencies and strengths. Just as therapists elicit hope for change with families, trainers elicit hope for trainee improvement. Conscious of the stage-oriented nature of training, the trainer begins assessment of trainee learning style, developmental level, and idiosyncratic strengths and weaknesses at this phase. This stage's essential mandate is the engagement of the trainee in the learning process and the establishment of the kind of relationship that will allow the challenges of the next phase to be withstood.

CHALLENGING AND CREATING REALITIES

In the section of the assumptive elements of the structural–strategic training approach, we outlined the essential ingredients of this model's theory of learning and change. The present section on challenging and creating realities with trainees reflects this theory of learning and change.

Minuchin and Fishman (1981) clearly state one of structural family therapy's major objectives. "The goal is always the conversion of the family to a different worldview . . . to a more flexible pluralistic view of reality—one that allows for diversity within a more complex symbolic universe" (p. 215).

Along synchronous lines the primary task of training is to challenge and change the trainee's nonsystemic, individualistic worldview. Several skills are required to affect this paradigm shift. Reframing behavior interpersonally and in terms of its complimentary aspects is a core supervisory skill. In this manner challenges are posed to a trainee's conception about themselves and the possibilities of a family's ability to change. The supervisor unbalances a trainee's conceptual framework through the procedure of enactment. Creating an intentionally pressured, emotional context facilitates memorable, intense events, which the supervisor maximizes for trainee learning. For example, supervisors help trainees withstand the intensity generated by unbalancing or focusing on a single theme so that the trainees will extend their range of conflict and intensity tolerance. Similarly, supervisors give directives before, during, and after live supervision sessions that are oriented toward altering the conceptual and behavioral range of a trainee.

Of course, trainers inevitably translate the techniques of training in personal, idiosyncratic ways. Therefore, just as there exists a *use of self* in the therapeutic skill domain, a parallel *use of self* category *for supervisors* must also be defined. A beginning definition would include a trainer's capacity to broaden and use his or her behavioral repertoire in the same way a trainee's range is expected to be broadened and utilized.

In sum, the theory of learning and change is clearly represented by the metaphor of enactment in which directives are given prior to, during and between sessions. Although we rely here primarily on live supervision, other kinds of learning experiences (video supervision, pre- and postsessions of case conceptualization) are inextricably linked to maximal trainee and family change.

CONSOLIDATION OF CHANGE

This set of supervisory skills corresponds to those therapist skills that are required after a family has begun to change. These skills address the sealing, generalizing, and transferring of the changes that have already occurred with the trainee. Further, this phase of training deals with the effects or the consequences of change on the professional and personal life of the trainee (Liddle, 1978).

Reading feedback from the training system continues to be a key assessment skill required throughout training. Supervisors closely track trainee behavior, as well as, of course, the behavior of the family over time. Desired trainee changes are supported, highlighted, and shaped through the various training tools (live supervision, videotape review, case conceptualization conferences). The pace of trainee change, in addition to the kind and degree of change, is also a subject of trainer concern. Too rapid or slow a change (which is of course defined relative to wide degrees of individual variance) might dictate alteration of the trainer's plan.

At this phase of training, trainers are sensitive to the ways in which trainees assert their clinical/conceptual independence and skill. The issue of supervisory input prompted by a trainer's disagreement with the trainee's personal style (rather than because of a judgment about the correctness of a trainee's strategy or intervention) now becomes a potential problem. Especially at this phase then, trainers require special skills of restraint. They must accurately differentiate between those trainee interventions that are ineffectual and those that are potentially effective but accomplished differently from the supervisor's personal style.

Finally, there also exists the issue of the transferability or gener- alizability of trainee skills to contexts external to the training setting. Related to this point is the degree of professional (political consequences in one's agency) and personal (new views of relationships) accommoda- tion necessary during and after family therapy training. Supervisors must be sensitive to these issues of termination and conceptualize trainee concerns, not as individual deficits, but as generic, develop- mentally appropriate inevitabilities that occur with most trainees during this final phase of training.

Summary

This chapter has sketched the isomorphic nature of training and therapy from a structural–strategic theoretical perspective. The principle of isomorphs is seen as both a phenomenon in need of further study and a conceptual device useful in understanding complex, interrelated, and interconnected entities such as training and therapy. Minuchin employs the metaphor of the zoom lens to describe the levels of assessment and intervention necessary for family therapists. A zoom lens would be capable of moving into a proximate position (e.g., to access the intrapersonal sphere) as well as of pulling back and observing the broader field (e.g., the interpersonal view). The principle of how structures are isomorphically related is a similar, perspective-widening lens for family therapy trainers. Although conceived and written from a particular theoretical orientation, this chapter can also be used as a guide for trainers from different orientations. As we have said, the principle of isomorphism transcends theoretical boundaries. It offers a descriptive schema or template that uncovers (and imparts) order, connections, and pattern at the levels of content and form.[11]

Because we have been influenced by Hofstadter in our understanding of how isomorphism applies to the realms of training and therapy, let us return to his outstanding text as a way of closing. Gödel, Escher, and Bach were for Hofstadter "shadows cast in different directions by some central solid essence" (1979, p. 28). His book, *Gödel, Escher, Bach: An Eternal Golden Braid*, was itself an attempt at reconstructing this central object. For our purposes, in an abstract sense the principle of isomorphism could be said to be this central essence. However, when we consider the isomorphic nature of training and therapy, the "central, solid, essence" becomes less abstract. This chapter has dealt with the ways in which the content and processes of these contexts are replicated in their counterparts.

We must always recall that these domains do not linearly or unidirectionally affect each other. Hofstadter calls this situation one in which a "tangled hierarchy" exists. Such a process occurs "when what you presume are clear hierarchical levels take you by surprise and fold back in a hierarchy violating way" (1979, p. 691).

The visual recursiveness in Escher's *Drawing Hands*, where the left hand is sketching the right while the right simultaneously draws the left, also applies at the process level to training and therapy. Each level

---

11. Here we are reminded of Heisenberg's uncertainty principle, which, in simplified terms, states that the observer alters the observed by the mere act of observation. Thus, Heisenberg questions objective reality. Similarly we must realize that we participate in the creation of our own realities (e.g., the principle of isomorphism).

constantly influences the other in a never ending spiral of recursiveness. Viewed a different way, again using Hofstadter's analogy, training and therapy might themselves be seen as shadows cast in different directions—perhaps with the central essence being their respective theories of learning and change.

In the final analysis, the principle of isomorphs must not be seen as a panacea or, at another level, not even as truth. Like any theory or view, the isomorphism concept has limitations. Just as physicists have come to use approximations to understand the interactive behavior of electrons and protons, so must we as family theorists and therapists devise similar approximating schemas to understand and utilize the interactive behavior of our world.

The principle of isomorphisms remains an area of potential creative exploration. The future may bring us to new levels of analyzing the connections between training and therapy. For example, if we could obtain a holographic image of training and therapy, each bit of that picture could only be understood as it relates to the collective bits of the entire picture, for such is the nature of a hologram. For now, however, the isomorph principle can serve as a useful, yet still underdeveloped schema.

A final point, made with the help of a story.

> In the 1940's, the Dutch psychologist Adrian de Groot made studies of how chess novices and chess masters perceive a chess situation. Put in their starkest terms, his results imply that chess masters perceive the distribution of pieces in *chunks* . . . the master . . . thinks on a different level from the novice; his set of concepts is different. . . . His mode of perceiving the board is like a filter: he literally does not see bad moves when he looks at a chess situation. (Hofstadter, 1979, p. 286)

The struggle to define the isomorphic nature of training and therapy is our journey to a new level of perception known to de Groot's chess masters. In specifying the recursion, mutual influence, and correspondence between these domains, we heed Bateson's advice about how to more richly understand the world, namely, through his principle of dual or double description. For Bateson, double description provides a class of information (relationship/process) not obtainable from the single, monocular view. Further, this description exemplifies the systemic perspective—the capacity to understand in their proper context what appear to be unitary phenomena. Thus, the isomorphic principle with its binocular vision leads us one step closer to developing models of teaching, training, and conducting therapy that are syntonic with a systemic epistemology. This chapter represents a beginning in our search for the "patterns which connect" (Bateson, 1979) training and therapy.

ACKNOWLEDGMENTS

Parts of this chapter appear in more detailed form in a forthcoming book by H. A. Liddle and G. W. Saba, *Training Family Therapists: Creating Contexts of Competence* (New York: Grune & Stratton, in press).

REFERENCES

Bateson, G. *Mind and nature: A necessary unity*. New York: Dutton, 1979.

Bohm, D. *Wholeness and the implicate order*. London: Routledge & Kegan Paul, 1980.

Breunlin, D., Schwartz, R., Selby, L., & Krause, M. Development of an evaluative instrument to measure acquisition of a family systems perspective. *Journal of Marital and Family Therapy*, 1983, 9, 37–48.

Bronowski, J. *A sense of the future*. Cambridge, Mass: MIT Press, 1977.

Capra, F. *The turning point: Science, society and the rising culture*. New York: Simon & Schuster, 1982.

Coyne, J., Denner, B., & Ransom, D. Undressing the fashionable mind. *Family Process*, 1982, 21, 291–396.

Doehrman, M. Parallel process in supervision and psychotherapy. *Bulletin of the Menninger Clinic*, 1976, 40, 3–104.

Dossey, L. *Space, time and medicine*. Boulder, Colo.: Shambhala, 1982.

Draper, R. From trainer to trainer. In R. Whiffen & J. Byng-Hall (Eds.), *Family therapy supervision: Recent developments in practice*. London: Academic Press, 1982.

Ekstein, R., & Wallerstein, R. *The teaching and learning of psychotherapy* (2nd ed.). New York: International Universities Press, 1972.

Fraser, S. Structural and strategic family therapy: A basis for marriage or grounds for divorce? *Journal of Marital and Family Therapy*, 1982, 8, 13–22.

Gershenson, J., & Cohen, M. Through the looking glass: The experiences of two family therapy trainees with live supervision. *Family Process*, 1978, 17, 225–239.

Haley, J. *Strategies of psychotherapy*. New York: Grune & Stratton, 1963.

Haley, J. *Uncommon therapy: The psychiatric technique of Milton H. Erickson, M.D.* New York: Norton, 1973.

Haley, J. *Problem-solving therapy*. San Francisco: Jossey-Bass, 1976.

Haley, J. *Leaving home: The therapy of disturbed young people*. New York: McGraw-Hill, 1980.

Hoffman, L. *Foundations of family therapy*. New York: Basic Books, 1981.

Hofstadter, D. *Gödel, Escher, Bach: An eternal golden braid*. New York: Basic Books, 1979.

Jantsch, E. *The self-organizing universe*. New York: Pergamon, 1980.

Koestler, A. *Janus: A summing up*. New York: Random House, 1978.

Levinson, E. *The fallacy of understanding*. New York: Basic Books, 1972.

Liddle, H. A. The emotional and political hazards of teaching and learning family therapy. *Family Therapy*, 1978, 5, 1–12.

Liddle, H. A. Keeping abreast of developments in the family therapy field. In A. Gurman (Ed.), *Questions and answers in family therapy*. New York: Brunner/Mazel, 1981.

Liddle, H. A. On the problem of eclecticism: A call for epistemologic clarification and human-scale theories. *Family Process*, 1982, 21, 243–250. (a)

Liddle, H. A. Family therapy training: Current issues, future trends. *International Journal of Family Therapy*, 1982, 4, 81–97. (b)

Liddle, H. A. Using mental imagery to create therapeutic and supervisory realities. In A. Gurman, (Ed.), *Questions and answers in family therapy* (Vol. 2). New York: Brunner/Mazel, 1982. (c)

Liddle, H. A. Review of *Family therapy techniques* by S. Minuchin & H. C. Fishman. *American Journal of Family Therapy*, 1982, *10*, 82–87. (d)

Liddle, H. A. Five factors of failure in structural–strategic family therapy. In S. B. Coleman (Ed.), *Failures in family therapy*. New York: Guilford, in press. (a)

Liddle, H. A. Toward a contextual/dialectical translation of structural–strategic family therapy. *Journal of Systemic and Strategic Therapies*, in press. (b)

Liddle, H. A. Breunlin, D., Schwartz, R., & Constantine, J. *An integrative model of structural and strategic family therapy*. Paper presented at the National Council on Family Relations Conference, Milwaukee, Wisc., October 1981.

Liddle, H. A., Breulin, D., Schwartz, R., & Constantine, J. Training family therapy supervisors: Issues of content, form, and context. *Journal of Marital and Family Therapy*, 1984, *10*, 139–150.

Liddle, H. A., Davidson, G., & Barrett, M. J. Evaluating live supervision/consultation: The trainees' perspective. *Zeitschrift für Systemische Therapie*, in press.

Liddle, H. A., & Saba, G. W., Systemic chic I: Family therapy's new wave, and systemic chic II: Can family therapy maintain its floy floy? *Journal of Systemic and Strategic Therapies*, 1981, *1*(2), 36–44.

Liddle, H. A., & Saba, G. W. On teaching family therapy at the introductory level: A conceptual model emphasizing a pattern which connects training and therapy. *Journal of Marital and Family Therapy*, 1982, *8*, 63–73. (a)

Liddle, H. A., & Saba, G. W. Adventures in famtherland: Episode 5—creating a context of change; and Episode 6—process of change. *Family Therapy News*, September and November 1982. (b)

Liddle, H. A., & Saba, G. W. *Training family therapists: Creating contexts of competence*. New York: Grune & Stratton, in press.

Liddle, H. A., & Schwartz, R. Live supervision/consultation: Conceptual and pragmatic-guidelines for family therapy trainers. *Family Process*, 1983, *22*, 477–490.

Lowenstein, S., Reder, P., & Clark, A. The consumer's response: Trainees' discussion of the experience of live supervision. In R. Wiffen & J. Byng-Hall, *Family therapy supervision: Recent developments in practice*. London: Academic Press, 1982.

Minuchin, S. *Families and family therapy*. Cambridge, Mass.: Harvard University Press, 1974.

Minuchin, S., & Fishman, C. *Family therapy techniques*. Cambridge, Mass.: Harvard University Press, 1981.

Minuchin, S., Montalvo, B., Guerney, B., Rosman, B., & Schumer, F. *Families of the slums*. New York: Basic Books, 1967.

Montalvo, B. Aspects of live supervision. *Family Process*, 1973, *12*, 343–359.

Searles, H. Problems of psychoanalytic supervision. In *Science and psychoanalysis* (Vol. 5: *Psychoanalytic education*). New York: Grune & Stratton, 1962.

Sluzki, C. On training to think interactionally. *Social Science and Medicine*, 1974, *7*, 482–485.

Spielberg, S. An Interview with Steven Spielberg. *American Premier*, 1982, *3*(5), 17.

Stanton, M. D. An integrated structural/strategic approach to family therapy. *Journal of Marital and Family Therapy*, 1981, *7*, 427–440.

Thomas, L. *The lives of a cell*. New York: Bantam, 1975.

3

Case consultation:
The systemic interactional perspective

GEORGE S. GREENBERG
Family Therapy Institute of Greater New Orleans, Inc., and
Louisiana State University Medical School

Case consultation is often viewed as an indirect approach to helping the client by typically addressing problems about which the consultee has some identified concern (Berlin, 1979, p. 353). The consultative process is most frequently carried out through consultant–consultee meetings or by the consultant examining the patient and reporting his or her findings.

Traditionally the emphasis of case consultation has been directed to helping the therapist/consultee identify and deal with his or her own internal difficulties that were conceptualized as interfering with the therapist's ability to help the disturbed patient (Berlin, 1979, p. 353). Toward these ends, a host of consultative goals have been delineated. These include

- Examination of ways feelings of the therapist are blocked or affecting his or her functioning.
- Attempts to reduce the consultee's rage, for example, regarding unmet dependency needs of the patient.
- Improving and building the therapist's knowledge in specific areas.
- Improving the therapist's skills.
- Increasing the therapist's objectivity and reducing his or her cognitive distortions and/or correcting misperceptions in judgment.
- Supporting and reassuring the therapist.
- Helping to improve the therapist's management of the case by offering one's superior knowledge and skills (as a consultant) in assessment of the problem; then recommending an approach (Berlin, 1979; Caplan, 1970, pp. 32, 127ff.).

In examining consultative goals, it becomes apparent that at a general level there is much similarity and agreement among consultants, particularly about concepts related to skills or educational improvement; diagnostic clarification; supportive and reassurance activities; problem solving; resource recommendations; and so forth. Additionally, we have found little disagreement that consultation and its processes are predominantly viewed to be different from psychotherapy and that the primary function of consultation tends to be characterized as dependent upon the information sought by the consultee, or what is frequently identified as the purpose of the consultation.

In short, case consultation can be described as comprised of four basic components.

1. The chief complaint(s) (Greenberg, 1980, p. 314): what the consultee identifies as the problem area, included stated beliefs about causes and effects, as well as any type of rationale employed in explicating his or her viewpoint.
2. Espoused goals or purpose of consultation: precisely what the consultee's expectations are or his or her hopes for the outcome of consultation.
3. The presenting problem (Greenberg, 1980, p. 314): the sense and order the consultant makes out of the data obtained.
4. The paradigm or theoretical framework that is utilized by the consultant as a frame of reference for making sense and order out of the phenomena that are presented and arise in the consultative session.

It is this paradigm (Greenberg, 1983, p. 139ff.) that will primarily determine the type of materials sought in the consultative session; the manner in which it is shaped and classified by the consultant; how the consultant will use the material to make recommendations to the consultee, while at the same time selectively and systematically intervening.

It is the purpose of this chapter to examine case consultation from a brief systemic interactional perspective[1] and to demonstrate how the paradigm influences not only the data gathered as well as their meaning but also the function of the consultant.

The Paradigm: Basic Premises

In recent years the basic premises of systemic interactional psychotherapy have continued to emphasize that the therapist's primary func-

---

1. The systemic interactional perspective has historically been identified as the family interactional viewpoint; the term "systemic" is more inclusive, and more accurately identifies the framework.

tion is to help influence the client in such a manner that the presenting complaint of the client is ethically resolved to his or her satisfaction (Fisch, Weakland, & Segal, 1982, p. 127).

This focus is generated out of fundamental assumptions that most problems that people present to psychotherapists are emergent products of behavior and communication with one's self or between people (Greenberg, 1980, p. 310). Problems are characterized as complaints typically involving a concern by one person about something pertaining to his or her own behavior or the behavior of at least one other person with whom he or she is significantly involved. Such behavior is depicted as undesirable, distressing, deviant, difficult, or harmful, often relative to normative expectations. The behavior persists despite efforts to eliminate it, and therefore professional help is sought (Fisch et al., 1982, p. 285; Greenberg, 1980, p. 313; Weakland, 1977, p. 24).

According to the paradigm, problems persist because people persist with the same viewpoints and/or the same or similar sets of behavioral operations which keep the context-generating problem situation unchanged or facilitate problem maintenance or problem amplification (Fisch et al., 1982; Greenberg, 1974, 1977, 1980; Haley, 1973, 1976; Watzlawick, Weakland, & Fisch, 1974; Weakland, Fisch, Watzlawick, & Bodin, 1974; Weakland, 1977).

Therapeutic Impasses and the Function of Consultation

The preponderance of consultation requested by trained, experienced psychotherapists usually occurs when the therapist is "stymied." This is frequently referred to as a therapeutic impasse. Such impasses occur early or late in treatment and seem to present most frequently at the following junctures: (1) when the therapist is attempting to generate or modify a treatment plan; (2) where a basic therapeutic goal has been achieved and gone unrecognized by the therapist or patient; (3) when a basic treatment goal is incorrectly believed to have been achieved; (4) where the basic goals or strategies articulated or deployed are utopian; (5) where the basic assessments (relative to the selected paradigm) of the location of the dysfunction or the focus of treatment is incorrect or is proving inadequate, that is, where the diagnosis is insufficient or where the diagnostic formulations are incorrect; (6) where a change has occurred in relationship or in relationship position between the patient(s) and the therapist and a concerted effort is being made by at least one member of the treatment set to return to a previously established pattern; (7) where the therapist is unclear about the paradigm or theoretical framework he or she is utilizing and is therefore fragmented in his or her thinking related to the treatment or evaluation; (8) where the paradigm itself is not applicable or is no longer an effective frame of reference; and so forth.

Such impasses are found in inpatient and outpatient settings alike. However, regardless of the timing of the impasses, it appears that they themselves can be conceptualized within the systemic interactional paradigm as consisting of a complaint by the consultee/therapist about his or her own persisting behavior or some behavior of another with whom the consultee or his or her patient is significantly or professionally involved; the persistent behavior is viewed (1) as a block to treatment or evaluation and (2) as distressing, difficult, deviant, or potentially or actually harmful; and the behavior (hence the problem situation) continues and persists despite efforts to eliminate it.

The problem is actually a feature of an interactional cycle between therapist and patient(s). The cycle consists of feedback loops of routinized, redundant behavior sequences comprising some undesired behavior(s) and/or viewpoint(s) and ineffective efforts to eliminate them (Weakland, 1977, p. 24; Greenberg, 1980, pp. 313, 316). In this context therapeutic impasses are the product or outcome of the behavior/communication between therapist and client and/or the product of the therapist or the patient's view.

Consequently, the basic function of the consultant becomes one of *making an interdiction in the problem-sustaining behavior* of the therapist/consultee and/or his patient(s) where appropriate and/or in some fashion *altering the consultee's or patient's* (or both patient's and consultee's) *views pertaining to the problem* (Greenberg, 1974, pp. 86ff., 190ff., 1977, 1980; Fisch *et al.*, 1982, p. 127; Watzlawick *et al.*, p. 77ff.; Weakland *et al.*, 1974) so that the presenting complaint of the consultee is "on the road" toward resolution or ethically resolved to his or her satisfaction or so that the consultee is no longer distressed or finds that there is no longer a need for consultative intervention.

Interactional Consultation: Basic Processes and Procedure

Unlike most of the paradigms of consultation with which we are familiar, the therapist using this type of consultation follows virtually the same processes and approaches that he or she would when evaluating and treating individuals or families. The consultative process can be described in a four-step procedure. The consultant

1. Locates or conceptualizes the presenting problem, which is simply the sense and order the consultant makes out of the information he or she obtains. This includes a clarification of the consultee's complaints and requests, and the consultant's per-

sonal hypothesis regarding the behaviors, interactions, or viewpoints comprising the problem or impasse. This personal overview may or may not be directly revealed to the consultee.

2. Clarifies his or her own personal goals and interventive strategies or tactics (vis-à-vis the impasse).
3. Intervenes (attempts to interdict the behavior and/or viewpoints comprising or sustaining the impasse.
4. Follows up and evaluates.

The examples that follow are merely brief illustrations designed to further clarify the nature, focus, and processes of systemic interactional consultation. Although the paradigm is rather simple to characterize and although its basic premises can be easily grasped, the leap from premise to application is neither simple nor easy. The reader should be aware that in our experience the most common reason why therapists reject a treatment or consultative paradigm is the experience of having unsuccessfully tried the viewpoint without sufficient prior experience and supervision. This usually leads to a rationalization that focuses upon the inadequacies of the theoretical perspective rather than the recognition of the need to develop skill in the application of the paradigm.

Example 1

The therapist is aware of increasing personal anxiety. He recognizes that as a result he has become variably overactive or underreactive in the therapeutic sessions. In presenting to the consultant, the therapist proposes that the patient reminds him of his mother and that the basis of his countertransference may be a direct result of his incomplete differentiation from his family of origin. He says that even though he believes he is on the verge of a major therapeutic breakthrough, he finds himself unable to maintain professional distance.

The consultant presses the therapist/consultee to describe where in the therapy session he begins to experience anxiety. He replies that he is not certain. Out of the consultative interchange, the following picture emerges: As the consultee begins to experience an elevation in anxiety, he becomes increasingly introspective and passive, but occasionally overreactive.

Typically, when a therapist/consultee presents with a psychoanalytic or psychodynamic perspective, there is a tendency on the part of many interactional therapists to become oppositional to such a viewpoint. Although in our experience this is changing, more traditionally oriented therapists have therefore either tended to avoid using interactionally oriented consultation or have referred family members of the patients they are treating to the family therapist, although often not consciously aware or at least publicly acknowledging that this maneuver was designed to alter a therapeutic impasse.

That the consultee is not a systemic interactional therapist is not a contraindication for consultation. However, as a general rule, the interactional consultant should have an understanding of and/or expertise in the framework utilized by the therapist/consultee, or the consultee should have a sufficient familiarity with the consultant's theoretical orientation(s) so that he can present within that frame. When possible, the interactional consultant is advised to use the "language" and, hence, the therapeutic frame of the consultee (Greenberg, 1980, p. 316).

In the above example, the consultant conceptualized the problem and impasse to be a consequence of the therapist's viewpoint—a view wherein the therapist's prerequisite for solving the impasse rested with the resolution of his own internal conflicts.

The consultant privately hypothesized that with such a perspective the therapist had identified himself as the patient, in effect behaving in a manner, that whether passive or overreactive, was focused on treatment for himself as a prerequisite for the treatment of his patient. In the process the therapist was viewed defining his passivity and/or overactivity as a spontaneous (unconsciously motivated) response to the insoluble anxiety. In other words, his loss of professional distance, his selection of therapeutic activity and direction, was viewed as secondary to the anxiety and underlying conflict and hence his personal behavior was defined by him as, if not directly out of control, at least not effectively in control.

The consultant moved to alter the therapist's view by attempting to modify the behavior by prescribing the behavior. (It is interesting to note that the consultant does not confront the therapist's viewpoint directly because a "be spontaneous problem" is best solved by what can later be viewed by the client as a spontaneous solution, and the therapist has clearly noted that it is the unconscious components that are generating the impasse.)

The consultant agreed with the therapist that he indeed had the problem described; that yes, it appears that he is at a critical point in treatment where major gains can be made. The consultant stressed it was obvious that for this to occur, the therapist must utilize his own personal needs for resolution lest he magnify the problem. He went on to point out that regrettably he had been unable to find any basic or fundamental differences with the therapist's approach or his formulation. Apologetically he noted that he had but an intuitive hunch. He verbalized once again his regret that his ideas were based on nothing more than intuition. Nevertheless, he recommended that during the next one to three therapy sessions, when the therapist became aware that his anxiety was highly elevated, he, at that point, intentionally become increasingly passive. The consultant went on to say that although the consultee's anxiety levels would probably remain high, it appeared that increased passivity would allow him to get a better handle on the nature of his own conflicts. Additionally, the consultant suggested, on the basis of the consultee's reporting, that there was a great likelihood that his high level of anxiety had probably fostered greater distortions than he was currently aware of and that in the consultant's opinion, increased passivity might allow him more time for introspection or at least more time to attend to the patient's productions. In any case, he contended that both avenues might lead to further insight into the matter. The consultation terminated with the consultant again emphasizing the importance of the therapist's trusting his own feelings and recognizing them as legitimate although reflecting conflict.

Several sessions following the consultation, the therapist phoned the consultant to report that although he had not gleaned any major new insight, his patient had made a therapeutic breakthrough. He suggested however, that he did recognize that his previous overactivity had intruded into the patient's productions and that a more passive stance had allowed for a positive change in the sessions. Nevertheless, he noted he was still having difficulties in dealing with the features of the countertransference.

Example 2

Consultation is requested by the therapist who reports that she has been treating a 20-year-old female who presents with a history of anorexia and bulimia. The consultee's chief complaint is that every time she attempts to define the problem that might be worked on, the patient seems at first to agree with the formulation, and then changes her mind. The consultation is requested to help clarify the diagnosis, about which the therapist appears quite certain, and more specifically, to help delineate what is blocking the process. A joint interview was arranged with the consultant, therapist, and patient.

Traditionally, the consultant's function has not been viewed as directly treating the patient. Within the interactional perspective, not only is this acceptable but it appears to have become a normative procedure for the consultant to observe the therapist treating the patient, and vice versa. The consultant, however, must not deviate from his or her primary function, which is to facilitate a change in viewpoint and/or behavior, thereby altering the nature of the impasse or altering the impasse itself.

During the 1½-hour consultative/treatment session that followed, the consultant viewed the impasse to revolve around the patient–

therapist interaction. The patient presented as intent, helpful, and desirous to find solution for a host of problems. Each time the therapist moved to restate the patient's formulation, the patient would move to top her by ever so slightly restating the problem or suggesting that yes, that was the problem, but there was a more important one. In short, the therapist persisted with the view that she could get agreement from a patient who would look like she was agreeing, but never would; and both persisted with behavior wherein the therapist had joined the patient in an ongoing power struggle.

The consultant's goal was to modify the viewpoint and interrupt the behavior comprising the power struggle. He did this by reframing the problem and then prescribing the symptoms and the behaviors. The consultant reported to the therapist in the presence of the patient that the nature of the problem was "trumpcarditis," that the patient would never agree to clear identification of her problem nor treatment because the diagnosis had been incomplete. The consultant noted that a more complete diagnosis, such as he was now offering, would focus on the centrality of how frequently the patient would play her trump card, which was the activity of *agreeing, then disagreeing* with the therapist. The patient agreed with the consultant that this was, well maybe, the problem. The consultant suggested to the patient that she would most likely change her mind between this consultation and her next therapy session and this would confirm the diagnosis.

The consultee, in conference after the joint session, agreed with the consultant and reported that now that she knew the problem, she was no longer going to continue to have to define the nature of it. Besides, she noted, "I'd be surprised if I could get a treatment contract from this patient."

Example 3

A typical request for consultation comes frequently from therapists who choose to continue to treat couples in conjoint marital treatment, even though nothing seems to change. The therapists work harder and harder to facilitate a change in the "marital condition," but the harder they work, the less they see accomplished. The following consultation was arranged around just such a circumstance.

The husband was described as hostile, bitter, and passive aggressive and the wife as soft-spoken, sensitive, with a history of depression and accompanying hysterical features. She had been treated individually for three months. Her depression was characterized as greatly reduced. The therapist then began a course of conjoint treatment. He indicated he would have initiated it earlier, but it was only into the third month of individual treatment that he was able to motivate the husband to attend. The conjoint marital treatment (once weekly) was now in its sixth month.

The reason for the consultation was that the therapist believed that he could accomplish no more. He complained of how difficult it was to hold the husband in treatment. In essence, he felt defeated, was worn down, and had recently thought it best just to stop treatment and refer his patients to individual therapists. The rationale for this was that (1) conjoint treatment was no longer effective; (2) further individual treatment with each spouse was indicated; and (3) he believed he had contaminated his alliance with the wife by moving into a conjoint format.

The basic questions posed by the consultee were (1) Do you concur that treatment should be terminated and the patients referred to other therapists? and (2) Are there any indications that a change of treatment strategy would be effective in modifying the impasse described?

The therapist/consultee resided several hundred miles away in another state. To avoid the costs of travel and so forth, the consultee was asked to forward a videotape of a recent session that would demonstrate the kinds of difficulties typically encountered. An agreement was reached that the consultee would later send a tape of the session following the consultation.

The advent of videotape has literally revolutionized aspects of treatment, training, and consultation. Not only can one directly observe the process of treatment and consultation, but a consultant can review tapes from consultees who are thousands of miles away. In addition, phone consultation even with large agency groups can be carried out by a conference phone hookup with the therapist/consultee and consultant almost simultaneously referring to and reviewing taped segments during the conference call.

The tape aptly demonstrated an interactional sequence where the therapist, for the most part, managed to block husband and wife from dealing with each other. It appeared on almost every occasion that husband and wife were beginning to talk and negotiate around issues of substance and anger was intimated or overtly presented, the therapist would interrupt, raise a question, or clarify a point. There was hardly a sequence of interchange between husband and wife that was allowed to continue beyond 30 seconds. The longest sequence before the therapist found a way to interrupt was two minutes, ten seconds.

The consultant conceptualized the impasse as an outcome of the therapist's behavior. The consultant's goal was to help the therapist get out of the middle of the spouse–spouse interaction. The attempted intervention was in the form of a letter.

Dear Paul:

In my experience, following a period of individual treatment with a female patient, when a shift is made to a conjoint format, the male often presents with increased passive–aggressive features and enters a power struggle with the therapist for his mate. Most often he is afraid, jealous, and feeling inadequate that he has failed where the therapist has succeeded.

He is typically relating a treatment plan and position of "I want my wife back. I am the husband." I don't know that this applies here, but a simple manner to test the hypothesis is to allow the spouses to deal directly with each other for longer and longer periods, supporting the husband to assert in places where you have asserted previously. You have already modeled this successfully in sessions for both husband and wife, and I believe the husband is now saying, "I am ready to assert more than you."

To support him in this, I would recommend that you not immediately get out of the middle between husband and wife. Rather, if you agree, this can be accomplished subtly by shifting the frequency of treatment from weekly sessions to one session every two, three, or four weeks.

I would add that you should consider modulating your activity in the sessions, staying in the middle for longer and/or shorter periods. I regret, however, to relate that after such modulation, most therapists often recognize that the couple is fighting more. This is frequently misinterpreted as regression rather than the next big step in the conjoint treatment process. When viewed as regression, the therapist leaps into the middle to try to hold the marriage together. This is obviously something that only the spouses individually could accomplish, but therapists get snookered.

When viewed as the next step in the treatment process, the therapist allows the couple to deal with each other. Looking forward to your follow-up tape and feedback.

                                                        Best regards,

Space does not permit an in-depth discussion of the second tape forwarded after the consultation. However, a few comments are in order: (1) The therapist used the first eight to ten minutes of the tape to discuss his view about the consultant's letter and (2) The tape demonstrated a definite shift in posture on the part of the therapist; he indeed began to avoid the seduction of interrupting, leaving the husband and wife to increasingly deal with each other.

Example 4

Within the emergency psychiatric unit of a large metropolitan hospital, the chief therapist seeks out consultation regarding a 25-year-old black male "paranoid schizophrenic patient" whom he has treated over the past 6 weeks. This morning the patient had been brought to the psychiatric unit by the police. He had been transferred from jail, where he had been placed 3 days before and was awaiting trial for stealing beef

from a major retail grocery outlet. He was described by the police as
"crazy as hell," uncooperative, increasingly agitated, screaming for hours
on end, and generally yelling about things that appeared incomprehensible.

The reason for the consultation was that the therapist had become
incensed during the 45-minute interview he was just completing. He
noted that he was unable to engage the patient in productive interchange. It appeared that no matter what he attempted, the patient
would consistently mumble a delusional refrain about the FBI and
something about the powerful machines the FBI had used on him to get
him to steal.

The therapist appeared to have encountered the same type of
behavior the police had described and thus had considerable difficulty in
making any recommendation other than hospitalization. His reason for
consultation revolved around his recognition that his rage and ineffectiveness in negotiating with the patient were not primary indices for
hospitalization. However, he noted that without further information,
he could not be certain of the patient's mental status and hospitalization
would be indicated for observation. Additionally, he queried whether an
"interactional approach" might facilitate matters.

Following a brief discussion with the therapist, the consultant
privately hypothesized that the impasse revolved around the therapist's
attempts to confront or attack the patient's delusional system. This, he
anticipated, had promoted an antagonistic interactional set and had
blocked any working alliance with the patient.

According to the hypothesis, the tactical error in the interview was
an attempt to invalidate the patient's perspective rather than utilizing
the view itself to enlarge or modify the perspective. This is a typical
problem most frequently seen with therapists treating patients who
present with fixed delusional systems. In our experience, the delusional
material may be conceptualized as one's worldview, and the therapist or
consultant may work within it as he or she would within the worldview
of "nondelusional patients."

The therapist and consultant agreed to a joint 10- to 15-minute
interview with the patient, who had remained in the interview room
while the therapist sought consultation. The basic ground rule that the
consultant requested of his colleague was that he not say anything
during the consultation unless asked. If he felt there were something of
great importance to be discussed, it was agreed he would ask for a
conference outside of the interview room. The reason for this request is
that often where joint interviewing occurs, the consultee will either go
in the opposite direction of the consultant or interrupt that direction
before the consultant therapist has an opportunity to develop his position and attempt intervention. This type of maneuver frequently results

in the therapist and patient aligning against the consultant. Such a joining maneuver can be promoted by the consultant himself, but in this circumstance, it was not in the consultant's plan.

Entering the room with the therapist, the consultant immediately and in a slow, understated manner, introduced himself to the patient. He then gently, but firmly, related, "I think it only fair that I clear some things up right from the beginning. I understand that the FBI has something to do with this case and I have no G— d— use for those m— f—s. All those bastards do is invade privacy, cause trouble, force themselves on others, and so forth. So if you think I am going to have one positive thing to say in regards to those m— f—s, forget it."

The consultee appeared startled. The tension in the room was broken by a wide smile that erupted on the patient's face. The consultant now turned to the patient (as if addressing him rather than the therapist) and said, "I heard from your doctor that the cops brought you in this morning. Have those m— f—s been hassling you?" The patient replied, "No!" The consultant continued, "You told your doctor the cops grabbed ya for stealing meat." The patient interrupted, "Yea, the FBI made me do it." The therapist continued: "I told you I hated those bastards. Would you mind keeping them out of the conversation for awhile? By the way, was that good meat you stole?"

PATIENT: Yes.

CONSULTANT: How do you know? Did you cook it up?

PATIENT: No. I just knew it.

CONSULTANT: So what happened?

PATIENT: The FBI hooked me to those big m— f— machines they have. They forced me, they made me do it.

CONSULTANT: (angrily) They did what?

PATIENT: They took me away and connected me to those giant machines and forced me . . .

CONSULTANT: (turning to the consultee) Did you ask the patient for his FBI ID card or badge, or at least a check stub to show the money he received for his work?

CONSULTEE: No.

CONSULTANT: (to the patient) Okay, please show us your badge or ID or check stub from the FBI.

PATIENT: I ain't got none.

CONSULTANT: (to the consultee) Those m— f— bastard FBI people have this poor m— f— working for them and they conned this poor SOB to work for nothing . . . Boy, it not only pisses me off, but I told you those G— d— people were not worth a damn.

CONSULTANT: (to the patient) Are you going to continue to work for those lousy, cheap bastards or do you want to be a man?

PATIENT: I want to be a man.

CONSULTANT: How are you going to show that?

PATIENT: I'm going to go to the local TV stations and tell them the FBI has connected me to those machines and made me steal. I'll get them to put it on the tube, and when it's known, the FBI will have to let me go.

CONSULTANT: That's a very good idea.

PATIENT: (*Nods agreement.*)

CONSULTANT: But I see one minor problem. I know the kinds of machines the FBI has and how powerful these FBI people can be . . . and if you go public with private information and breach their security, they will stick their meat hooks deeper and deeper into you. You break security and they'll never let you free. Do you want to work for those m— f—s or do you want to be a man?

PATIENT: I want to be a man.

CONSULTANT: I'll tell you how to be the real man that you say you want to be, but only a real man would be able to pull it off. It would be difficult and stressful. You might even feel as if they were driving you crazy when you do it, but only a real man would try it and only a real man could succeed.

PATIENT: What? I coud do it!

CONSULTANT: Well, you would have to tell the FBI to take their G— d— machines and to stuff them up their . . . They will continue to use those machines. It will be difficult as hell 'cause those m— f— FBI people do favors for no one. Do you want to work for the FBI or be a free man?

PATIENT: A man!

CONSULTANT: Well, let's stop here to see what you do. The way I figure it, though, (*turning to the consultee*) is that he would rather be a slave for those people and work for nothing.

PATIENT: No!

The following day the consultant returned to the psychiatric unit and ran into the patient, who had returned to pick up an item he had inadvertently left when discharged by his therapist from the emergency unit following the consultation. The consultant asked him if he were still working for those bastards. He said no. A 3-month follow-up with the therapist/consultee suggested the following: The patient had quit working for the FBI, appropriately reduced therapeutic contacts, and began working part-time elsewhere.

Summary and Conclusion

The primary function of the interactional consultant is to influence, where appropriate, a change in the behavior or viewpoint of the therapist/consultee, his or her patient(s), or both, thereby altering the nature of the therapeutic impasse or the impasse itself. To accomplish this, the consultant must be able to rather rapidly gather enough information to conceptualize the nature of the impasse. The conceptualization itself must be formulated in such a way as to make the impasse approachable to intervention. The consultant's formulation must first take into account a clear picture of the consultee's complaint(s) and requests and, secondly, his or her own hypotheses (in the form of a clear, private statement to himself) on the viewpoints and behaviors that constitute the impasse, his consultative goals, and interventive tactics.

Regretfully, in writing about the consultative process, which is virtually the same process employed in other forms of brief systemic interactional therapy with families and individuals, the reader is often left with the incorrect idea that the interactional therapist is insensitive, nonempathic, or solely cognitive, and furthermore that the process is a one-move or one-shot operation. Whether or not the consultative format entails one session or five, one must be aware that consultation is an empirical process wherein the consultant is consistently utilizing his personal sensitivities while establishing and modifying his or her own thinking. Hence, conceptualizations are modified and reformulated as the consultant tests his or her hypotheses and interventive tactics.

When the theory, processes, and techniques that constitute the systemic interactional perspective are mastered, they can be integrated into almost any therapeutic or consultative format providing the following conditions obtain:

1. The therapist and/or consultant are clear on their own theoretical perspectives. Therapists trained in several therapeutic perspectives often will attempt to consult or treat out of one framework while shifting to a second. The result is that they lose sight of the paradigm, which if properly utilized, helps to define the nature and meaning of the material gathered and suggests interventive directions. When the paradigms are mixed, the therapist finds him- or herself in a confusing situation that often leads to a consultative or treatment impasse.

2. The consultant and/or therapist should be flexible and have a working familiarity of the paradigm they are using. In consultation the consultant should have an understanding of and/or expertise in the framework utilized by the therapist/consultee or the consultee should have a basis of familiarity with the consultant's orientation such that he can present within that frame. Where possible, the consultant should use the language and, hence, the therapeutic framework of the consultee.

3. Interventive tactics must be based on appropriately gathered information. Impulsive recommendations or cookbook approaches based solely on "clinical hunches" or "citations in the literature" or "on activities one has observed other therapists doing" are not considered a sufficient rationale to validate intervention.

4. The consultant and therapist must be aware there is a potential risk with any intervention and one must cautiously measure the potential danger to the patient, family, consultee, and other members of the social network before intervening.

REFERENCES

Berlin, I. N. Mental health consultation to child-serving agencies as therapeutic intervention. In S. I. Harrison (Ed.), *Basic Handbook of child psychiatry* (Vol. 3: *Therapeutic interventions*). New York: Basic Books, 1979.

Caplan. G. *The theory and practice of mental health consultation.* New York: Basic Books, 1970.

Fisch, R., Weakland, J., & Segal, L. *The tactics of change: Doing brief therapy.* San Francisco: Jossey-Bass 1982.

Greenberg, G. S. *Conjoint family theory: An entree to a new behavior therapy.* Doctoral dissertation, Tulane University, 1974.

Greenberg, G. S. The family interactional perspective: A study and examination of the work of Don D. Jackson. *Family Process*, 1977, *16*, 358–412.

Greenberg, G. S. Problem-focused brief family interactional psychotherapy. In L. R. Wolberg & M. L. Aronson (Eds.), *Group and family therapy.* New York: Brunner/Mazel 1980.

Greenberg, G. S. The beginning family therapist and dilemmas in diagnosis. In J. C. Hanson & B. P. Keeney (Eds.), *Diagnosis and assessment in family therapy: The family therapy collections.* Rockville, Md.: Aspen Systems, 1983.

Haley, J. *Uncommon therapy: The psychiatric techniques of Milton H. Erickson, M.D.* New York: Norton, 1973.

Haley, J. *Problem solving theapy: New strategies for effective family therapy.* San Francisco: Jossey-Bass 1976.

Watzlawick, P., Weakland, J., & Fisch, R. *Change: Principles of problem formation and problem resolution.* New York: Norton, 1974.

Weakland, J. H. OK—you've been a bad mother. In P. Papp (Ed.), *Family therapy: Full length case studies.* New York: Gardner Press, 1977.

Weakland, J. H., Fisch, R., Watzlawick P., & Bodin, A. M. Brief therapy: Focused problem resolution. *Family Process*, 1974, *13*, 147–168.

4

Social networks and family therapy

ROSS V. SPECK
Jefferson Medical College

> *Extreme remedies are necessary for extreme diseases.*—Hippocrates

History

Early in my psychiatric residency training (1953) in New York State, an edict was issued from the Department of Mental Hygiene that group therapy would be done in all New York State Hospitals. This order was passed down from the director of the hospital, to the assistant directors, to the clinical director, and down through all the levels of the system to the first-year residents at the bottom. Before long I found myself facing a group of about 25 psychotic women on a chronic service. Another group assigned to me were postlobotomy patients. In a few months, my anxiety had subsided, and I was beginning to learn something about the workings of large groups. What one learns early in a career tends to have a determining direction for the future.

Later at the Philadelphia General Hospital and in the army at Brooke General Army Hospital, I continued working and learning in group therapy with many groups.

In order to get the best existing training, after residency and the army, I started my psychoanalytic training in Philadelphia and graduated some 8 years later as a psychoanalyst. However, during this entire period, I was a research psychiatrist in family therapy of schizophrenic families.

I began working with schizophrenic families in their own homes in 1958, on a National Institute of Mental Health (NIMH) demonstration project, "Family Treatment of Schizophrenia in the Home," with Alfred S. Friedman, PhD, as program director. During the next 7 years, our cotherapy teams saw several hundred families, each with one or more diagnosed schizophrenic family members. The goal was to study and treat the family on a regular basis, avoid hospitalization, and in the great majority of cases, to use no medication.

Early in our work with these families, our cotherapy teams observed that certain families failed to make progress because the healthiest-appearing member of the family would be absent from the home on the night of the family therapy. Frequently, a trivial reason would be given, such as he or she went to the movies, had a date, was studying for an examination, and so forth. The family would collude with the absent family member, and we found this a potent resistance to family change. We named this resistance the "absent member maneuver" (Sonne, Speck, & Jungreis, 1962).

In other families we found extended family members, such as aunts, uncles, grandparents, and even family advisors, such as lawyers, priests, doctors, could have a potent resistant effect upon the course of family therapy if they absented themselves from the family sessions. One uncle made a secret contract with a family that he would pay for their therapy if after each session the family would report back to him for a type of debriefing. This uncle steadfastly refused to attend the family therapy sessions, and even took the precaution of inventing a pseudonym so that he could not be contacted. In another family the parish priest colluded with a 19-year-old schizophrenic boy by agreeing with the family's opinion that the boy was infested with demons. He further stated that the problem was one for specialists in the Vatican, rather than for family therapy.

We began to see that difficult family problems often stretch beyond the family into larger extended family groupings. One way of resolving therapeutic impasses in a family is to expand the group by inviting family relatives and friends to the therapy sessions in the home.

At about this time, in 1964, I read Elizabeth Bott's (1957/1971) *Family and Social Network.* It reported an important research project's study of 20 "ordinary" British families and their surrounding social networks. The concept of a social network, or "tribe," mediating between the family and the larger society seemed an important step forward in dealing with families having gotten stuck in problems of symbiosis, suicidal preoccupation, marital impasse, or schizophrenia.

The work of British anthropologists (see Barnes, 1954) gave me a concept that I could translate into clinical terms, so that by 1966, I had assembled a "family of families," as they called themselves, a network, a tribe, and I was conducting weekly network meetings with a family having a young chronic schizophrenic member. Since then, my col-leagues Joan Lincoln Speck; Carolyn Attneave, PhD; Uri Rueveni, PhD; David Trimble, PhD; Muriel Wiener, MSW; and others have done social network interventions (also called "network therapy") on over 50 networks. Network size varies from 40 to over 100 persons. Thus, several thousand persons have participated in network meetings.

Technique

We usually meet in the house of the family that requests network intervention. The intervention team has a leader, called intervenor, an assistant who is skilled in rapid and brief encounter techniques, and two or three other team members whom we call consultants. It is necessary to have a team because of the great complexity of having 40 to 60 people simultaneously interacting. The team wanders about, collects gossip and group process, and is the catalytic agent that encourages the network to take on its tasks. The team's role resembles that of the shaman or medicine man—not the tribal chief. It is the network that helps the family to change.

The family contacts a member of the intervention team, usually when other methods have failed—hospital, therapy, family therapy. The team usually does a home visit with the family to assess the problem, get acquainted, to see the layout of the house and what furniture might have to be moved, and so forth. The family is instructed to call all their friends, relatives, neighbors, and anyone else who might be helpful to them. A time is set, usually for 7:30 P.M., in about a week. They are instructed to call support persons for every family member and just to tell them that a tribal meeting is being held and that the family needs the network's help to solve the difficult problem and that a professional team will assist the tribe to do the work. We have found, empirically, that a minimum of about 40 persons is necessary and we inform the index family of this.

The following phases of a network intervention session occur in a spiral, as described in *Family Networks* (Speck & Attneave, 1973):

1. The intervention team arrives about an hour early at the family home to meet people as they arrive, move furniture, get permissions for recording or generally get acquainted. We now do one to three network meetings (at 2-week intervals if three sessions are contracted). When the tribe has assembled, the intervenor gives a short talk on tribes and the reasons for assembly. Then, the group is asked to hum or sing a song (usually ethnic to that group), or I prefer to war whoop and jump up and down and then follow this with silent swaying, holding hands. There are many ways to transform a crowd into a working group. A common bond developes. This phase is called *retribalization*.

2. Now we put the index family in the center of the room and ask each member to tell what he wants help with. We set up inner and outer competing subgroups—age versus youth, political differences, power versus powerlessness, male—female, and so forth. This produces *polarization*. People begin to speak out.

3. This leads to *mobilization* of the activists in the group. A group of

40 has about 6 indigenous leaders. They will also help organize and lead support subgroups.

4. Somewhere along, in any large-group process, comes a phase we call *resistance–depression*. The intervention team helps the group through this phase by changing the tempo of the meeting, encouragement, brief encounter techniques, or moving back to retribalization and polarization.

5. When network goals are reached, the whole tribe feels *break-through* has occurred.

6. This is followed by a feeling of satisfaction, *elation–exhaustion–termination*.

We find it very easy to identify what phase we are in, using the above scheme. Our goal is to progressively move through the six phases.

Definition of Networks[1]

Social network intervention is a clinical approach to difficult problems within a person or within his or her family, utilizing a professional team of two or more members as the catalyst, and from 40 to 100 friends, kin, or neighbors as the therapeutic agent. Certain editors have labeled the approach "network therapy," but there is consensus among workers in this field that network intervention is a more accurate term, in the same sense that crisis intervention is preferred to "crisis therapy."

I define a social network as that group of persons, family, neighbors, friends, significant others, who can play an ongoing important role in supporting and helping an index person or family. It is the layer surrounding the family unit that mediates between the family and the larger society. It is the remnants of the tribe in primitive societies. More modern equivalents are people who assemble at family reunions, cousins' clubs, weddings and funerals, or the older "shtetl" society.

Because little common language seems to have evolved among the network of network therapists that is rising to the surface of the therapeutic caldron, the following lexicon is proposed as a first step toward articulating theory.

Social matrix: The totality of social contacts and contexts of a person. The social matrix may be organized but also includes amorphous and unarticulated relationships, as well as various structures.

Nexus: That group of relatively enduring human relationships that maintain themselves in face-to-face contact. Such phenomena include, as type examples, the nuclear and commune family as well as work associations on an everyday basis. Also included are friends and neighbors and tradesmen who are highly visible in terms of both time and space. For instance, the woman who visits a neighbor for coffee every

1. Derived from joint work with Carolyn Attneave, PhD.

morning, or the man who stops at the bar or gas station regularly, have *nexus* relationships that can involve them in many aspects of one another's lives.

The primary contact of the *nexus* often gives entry into secondary human groups, so that there are at least two levels of contact that might be termed *nexuses*: the most intimate and personally idiosyncratic relationships of family and the enduring but less highly charged friendships and associations.

Vincula: The *vinculum* is the bond or tie connecting persons. The *vincula* between persons making up the nexus possess the most highly charged bonds and binds in human relationships.

Groups: *Groups* are human relationships in which vincula are arranged more or less loosely but which operate within tight formal roles. A *group* may have formal expression of its rules in a constitution and bylaws, or it may exist in a tradition shared and obeyed at an almost subliminal level. However, when called upon, any member can express fairly accurately the criteria for membership and exclusion and the typical activities engaged in by the associates.

Cluster: A *cluster* is an interface (interphase) between the nexus and the group. In a *cluster* human relationships have charged vincula which have more intimacy than in the total group, and less love–hate bonds and binds than in the family. *Clusters* can rapidly oscillate between the nexus and the group. They are less subject to codified rules and can sometimes dissolve entirely.

For example, in a psychiatric hospital, the medical director and the clinical director call a committee meeting (group) in which various department heads are asked to attend. The medical director and the clinical director and the research director are often personal friends and have social nexus relationships, including their wives and children, as well as the work associations. The purpose of the meeting may have been discussed in the home, over cocktails. After the formal meeting of the committee, in which each played assigned group roles, they may meet informally as a cluster to revalidate their experience. They now reexperience their experience of the meeting and will then tell the group what the group's experience has been. There are three relationships involved in this operation: the nexus, the cluster, and the group.

To see the relationships more clearly and particularly to see *clusters* in operation, watch who has coffee together, who is on the telephone to what persons, and who acts in a less visible way with other members of the formal group than those holding the normally ascribed roles. If one were to look for a photographic example of a group, one could hardly find a better illustration than the typical picture of the formal hierarchy of the Russian Communist Party on May Day anniversaries. To find a photographic representation of human clusters requires candid photos that reveal messages of intimacy, side views, huddles, rear views, corners of the room, and constantly shifting status and role relationships.

Plexus: A *plexus* is a person or small nexus that is the central focus or nucleus of relationships in a group, cluster, or network.

Network: A *network* is the total relational field of a person or plexus that usually has space–time representation. Although a network has a low degree of visibility, it has a high degree of information exchange properties. A network has few formal rules but consists of relationships between many persons, some of whom (plexuses) are known to many others in the network, whereas others merely form a *linkage* between persons, this linkage often being unknown to the two persons linked by the third person. (A may know B and B may know C, but B's common relationship to A and C may be unknown to both A and C.)

A network is much larger in size than a cluster or most groups. Funtionally network size runs from a minimum of about 15 to upwards of 100 persons. Over time, networks are represented by the multi-generational extended family; in contemporary space, networks are represented by friends, peers, and neighbors. Any individual's network is the sum of human relationships that have a lasting significance in their lives. Networks allow for relative freedom of mobility from the more fixed, codified, and regulated nexuses and groups. One might say that a cluster is to a network as a nexus is to a group.

Is the Nuclear Family a Myth?

Major shifts have been occuring in theoretical, practical, and psycho-therapy procedures in the last 25 years. The aim of therapy has switched from the individual to change in the family system. There is a turning away from earlier sociological concepts about the family to newer con-cepts out of systems theory and/or cultural anthropology. There is still a struggle for a family typology, nomenclature, or even a family diag-nosis system.

In the past families have been classified as nuclear, origin, procrea-tion, or extended. These terms are not as clear cut or descriptive as every day usage would suggest. The extended family bears some similarity to the term *tribe*, which most lay people at least assume is a kinship system, rather than a network of persons who share a common worldview.

The extended family system is usually thought of as most active in Asia, Africa, India, or in certain simpler societies. The "nuclear family" is thought of as descriptive of Western families and consists of the father and mother and minor children born to or adopted by the parents. The "family of origin" is the nuclear family one is born into, whereas the "family of procreation" consists of the conjugal couple and their children (adult and minor and adopted). The nuclear family structure has been thought to characterize modern (particularly Western) societies, whereas in simpler societies, the multigenerational and other kinship and friendship groups play a more important role in life.

Many family therapists have defined a "family" as all those persons living and interacting in the same household, although this does not account for married offspring or other close kin living out of the home. A further complication today in the Western family is the high divorce and remarriage rate in the United States, with some families having three or four marriages of each spouse and children from multiple liaisons, entering and leaving the various homes to stay, visit, or holiday. One such family reportedly had over 20 marriages of the (adult) child's parents.

African traditional society includes in the family children, parents, grandparents, uncles, aunts, brothers and sisters with their children, other relatives, and dead relatives—the "living dead." The latter are alive in the surviving family member's memories and are thought to be still interested in the affairs of the family. The extended family is thought of as a loving surround of the individual enveloping him or her in love and care, supplying a network of social duties, responsibilities, and expectations.

The Western family is often described in nuclear terms—the mother, father, and children. The extended family is often invisible. Emphasis is on conjugality rather than consanguinity.

According to Uzoka (1979), Ferreira has shown that family myths are to relationships within and about the family as the concept of personality defense mechanisms are to the individual. Uzoka advances the brilliant thesis that the early Industrial Revolution produced radical family separations in the 17th to 19th centuries in Western Europe. Because myths may function as defense mechanisms in times of family chaos and disorder—what we now know of psychological defenses following separations, death and divorce—it does not seem too preposterous to suggest that the Western Industrial Revolution created a massive repression and denial process that emerged as the modern nuclear family. The myth of the nuclear family was thus the attempt to heal the pain and utter anguish of separation by denying the existence of the extended family network. It may be that the high divorce rate today is a reaction to a disappointment with the myth of the (non-existent?) nuclear family. And maybe we are headed back to a larger, extended, new kind of network family—friends, neighbors, kin, other support persons. But first, the loneliness, the anomie, the loss and abandonment increases in the form of a single parent, the swinging singles, the unmarried—until a generation or two has experimented with enough human groupings to come up with a new family type and style, content and context. There is every indication that the new family will be a network family and much more similar to the older extended family than to the present disintegrating nuclear family.

One must ask why so many family therapists today have just discovered the nuclear family when it is about to disappear (if it ever existed). But why are therapists so reluctant to explore the extended family, the tribes, and networks as a logical sequel to understanding the human condition? Litwak (1959), Sussman (1959), and others have reported that the nuclear family is usually embedded in networks of extended kin, supplying functions of mutual aid both physical and financial, support during rituals or crises, help with child care, shopping, building, or household tasks. Family members turn to kin before social agencies are contacted.

The social and existential philosopher and psychiatrist David Cooper (1970) has observed that people are glued to each other in the family, and the process of separating requires coming to terms with one's entire family past. This involves getting rid of internalized parts of people and relationships—a process that Cooper calls "a progressive depopulation of the room." Presumably this process occurs within the therapist as well. Finally, two people—the therapist and patient—are left in the room, free to decide whether to embark on further therapy.

I have known Cooper and some of his work since 1964, and feel that he deals with intrapsychic networks in a very similar way to those of us dealing with the kin–neighbor–friend–helpers-we-know networks. Accordingly, a repopulation context of therapy, suggested originally by Uzoka, is also an appropriate treatment orientation. Therapists with an individual belief system will ask family members to leave the room, whereas therapists with a family intervention orientation will encourage the patients to bring into the therapy as many persons as possible who may help the problem. The entire social network of a person or family— all those persons who may be called upon to help in a difficult crisis—as many as 100 or more persons may assemble.

Clinical and Theoretical Implications of Network Therapy

In the earlier years of social network intervention, I met with the network for much longer periods of time than is now customary. It was a transition from large group psychotherapy and multiple family therapy to our present network method. Much can still be learned from long-term work, although it is not time-economical for 40 or more persons to meet weekly to help someone.

The "A" family consisted of a 19-year-old son and his 55-year-old mother. There had been trouble since his birth. The mother said that when she was handed the baby at his birth, he let out a piercing scream and cried continuously for the next 6 months. "It was hate at first sight." Her husband had died suddenly while she was pregnant. The pregnancy had not been planned. At 6 months of age, the son was diagnosed at a well-known clinic as having infantile autism. Dozens of psychiatrists and psychologists were consulted over the years. Mother and son argued and quarreled constantly. He had no friends but became an expert on the local transportation system from an early age. From the age of 17, he refused to leave their small row home. He learned to tie his shoes at 12 and his tie at 17 and did little for himself and nothing for the household.

After a home visit in which he was reluctantly interviewed in the basement, I made arrangements with his mother to have everyone she and her relatives knew come to their home in the evening about a week later. The stated goal was to do something for the son and mother. Although it was not clearly articulated, both seemed to be asking for separation from their symbiotic state.

At the first meeting, about 40 persons showed up, filling the hall, stairs, dining room, and living room. Most of the group were friends of extended family or friends of their friends. A few were almost total strangers who had heard about the meeting. It would turn out to be a novel way for them to get a "back door" entrance into psychotherapy.

The group talked animately about how to solve the family's problem. They arranged future meetings, meanwhile learning about the extent of the problem. They began to refer to themselves as a family of families. The network grew, so that by the third meeting, the front door had to be closed on several people lined up to get in. A few people shouted that they did not have a network. We continued meeting for 2 to 3 hours and the group stayed on when I left, to continue discussions.

The meetings were lively and sometimes acrimonious. Leaders appeared in the group who were labelled activists. By the tenth session, a subgroup formed who announced they would bring cars, move the son and his belongings, rent an apartment, and act as a continuous support group to both the son and mother. The son looked dazed; the mother was alarmed. She cried that he could not even open a can of food for himself, "He'll starve." Nevertheless, he was moved into a small apartment. The group set up a schedule of visits and planned outings.

In a few weeks, group discussion focussed on employment for this hapless, seemingly hopeless boy. Someone in the network knew someone who had an uncle who had a friend who supervised cleanup in a public park. The job paid $1.00 per hour for 10 hours weekly. Even that was overpay because he did not know how to work or apparently did not care to know. He slept on the job, usually when the boss came around. However, as part of the job, he got a large badge that said "Recreation Department." He promptly pinned this over his genitals. The network and others tried to point out that this was not appropriate. "Badges belong over the heart."

The following episode taught me how networks produce change— if only by the overwhelming alternatives they make possible. A fortyish woman arrived a little early at one of the network meetings. She was very anxious and hypomanic. Having heard about the network in a mental hospital from which she had been discharged that day, she came looking for help for herself. She asked me for permission to attend the meeting and then suddenly took both of my hands and cupped each on her breasts, looking up at me like a little girl while she clasped her hands behind her back. And there I was, greeting new arrivals at the meeting. When I slowly removed my hands, the lady saw the recreation button and grabbed for it. The boy turned scarlet, bent over, and in less than 5 minutes, his button was pinned over his heart.

After further meetings the network found several different supervised jobs for him. Two years later he was a cab driver. In this network during a 6-month period, 11 persons changed jobs and 3 temporary marital separations occurred, while 4 persons requested referral for psychotherapy.

What Is a Network?

As Jay (1964) indicates, there are two different uses of the term "network" in the literature. In the sense that a network is conceived as a piece of a totality of relationships, it is similar to the formulations of Bott's (1957/1971) and also to Lewin's (1952) concept of social field. It consists of a unit looking outward at other units, some of which are also looking towards each other, some not. From the point of view of any given unit, the system is boundless, because A may have a relationship with B, and beyond that B may relate to C. But A may have no relationship with C, and C may have relationships with other units, D and E. Only if we traced out all relationships would we arrive at a definite boundary. In one sense the boundary of the system of A's point of view is B; from C's point of view, it is B, D, and E. These are the limits of A's and C's interactions. But they are not true boundaries, as the interaction patterns can go on indefinitely in many directions. All the units in this type of system are considered equivalent; there is no hierarchy and no real center. Every unit is a center, in an "egocentric" sense. A network can also be defined as the totality of all units connected by a certain type of relationship, nonegocentric, with definite boundaries, and units that are not necessarily equivalent. For our purposes "networks" can be both bounded and unbounded, with equivalent or nonequivalent units, noncentered, centered, or artificially centered.

Change: Hypotheses and Goals

I have tried to show changes in part of the network at the time of the initiation of the network meetings and a period of 6 months later.

"Change" is meant as an overall subjective impression of physical and emotional closeness or distance, including the following: actual physical separation; attempted physical separation; threatened physical separation; seating arrangements in the network; direct or indirect verbal rebellious attempts to separate; statements about separation; verbal attempts at closeness; increased physical contact; statements about perception of closeness; directed communications; and affect changes including tonality changes, behavioral changes, cooperation and disruption in the total network, and changes in the network climate.

Beside the changes between various units of the partial network, it can be seen that the "knittedness" of the partial net became more complex. My hypothesis was that in any social organization, the maintenance of the organized state occurs not only by conforming to overt rules but also by collusive bonds and binds, secret alliances, and relationships that are shared by various members of the organization, resulting in advantages and power, or status positions, which occur in the market place of human relationships. Thus, where A may know B, and B knows C, A knows nothing of the relationship between B and C. Over time, in network meetings, the relationships among various persons in an individual's environment tend to shape the relationship that the individual has with them, and consequently, his or her behavior. My plan was to make the social field of the mother and son, referred to previously, as explicit as possible and to break up as many binds and collusions that rendered the pair of them underprivileged.

During the 6-month period, many changes occurred, not only in network relationships but, for example, in group process, focal themes, and the exposure of secrets and collusions. Over time, network members became more intimate and specific about their problems. From an initial group of 30 members, a stable group of 15 to 20 members evolved. Some of the topics discussed involved parental authority, adolescent autonomy, symbiotic binds between parents and children, similarity of temperament among various members of the family, husband and wife interaction in disciplining children, the alienation of the modern family, and such family roles as family boss, family angel, head of the clan, family sinner, and the sick child. Perhaps the most significant change was the loosening of the symbiotic bind between the schizophrenic son and his mother and the maintenance of some distance between them. This could be greatly attributable to the closer relationships the mother formed with some other members of the network. The network was able to support her by helping her to contain her anxiety. The son was able to form separate attachments in the network more fully as an individual, and he made attempts to grow in several ways: He obtained his own apartment, obtained a new job, asked questions concerning the dating of girls, and so forth.

In a network, many of the binds within the individual family and between the individual family and the therapist can be short-circuited through the intervention of extrafamilial members. Further, role models are experienced across families, involving a greater and more diversified learning experience than from simply the therapist as a role modeler.

On norms, ideology, and values, Bott has indicated that "ordinary" people do not acquire these solely by internalization or introjection. Internalized standards are reworked and conceptualized in a new form and projected back onto the external situation. Perhaps this reworking may be less true of "abnormal" people. But it may be that the more varied people's social experiences are and the more unconnected the standards they internalize, the more internal rearrangements must be made. Thus, where networks are "too tight," it might be said that a high degree of internalization and the status quo of norms and ideology are likely; and where networks are "too loose," a high degree of projection, construction of reference group standards, and abstract categories of persons as referents of norms and ideology are likely. Thus, one goal of the therapist conceivably can be reworking the knittedness of networks to afford optimum emotional support and the realistic evaluation of projections and introjections. On a more conceptual level, therapists may be able to derive relationships between social structure and psychodynamics. My emphasis, and perhaps this is necessary with large groups, has been on the interpersonal, transactional, on-going phenomena, rather than on intrapsychic processes, although the latter have also been worked on in network meetings. And as in family therapy, many of the key figures on which transference and introject phenomena are based are actually present in the here-and-now setting.

Implications for Social and Preventive Psychiatry

In terms of preventive psychiatry and the community and community mental health center, Smith and Hobbs (1966) and Reiff (1966), among others, have stressed the importance of studying, changing, and maintaining various social systems in coping with mental health needs. As Smith and Hobbs have stated,

Certainly mental disorder is not the private misery of an individual; it often grows out of and usually contributes to the breakdown of normal sources of social support and understanding, especially the family. It is not just an individual who has faltered; the social system in which he is embedded through family, school, or job, through religious affiliation or through friendship, have failed to sustain him as an effective participant. . . . For the disturbed person, the goal of community mental health programs should be to help him and the social systems of which he is a member to function together as harmoniously and productively as possible. Such a goal is more practical, and more readily specified, than the elusive concept of 'cure,' which misses the point that for much mental disorder, the trouble lies not within the skin of the individual, but in the interpersonal systems through which he is related to others. (p. 503)

Reiff points out the manpower problem in changing social systems for the benefit of whole communities and societies.

The fact is that there is hardly anyone in the mental health profession of the behavioral sciences who is trained in a body of knowledge, a set of concepts, or an adequate theory on which to base such training. But, this is the greatest need and most promising approach. What is needed is a new profession of experts in changing social systems for the prevention of mental illness and for the improvement of the psychological effectiveness of all individuals in society to deal with the problems of living. (p. 546)

Until the larger society's economic and educational networks are changed, it will probably be difficult, if not impossible, to work therapeutically with many families who are of low socioeconomic status and impoverished materially and educationally. However, a treatment approach involving several larger societal units than individual or family appears feasible at present. One kind of such a larger unit is a social network involving family, extended family, and friends of both family and extended family.

We do not feel that our concept of network therapy is completely different from Maxwell Jones's idea of milieu therapy, except that we are working in the community, in homes rather than in a mental hospital or an institutional setting. Another essential difference is that in the network we have been working with, the composition of the group is made up of friends and relatives rather than patients and institutional staff personnel.

Clinical Example

Mrs. Jones contacted the network intervention team because of family problems that mainly involved her inability to manage or control the behavior of her 14-year-old daughter, Betty. She had taken Betty to a number of psychiatrists but Betty was uncooperative, blamed the psychiatrists for her difficulties, and refused the numerous medications that had been offered. Finally, the whole family had been put on mega-vitamin therapy by the last psychiatrist seen and he had made a diagnosis of schizophrenia and hypoglycemia and advised a diet for Betty. As my wife, an anthropologist and psychotherapist, and I see all families con-jointly, we started by seeing the entire Jones family, who reside to-gether. This consisted of Mrs. Jones, a 40-ish woman who looked much younger and seemed more like one of the children; Jane, 17; Bill, 15; Betty, 14; Jerry, 12; and Dorothy, 9. Mr. and Mrs. Jones had recently divorced and Mr. Jones lived in a different city with the woman he was about to marry. A striking feature of the family unit was the hopeless-ness and exhaustion in all family members. Betty had dropped out of school some months previously. She refused to bathe, did not eat with the family, stayed up all night and then insisted on quiet during the day so she could sleep, left rotting food hidden around the house, and constantly littered and dumped garbage about the house. At times, she attacked her mother or Dorothy. In the family therapy sessions, Betty would sit mumbling or complaining about the family, with her hair completely concealing her face, except when she rubbed her eyes with a mixture of water and spittle, which she kept in a jar in her purse. Jane and Bill gave much history and behaved in a parentified way. Both said that they couldn't take the tension and disruption in the home. Both wanted to move out. Jerry wanted to move in with his father. Dorothy was frightened of Betty but wanted to stay with her mother.

About six family therapy sessions were held. Mr. Jones attended one of these meetings. He tended to blame Mrs. Jones for not under-standing Betty, for having been absent in the past, and for being a slovenly housekeeper. He was glib, used much denial, and could not be convinced that Betty showed any symptoms of a psychotic disorder. He also seemed like one of the children.

Because of the amount of family disorganization, and total exhaus-tion, social network intervention was suggested to help build up sup-port systems for each family member. An additional factor was the 3-hour drive, dangerous to all because of Betty's aggressive impulsivity, that the family had to undergo to visit us.

A single, 4-hour, social network intervention was planned in their home. Mrs. Jones and the rest of the family were asked to compile a list of all the people they knew who might be willing to meet in their home and help to change their predicament. Mr. Jones was also seen with his new wife. They agreed to attend, and Mr. Jones's sister was invited from a distant state. Mrs. Jones invited her parents and several of her siblings from out of state. Mrs. Jones and Jane and Bill invited their friends. By the time of the meeting, 10 days hence, they had invited over 60 persons.

The intervention team consisted of six persons with myself as team leader; Dr. Uri Rueveni, as encounter specialist; Joan L. Speck and Mira Rueveni, as group-process consultants; a young psychologist as trainee and process consultant; and an audiovisual expert, who videotaped the network intervention.

The team arrived at the family home at 7 P.M., about one-half hour before the meeting was to start. Already, a few of the invited network members had begun to arrive. We made a tour of the house and selected the living room and archways spilling into the hall and into the dining room as the space to be used for the main session. We met with Betty, who refused to attend and was hiding in the garage. She said she might listen to the meeting from the basement, where there was an "escape" door. A team member was assigned to get written permission from everyone for videotaping. Only one couple refused "because they were in politics." After consultation with Mrs. Jones, they were encouraged to leave, as it was doubtful that they would be of help anyway.

By 7:45 P.M., 60 persons had arrived and we decided to begin. As I mentioned before, there are six recognizable stages in social network intervention: retribalization, polarization, mobilization, resistance–depression, breakthrough, and exhaustion–elation–termination. I pointed out that the Jones family was emotionally drained, that friends, neighbors and relatives should begin to think of ways to help the various family members, that support committees for each member would have to be set up, and that the group could help in making the divorce of the Joneses more effective. (Mr. Jones had been appearing unannounced for dinner, criticized Mrs. Jones's housekeeping, and had taken pictures of the interior, which he threatened to take to the public health department.)

Each network member was asked to introduce him- or herself and tell his or her relationship to the network. Then, the Jones family was asked to sit in the center of the group and tell the group what the trouble in the family was and what they hoped from the network intervention.

Betty remained in the garage and, later, in the basement. The team decided not to force a frightened and hostile 14-year-old to sit through the long session. She would undoubtedly have tried to escape and the resulting disruption would fragment the network rather than unite it as a functioning social system.

Jerry said that he could not stand being called "dirt" at school and that he wished he could have a chance to live with his father "to see if he liked it there." Jane said that it was impossible to live in the same house with Betty and that she wanted to move out, either to California or to go to college. Bill said he was sick of Betty drinking out of milk and juice bottles and her smelling up the house. He, too, would like to move. Dorothy said the house would be all right if Betty weren't there. Mrs. Jones said she could no longer put up with Betty and wanted help in getting her into a school. Mr. Jones said the problem with Betty was exaggerated and that Mrs. Jones, with her untidy housekeeping, was the real problem.

The polarization phase had now begun. Dr. Rueveni began to confront Mr. Jones about inconsistent statements he had made. The polarization continued about whether Betty was sick and about blaming Mr. Jones for the family problems, and then focussed on the unresolved divorce between the Joneses. At this point the larger network was called upon for their reactions to what had happened in the meeting to this point. The majority of the network was very supportive of Mrs. Jones, and there was some hostility to Mr. Jones. His new wife became very angry, took his side, and attempted to align Jerry with her and Mr. Jones. She invited Jerry to come live with them.

A few network members began to make suggestions about school or new living arrangements for Betty. This began the mobilization phase of the meeting. At this point the intervention team asked the assembled network members to each pick one of the seven Jones family members and to form a small group to discuss in greater detail what assistance might be needed. The small groups met for the next hour in different rooms in the house, with the intervention team members sitting in or "floating" from group to group. Each group chose a member to report back later, in summary form, the results of the small group meetings to the entire assembled network.

After several hours of group work, there commonly is a feeling of depression–resistance that appears when the work of polarization and mobilization is met with a sense of frustration and difficulty in solving the tasks.

When the groups reported back, there were numerous suggestions about different alternatives to help individual family members. The groups volunteered to act as committees who could be turned to, over the next several weeks for advise and help. An aunt offered to take Betty into her home with her own children. A lawyer present suggested that Mrs. Jones needed legal help to get Mr. Jones not to barge into the house whenever he felt the need. A teacher offered to help Betty prepare for the grade eight exams. An artist offered her art lessons. Many offers were made to other individual family members. It was pointed out that the unresolved divorce between the Joneses threatened Mr. Jones's new marriage, and marital counseling was recommended.

As the meeting ended, Betty appeared (after having met with her small group) and offered to go with several people to get pizzas. The team left at this point, but the network stayed together discussing what had happened until nearly 2 A.M.

A follow-up, 3 months later, indicated that Betty went to live with her aunt but after about 10 weeks was causing too much trouble and was uncooperative, so arrangements were being made for residential care. The rest of the Jones family were much relieved. Jane was starting college and the rest were back in school. Mr. Jones seemed much happier and his new marriage seemed intact.

Social Network Intervention in Crisis Situations: Theoretical Model

Social network intervention is one of the alternatives available to the professional family or group therapist in difficult, acute, or chronic crisis situations. It has also been called network therapy, network intervention, and networking. Dr. Harold Wise (1980), an internist with extensive psychotherapy training, has developed a theory and technique using network principles, which he has named therapeutic family reunions. This method aims at using the network to heal physical as well as emotional problems.

The crisis model: (1) advocates immediate short-term interventions; (2) emphasizes the increased receptivity to influence in individuals, families, groups and institutions during periods of turmoil when significant situational change is occurring; and, (3) causes increased motivation to help and support persons by third parties not ordinarily involved or central to the situation.

The network model of "healing" a crisis situation has a time and space orientation. The vertical dimension may be thought of as time, when family members from several generations, friends and neighbors from years of involvement with the nuclear problem person or persons, and others with varying time exposure to the network assemble to intervene in the crisis. The horizontal or space dimension includes all who assemble, including helpers, friends of friends, or other interested people. The central questions are: What is here? and What is now? The network is the intervenor or healer. The professionals are catalysts who prepare, speed, and choreograph the network group process.

The concepts of "healing" and "change" will be used arbitrarily as synonymous in this discussion of social-network intervention in crisis situations. There are at least four varieties of healing: (1) organic–biological, (2) psychotherapeutic, (3) mystical–faith, and (4) social action.

My experience is that all four levels may be involved in working with networks, but in different degrees, dependent on content, context, and definition of the problem. Change, or healing, may occur as a result of redefinition of messages, a re-cognition. One of the rules of healing is a hierarchical status differentiation. The "healer" has a higher or more powerful status than the "healee." This is manifested in mien, attitude and general behavior, inflections of speech, the making of an appointment, request for help, and payment of a fee. In network intervention there are multiple levels of power—in the index family, in the network, and in the intervention team.

The intervention team observes the assembled network for customary events and watches for those things that stop or destroy the behavior, so that people leave or the behavior does not compete. Behavior in groups may be seen as steps in a program, for example, the football game with assembly of the crowd; arrival on the field of the teams, the referees, cheerleaders, the band, and procession; opening whistle and kickoff; and so forth; The program could be destroyed or radically modified by a plane crashing on the field, a sudden flood or other act of God, or an atomic attack.

Boundaries are also identified as what happens when someone crosses one. The potential healee is caught in some incongruity of frames. The healer gets the person or persons back into some frame—religious, ethnic group, or value system. There is a shift to consonance and affiliations. A new behavior may be changed to an old one, an old one to a new, or something totally different may be introduced. The network team does not permit itself to be indoctrinated into the system.

Network intervention is useful in many human situations where a plateau or stalemate has occurred. It has been successful in preventing suicide and hospitalization. Difficult paranoid and other schizophrenic situations can be alleviated; no claim for cure is made here. Networks are the best employment agencies. I know of no better solution for problems of symbiosis. We have also used network intervention on professionals organizations looking for change and in some professional, racial–ethnic stalemates.

Some Additional Evolving Network Therapies

Network analysis is an active field of research in anthropology, sociology, political science, mathematics, and many other disciplines today. We are on the verge of seeing research studies on the network therapies, as different as this still seems. All psychotherapies from the individual approaches to networks suffer from an ascending, perhaps asymptotic, degree of complexity in evaluating their effectiveness. David Trimble (1980) has categorized the developing network therapies.

The full-scale network assembly is the model developed by this author and the main topic of this chapter. It is described in detail in Speck and Attneave's (1973) *Family Networks* and in Rueveni's (1979) *Networking Families in Crisis*. This approach is a rediscovery of the tribal healing ceremonies in many primitive societies, usually using shamans or medicine men.

The therapeutic family reunions, pioneered by Harold Wise in the treatment of certain medical conditions, uses a similar tribal healing model and marathon-type sessions, such as used by various American Indians and the !Kung of the Kalahari Desert.

Murray Bowen (1978, pp. 529–547) has investigated and treated his own family network by serial methods (rotating visits with different small clusters of the network). Attneave (1969, 1971) has used similar serial network methods, working in rural and in inner-city poverty areas.

John Garrison has developed, after Norris Hansell, a screening–linking–planning network session. It uses a different metaphor than the tribal healing ceremony. It uses a negotiating process, "a laundry list of complaints," and works on a somewhat more conscious, rational, problem-solving, and contractual basis. The convenor catalyzes and mobilizes the resources of the assembled members of the network and mediates with them for agreement on how to help the distressed person. The network size tends to be smaller (usually 20 or less) and the process tends to accentuate negotiation and making contracts.

The team problem-solving approach of Robert Curtis is a systems management method. Group size may be as small as three or four persons. Six steps are described: (1) the index person invites all persons who influence his or her problem to a meeting; (2) the problem must be defined; (3) resources for change are identified in the network; (4) contracts are negotiated in the network for action; (5) at a second session, an evaluation of the success of the contracts is made; and (6) termination—the network is encouraged to continue problem solving. The case manager's job is to identify and organize personal supports, volunteers, and caseworkers in their efforts to provide help.

Edgar Auerswald has developed an ecological system-intervention approach. This is particularly helpful with multi-problem families where health care delivery is poor, partially because of multiple overlapping systems. The family is appointed as chairman of a meeting involving all agencies active in the case. Information is shared and the family picks the one agency that it finds the most useful. Skills in doing an ecological analysis of the systems involved is important in this approach.

Papers are appearing on community network intervention, network construction, and consultation to natural networks.

Attneave (1976) has developed a sophisticated method of network mapping to make social networks more visible to both therapists and clients and to help decide whom to include and whom not to include in network sessions.

The future of social network research is exciting. It uses a systems approach that is far broader than the medical model of healing or the individual psychotherapeutic one. Ari Kiev (1968) has suggested that in primitive healing, psychotherapy is a public affair. What we are calling a system model of psychotherapy (network therapy) is the oldest model—that of medicine man, folk healer, or shaman. In modern society, people are caught between naturalistic "old time" healing and the mystique of the technological, "scientific world". Perhaps we have to be as daring as Harold Wise in New York City and even A. Issels in Germany, revaluate modern science, even antibiotics versus "fever" therapy, and then decide what the broadest system approach might be to such diseases as schizophrenia, suicidal behaviors, and cancer. If we change the context of events in a person's life, can we change the system? If we change the system, will it change the context? Let us hope the future will consider the past as well as the present if new ideas are to flow over old "scientific" tenets.

ACKNOWLEDGMENTS

Parts of this chapter represent collaborative work with the following close network colleagues in the past and also recently: Joan Lincoln Speck; Carolyn L. Attneave, PhD; Jerome Olans, PhD; Uri Rueveni, PhD; Albert E. Scheflen, MD; and David Trimble, PhD.

REFERENCES

Attneave, C. L. Therapy in tribal settings and urban network intervention. *Family Process*, 1969, *8*, 192–210.

Attneave, C. L. Y'all come: Social networks as a unit of intervention. In P. Guerin (Ed.), *Family therapy: Theory and practice*. New York: Gardner Press, 1976.

Barnes, J. Class and committees in Norwegian island parish. *Human Relations*, 1954, 7.

Bott, E. *Family and social network: Roles, norms and external relationships in ordinary urban families*. London: Tavistock Publications, 1957; New York: Free Press, 1971.

Bowen, M. *Family therapy in clinical practice*. New York: Jason Aronson, 1978.

Cooper, D. *The death of the family*. New York: Pantheon Books, 1970.

Jay, E. J. The concepts of "field" and "network" in anthropological research. *Man*, 1964, *9*(10) 137–139.

Kiev, A. *Curanderismo: Mexican American folk psychiatry*. New York: Free Press, 1968.

Lewin, K. *Field theory in social science* (D. Cartwright, Ed.). London: Tavistock Books, 1952.

Litwak, E. The use of extended family in the achievement of social goals: Some social implications. *Social Problems*, 1959, 7, 177–187.

Reiff, R. Mental health manpower and institutional change. *American Psychologist*, 1966, 21, 540–548.

Rueveni, U. *Networking families in crisis.* New York: Human Sciences Press, 1979. (Contains a recent bibliography on networks.)

Smith, M. B., & Hobbs, N. The community and the community mental health center. *American psychologist*, 1966, 21, 499–509.

Sonne, J. C., Speck, R. V., & Jungreis, J. The absent member maneuver as a resistance in family therapy of schizophrenia. *Family Process*, 1962, 1, 44–62.

Speck, R. V., *et al. The new families.* New York: Basic Books, 1972; London: Tavistock Books, 1974.

Speck, R. V., & Attneave, C. L. *Family networks.* New York: Pantheon Books, 1973.

Speck, R. V., & Speck, J. L. On networks: network therapy, network intervention, and networking. *International Journal of Family Therapy*, 1979, 1, 333–337.

Sussman, M. B., The isolated nuclear family: Fact or fiction? *Social Problems*, 1959, 6, 333–340.

Trimble, D. W. A guide to the network therapies. *Connections* (Bulletin of the International Network for Social Network Analysis, Department of Sociology, University of Toronto, Canada), 1980, 3,(21). (Contains a network bibliography.)

Uzoka, A. The myth of the nuclear family: Historical background and clinical implications. *American Psychologist*, 1979, 34(11), 1095–1106.

Wise, H. Personal communication, 1980.

Family and human service organizations

5

Familiar institutions: How the child care system replicates family patterns

HELEN B. SCHWARTZMAN
Northwestern University

ANITA W. KNEIFEL
Chicago, Illinois

Families and bureaucratic organizations have historically been viewed as having contrasting and even antithetical atmospheres (e.g., Toennies, 1940; Parsons, 1949). It has also been suggested that the activities or functions of the family are, for the most part, directly replaceable by the bureaucracy (Litwak & Meyer, 1966, p. 35). In contrast, a number of studies focusing on "helping" organizations (i.e., social service institutions) for children suggest that the similarities between families and bureaucracies may be more important than their conflicts and differences. In this chapter it is suggested that helpers, and the helping institutions that compose the child care system, frequently replicate functional and dysfunctional family patterns in their interactions with each other and with the children and families whom they serve. Reasons for this replication and the positive and negative therapeutic consequences of it are discussed and examined. Three types of family patterns are identified here and their analogues in the child care system are described and illustrated using case examples from the psychiatric literature as well as those collected in an anthropological investigation of interactions between families and children's helpers (e.g., therapists, caseworkers, teachers, ward aides, probation officers).

Families and Bureaucracies

Families and bureaucracies share many features. Both groups are hierarchically organized (families use generational and sex-role ordering and bureaucracies use skill, merit, and experience-ordering procedures); and both groups develop shared beliefs and practices about what con-

stitutes proper group functioning. Bureaucratic organizations are typically believed to be faceless, impersonal, monolithic enterprises in contrast to the personal, face-to-face contact thought to be characteristic of
families. However, ever since the classic Western Electric "Hawthorne"
study documented the influence of informal work group relationships
on plant productivity, it has been realized that bureaucratic organizations are actually composed of small, personal, face-to-face formal and
informal social systems that may expedite or inhibit the task/goal of the
organization (see Roethlisberger & Dickson, 1939). The small groups
that ultimately compose the organization often take on family-like or
kin-group qualities—sometimes marking this by designating individuals
or units in the system with specific kinship labels, such as fathers,
mothers, grandparents, brothers, sisters. For example, at the Hawthorne
plant, the American Telephone and Telegraph Company (the "parent"
company for Western Electric) was referred to by workers as "Ma Bell,"
the plant manager was called "Daddy Rice," and the Western Electric
Company was itself labeled "Charlie Western," an avuncular-sounding
designation (see Dickson & Roethlisberger, 1966).

The "familiarizing" tendency of bureaucracies is generally an attempt by individuals and groups to personalize relationships that are
structured to be impersonal. This phenomenon may improve morale,
increase group loyalty, and raise productivity. However, this tendency
may also encourage group rivalries, territoriality, and conflict, as well as
decrease productivity and create difficulties in coordination and cooperation to achieve organizational goals.

Child care institutions such as schools, children's wards in mental
hospitals, therapeutic schools, child guidance clinics, and so forth, are
particularly interesting contexts for evaluating the effects of "familiarizing" in organizations. The re-creation of family dynamics by helpers is
frequently believed to be an important feature of their help. This is especially true of mental health workers because, in one sense, this is
the essence of the transference phenomenon. However, frequently this
re-creation backfires for helpers especially when it occurs in settings,
and among individuals, who were not intended to become part of the
"family" constellation. The process by which helpers (generally unin-
tentionally) replicate problematic family dynamics has been reported by
a number of researchers and clinicians as it has been observed in a
variety of institutions, especially hospitals and schools. We are unaware,
however, of any systematic review of this literature that attempts to
draw the clinical implications of the variety of reports and comments
that have appeared over the years in the literature. This is one of the
purposes of this chapter.

Szurek (1951) presents an early discussion of family–staff relationships on a children's ward in a mental hospital, and he suggests ways in

which patients and their families may manipulate hospital-staff divisions. Harbin (1978) presents an updated discussion of this issue and specifically describes how structural pathologies in families may be repeated by hierarchical arrangements in hospitals where "personnel lower in the administrative hierarchy have multiple supervisors so that there are no clear-cut lines of authority" (p. 1497). Parallels between pathological family patterns (chronic conflict, paradoxical communications, conflicting authority) have also been described by Fleck, Cornelison, Norton, Lidz, (1957), Haley (1969), Steinfeld (1970), and Bradshaw and Burton (1976). For example, Bradshaw and Burton suggest that

> a patient entering a psychiatric ward seldom (if ever) has warm, realistic parent images and will soon reconstruct his transference pathology with the milieu's authority figures. The ward staff, in their desire to relate to the new patient quickly, will often accede to the patient's unconscious wishes for parental surrogates; as a result the patient recreates the internalized family pathology on the spot. The nurse becomes the mother, the doctor the father, and other staff members are included in various family roles. If the primary therapist is a social worker or psychologist, he also assumes a parental position in the eyes of the patient. The family pathology may produce conflict between parental surrogates, just as the actual parents of the patient were split or in conflict, with the patient often having been used as the pawn in such struggles. Many patients are keenly aware of subtle conflicts among milieu staff members and, although unaware of their interaction, may skillfully foster the conflict to perpetuate their pathology. (1976, pp. 667–668)

Schools and other child care institutions have also been found to replicate the family dynamics of children. Aponte (1976a, 1976b), in an important discussion of "context replication" between school and home, describes how this occurred for one particular child.

> Jerry is an insecure youngster with a tough exterior. He was in a powerless, somewhat isolated position at home, where his father, whom he respected, was not involved in his care, and his mother, who had little control over him, was responsible for him. His brothers, who are older, out-fought him in the competition for each to have things his own way at home. In the larger class at school, Jerry fought his classmates for similar reasons, which only put him in trouble with his teacher and, like his mother, this teacher did not have the strength to handle the challenge Jerry presented. The principal sided with the teacher. Jerry's good work with his other teachers was less conspicuous and was not enough to offset the troublemaking reputation he had already earned. In her effort to help Jerry, the counselor overprotected him and prevented the school and his family from working on Jerry's problems. (1976a, p. 310)

Parallels between the triangling process (an inappropriate crossing of generational hierarchies) that has been observed in families (see

Bowen, 1966; Haley 1969) and triangling that occurs in a variety of organizational systems has been suggested by Bowen (1974), Kerr (1973), Hirschhorn and Gilmore (1980), and Minard (1976). Minard (1976) has specifically used Bowen's approach to analyze triangling problems that developed in a day care center for preschool children. The pervasiveness of conflicts and the potential for triangling in child care institutions is also suggested by Ebner (1979) in his discussion of differences between "hard-hat"-oriented child care workers and "soft-heart" workers. In delinquency treatment programs, pervasive differences between cottage parents and caseworkers or professionals and paraprofessionals have also been reported in the literature (see Piliavin, 1970; Weber, 1950).

This pattern of replication of certain types of family patterns is found not only *within* specific institutions, but it also extends to the larger treatment system as well and the relationships that develop between agencies involved in the care and treatment of children. Kaplan (1952) presents one of the earliest descriptions of this process in his discussion of problems that developed between a referring source and a child guidance clinic over the treatment of emotionally disturbed children. He suggests that a social agency referral (a court, school, welfare system) of a child and his or her family to a clinic has many important implications for the child, the family, the referring agency, and the clinic.

> The relationship is not only between the family and the referring source, but also between the family and the child guidance clinic and, through the family as well as directly, between the clinic and the referring source. One can think of this as a triangular situation involving groups somewhat analogous to the family triangular situation exemplified by the oedipus complex. (p. 118)

Kaplan notes that problems, confusions, and misunderstandings frequently creep into the agency relationships created by a referral and that many of the agency conflicts and problems may be acted out by the patient (or may be exacerbated by the patient and his or her family) because the helpers do not meet directly. For example, a referral may be initiated because of disagreements between two organizations involved with a case (e.g., a child care agency and the court) and the referral is initiated because it is hoped that the clinic will support one agency against the other agency.

More recently Schwartzman and Bokos (1979) have outlined how the structure of specific methadone maintenance clinics and the methadone maintenance system as a whole recreates structural flaws in the addict's family and functions to maintain the symptom. A pattern of parental disagreement about the addict, and the overinvolvement of one parent with the addict, is paralleled by pervasive differences in methadone maintenance clinics between professionals and paraprofessionals about how best to treat drug addicts. In these instances the paraprofessionals (often because they are ex-addicts themselves) are overinvolved and overprotective of the addicts. At another level of the system, differences were found to exist between professionally staffed (hard-hat) clinics and paraprofessionally staffed (soft-heart) clinics and these differences were exploited by addicts as they cycled through the drug treatment system (approximately 40 facilities in this study).

> In the facilities observed, certain clients were transferred from clinic to clinic because they had continuously broken clinic rules or had conflictual relationships with certain staff members, generally concerning the enforcement of these rules. Clients maintain the social system both by the messages they transmit about other clinics and the messages that they themselves *are* defined as "unsuitable" as clients at other clinics. Each client transferred from one clinic to another implicitly creates a perverse triangle by creating a relationship with the facility to which he transfers against the clinic from which he has been transferred because he has not been a "good" client. (Schwartzman & Bokos, 1979, p. 351)

Types of Family Patterns

The studies cited above suggest that specific patterns of family interaction that are believed to produce dysfunctional behavior *within* families (such as chronic conflict, perverse triangles), may also occur within and between child care institutions. To expand on these studies and also to systematize the research that has been conducted so far in this area, it is necessary to turn briefly to a separate research tradition in the family therapy field. Family theorists and therapists have been attempting to develop typologies of family symptoms, interaction patterns, structures and processes for some time now and with somewhat mixed results. There are, however, at least two very general types of dysfunctional family patterns that have been identified over and over again in the research and clinical literature. In Hoffman's (1981, pp. 67–85) recent review of family typologies, two family system types are portrayed drawing on the work of Ashby (1969) and Bateson (1972). The "too richly cross-joined family" is said to be stifled or dysfunctional because its parts and subparts are too closely interlocked, and systems of this type are said to find it especially difficult to negotiate changes in their environment (Hoffman, 1981, p. 74). These are families that have been described elsewhere as enmeshed (Minuchin, 1974), undifferentiated (Bowen, 1960), centripetal (Stierlin, 1974), pseudomutual (Wynne, 1958), and "sticky-glue" (Hoffman, 1981) systems. In Reiss's terms (1971a, 1971b) these are consensus-sensitive families that are internally well-connected and externally poorly connected.

In contrast, the "too poorly cross-joined family" is characterized by loose internal interlocking relationships and because of this it often becomes "locked in with social institutions that form a more enclosing kind of enmeshed structure, with agency personnel acting as surrogate parents" (Hoffman, 1981, p. 79). Reiss (1971a, 1971b) describes these families as interpersonal distance sensitive families that are externally well-connected and internally poorly connected. Minuchin (1974) describes these families as disengaged, and they have also been portrayed as fragmented (Hoffman, 1981), underorganized (Aponte, 1976b), expelling and centrifugal (Stierlin, 1974), pseudohostile (Wynne, 1958), and as "colliding molecules" (Hoffman, 1981).

Characteristics of functional or normal families are extremely difficult to identify. In the literature normal families have generally been defined in one of four ways: (1) absence of pathology, (2) ideal or optimal functioning, (3) as a statistical average with the middle range as normal, and (4) as a dynamic process changing over time (Walsh, 1982, p. 16). There are, however, some more specific characteristics that many family therapists and theorists have identified as associated with normal family functioning. These include the family's ability to be extremely flexible and open to its environment (Walsh, 1982); to allow individuals to establish clear boundaries and hierarchical relationships (e.g., Minuchin, 1974; Olson, Sprenkle, & Russell, 1979; Haley, 1980); and to encourage differentiation (Bowen, 1978). Reiss (1971a, 1971b) refers to these as environment-sensitive families, and Stierlin (1974) describes the normal families' achievement of a centripetal and centrifugal balance. For the most part, however, normal families seem to be defined by what they are *not*, that is, they are not enmeshed, they are not disengaged, they are not binding, they are not expelling, and so forth.

As families develop their own internal rules, dynamics, and patterns of interaction, helpers representing the child care system also develop their own patterns of interaction based on the history of their relationships with each other and on the nature of the family that brings them together. In this chapter it is argued that helper patterns of interaction frequently re-create the above three family pattern types that have been reported in the literature. The remainder of this chapter describes how the child care system replicates these patterns and the treatment implications of recognizing this replication.

Too Richly Cross-Joined Systems

Too richly cross-joined systems are characterized by a sharp separation between the institution(s) and its environment, a belief that all rewards come from within the group, a confusion or blurring of authority and role relationships, and a fear of internal opposition or disagreement (see Wynne *et al.*, 1958; Minuchin, 1974; Gustafson, 1979; Hoffman, 1981). The creation of encapsulated, insulated, "family-like" settings (such as hospitals and therapeutic schools) for the treatment of emotionally disturbed children was one of the earliest treatment techniques developed by helping professionals. The importance of creating a sense of "community," "society," or "family" in the hospital in order to make therapeutic use of carefully organized, personal environments (and also to separate the patient from the pressures of the outside world) was perhaps first systematically developed by Henry Stack Sullivan in his work with adolescent male schizophrenic patients at Sheppard and Enoch Pratt Hospital in Towson, Maryland, between 1929–1931 (see Sullivan, 1931). The development of "artificial families" in the hospital treatment of children by Anna Freud and Dorothy Burlingham (1943), and the recognition of the importance of the "therapeutic milieu" for counteracting the effects of "hospitalism" in children (e.g., by Bettelheim & Sylvester, 1948), are also examples of the conscious manipulation of the organizational context as a means for the psychotherapeutic treatment of children. One of the clearest examples of the effect on staff of drawing rigid boundaries between the treatment institution and the outside world is reported by the anthropologist Jules Henry (1957) in his analysis of the Sonia Shankman Orthogenic School.

> The beginning counselor is immediately confronted with the choice of the areas of life in which she shall seek gratification—the School or the "outside"; and what one sees in the successful counselor is the gradual, usually hard, decision in favor of the former. . . . The dominating dichotomies are *this* world and *that* world; the way *they* (outsiders) think; and the way *we* think; *their* ideas about interpersonal relations and *our* ideas about interpersonal relations. (p. 54)

Along with making a sharp distinction between the inside and outside world the treatment approach utilized at Sonia Shankman (and analyzed and reported by Henry, 1973, as well as by Bettelheim & Wright, 1955, and Bettelheim, 1974) stressed the extreme involvement of staff with patients. The boundary between staff and patients was blurred in several ways as staff were encouraged to involve (over-involve?) themselves with patients because this would be the only way to successfully treat these patients.[1]

> Since the counsellors have major responsibility for the rehabilitation of the children, and indeed for almost all aspects of their lives, deep *mutual* involvement of counsellors and children comes as a consequence, and with this massive outlays of time that extend far beyond the four days on

---

1. Henry (1973, pp. 5–6) notes that the average length of stay of staff was similar to that of patients.

dormitory duty. As a result of involvement, feelings of mutual equality are
to be expected, and attitudes of submission and dominance recede into the
background. (Henry, 1973, pp. 4–5)

In an effort to reinforce this "mutual involvement," counselors were
required to live at the school with the children.

A particularly revealing example of the blurring of roles between
staff and patients encouraged by the treatment approach used at the
Sonia Shankman Orthogenic School appears in Bettelheim and Wright
(1955). In this article the authors analyze a drawing test given to a
counselor at the beginning of her relationship with a child and at a later
stage of her work with the same patient. The first picture depicts a
young woman of similar age to the counselor, wearing an adult dress
and low-heeled shoes, looking at the world in a "questioning, interesting
and non-commital way" (p. 711). The second drawing is of a gawky girl
in a childish dress, with a ball extended over her head. The girl is smiling
in an uncritical way. The authors' analysis illustrates the value that a
"too richly cross-joined system" may place on role fusion and identification with patients. In this context the change from the first to the
second drawing is interpreted as a sign of growth and healthy adjustment for the counselor.

> The contrast between the two drawings suggests that she [the counselor]
> has become increasingly able to accept and gratify her own unfilled needs
> to receive and be like a child. Her identification with a childish image
> suggests greater emotional closeness between her and the children, a close
> relation to, if not identification with, the children under her care which is
> made explicit in her remark about whom she is going to draw. Such
> temporary diffusion of the boundary between their own and the children's
> personalities seems characteristic of workers who are able to relate to
> deeply withdrawn children (autistic, withdrawn, schizophrenic, pseudo-
> idiot), and through this relation to help them.
>
>   The second drawing shows her in a state of flux, but more accessible
> to emotional experiences. It suggests that there is growth in the direction
> of an easier, warmer, more expressive and more natural emotional adjust-
> ment. These changes in personality were made possible by her gaining
> interpersonal gratifications through her work. (pp. 712–713)

The too richly cross-joined system created at Sonia Shankman, as
well as many other types of mental health agencies, may be likened to a
closed family system. According to White (1978) "closed family" agencies
are characterized by the presence of professional, social, and sexual
incest-dynamics. "Professional incest" occurs when an agency staff
isolates itself and becomes a closed ideological system. This is characterized by a lack of outside professional contacts, homogenization of
staff, intense socialization of staff, and extrusion of problem staff
(generally labeling them as having psychological problems) (pp. 7–8).
"Social incest" occurs when staff begin to meet the majority of their

social needs with other staff members and when "one's relationships outside the program simply become a continuation of the work relationship" (p. 13). "Sexual incest" is a continuation of the above dynamic as staff in a closed organizational system begin to meet their sexual needs with other staff and/or patients. White claims to have observed these dynamics in a number of social service institutions, including free clinics, youth programs, residential psychiatric programs, and alcohol and drug abuse programs.

Features of a too richly cross-joined system have also been observed by the authors in state hospitals for children and adolescents (see Schwartzman, Kneifel, Barbera-Stein, & Gaviria, 1981). In one hospital, staff were extremely concerned with and knowledgeable about the minutiae of a child's behavior on the ward, and yet many staff were unaware of where the child had come from or where he or she would go upon discharge.[2] It was "as if" the child existed in a vacuum before admission and fell off the edge of the earth when he or she left the hospital. This is perhaps one reason why divisions often develop between hospital staff and families as well as other treatment organizations (see Schwartzman et al., 1981).

A too richly cross-joined system, as described here, may also develop across institutions/agencies, for example, when a particular treatment philosophy binds together day schools, treatment schools, and hospitals who refer back and forth among each other but leave patients and families open to a type of "culture shock" when they are forced to move outside the system to continue treatment (see Barbera-Stein, 1981).

Clearly these are systems that make a therapeutic virtue out of being internally well-connected and "together" while having poor external connections. Hospitals and long-term institutional placement facilities for children are the most likely contexts for the development of a too richly cross-joined pattern, and these are frequently the places that children diagnosed as psychotic/schizophrenic are placed. The literature in family therapy suggests that these are children who come from family systems that are themselves too richly cross-joined, enmeshed, or pseudomutual and so, in this way, the pattern is repeated at the helping level.

Too Poorly Cross-Joined Systems

Too poorly cross-joined systems are characterized by loose internal interlocking relationships. These are systems that Reiss (1971a, 1971b) has described as externally well connected and internally poorly con-

2. In one instance a child was admitted to the ward from another hospital in the same state system, and several staff were unaware of this hospital's existence.

nected. If too richly cross-joined systems are placed on one end of a continuum of family or system types, then too poorly cross-joined systems may be considered as their logical opposite.

In the child care system, examples of too poorly cross-joined systems are quite numerous. Such a pattern may be found *within* an institution (such as a hospital, school, or an out-patient clinic) as well as *across* institutions (e.g., the nature of relationships that may develop between families, hospitals, clinics, and schools). In fact, the current state of the child care system is frequently described using terms applied to too poorly cross-joined systems by Minuchin, Aponte and Stierlin. The major service delivery problems today are said to be characterized by fragmentation, conflict, lack of organization and coordination, and expelling and shuffling of children from placement to placement (see Children's Defense Fund, 1978).

It is suggested here that too poorly cross-joined families interact with a too poorly cross-joined child care system to perpetuate and sometimes exascerbate the problems of the patient and the system. As Hoffman (1981) suggests, a too poorly cross-joined family may become "locked in with social institutions that form a more enclosing kind of enmeshed structure, with agency personnel acting as surrogate parents" (p. 79). These are families frequently with many needs and few resources or connections to solve their problems internally, and so helpers in the social service and child care system may be drawn into the family, developing a variety of relationships (frequently involving triangling) with family members. Social workers may ally themselves with the child against the parents, parents may ally themselves with a priest or therapist against the other helpers, or the parent may seem to ally him- or herself with all helpers while exploiting the differences between them. The numbers of helpers that may become involved with cases such as this can sometimes be quite extraordinary, as was discovered in one study of 12 children hospitalized at one state mental hospital and followed 18 months after discharge. It was found that the average number of helpers involved with each case was 40, and overall 490 helpers were involved with the children (see Schwartzman *et al.*, 1981).

The too poorly cross-joined pattern appears within specific treatment institutions for children as well. If families of this type are characterized by disengagement, underorganization, disorganization, and fragmentation, it has been found that many treatment institutions develop similar characteristics, although for different reasons. Residential treatment facilities, hospital wards, classrooms, and so forth, may develop fragmented and disorganized/underorganized systems because of staffing shortages, staff turnover, lack of a consensus about proper treatment practices, as well as the demands of the specific children in treatment. Montalvo and Pavlin (1966 comment on this problem in their analysis of problems in the structure of a residential treatment center (the Wiltwyck School for Boys).

> It should be obvious that the social system of the treatment center must be better than that of the children's own homes if it is to evoke improvement in the children under its roof. A counselor as overwhelmed as a mother with a disorganized collection of 10 or more children, all demanding individual attention, nurture and protection, can hardly do more than that mother was able to do. (p. 711)

In another study of a children's ward in a mental hospital (see Scheinfeld, 1981, 1982; Krause, 1982), the ward atmosphere was consistently described as fragmented, extremely loose, drifting, and inconsistent. Patients (when not in school) were allowed to mill around in their dayroom, with few planned or organized activities. Staff described their role as responding to patients when they acted out negatively, but rarely as one of initiating, coordinating, or planning activities. Staff were also very concerned about developing and using an appropriate order maintenance system for the ward, but they somehow were never able to develop and enforce one. The ward seemed to drift from activity to activity, system to system, and in the process the authority structure of the ward deteriorated, making it even more difficult to organize or coordinate activities.

This fragmented, disorganized, and drifting pattern may also be observed outside the hospital. A too poorly cross-joined system produces child welfare caseworkers who carry huge caseloads (60 or more) and because of this are never able to even personally meet each child and find it impossible to follow-up on cases except the most serious. In addition, caseworkers may change frequently, making consistency and continuity difficult, if not impossible, to achieve. Correctional institutions also face many of these same problems, as probation officers carry large case loads and report that they are overwhelmed by the numbers of juveniles they must try to serve. Lack of consequences and inconsistent consequences are also found in the juvenile justice system, as a child may receive numerous "station adjustments" and must move to more serious acts of disturbance/violence before the system responds (and then frequently arbitrarily). Again the question asked by Montalvo and Pavlin appears here, for how can we expect a system that repeats the worst flaws of what we now know to be problematic family patterns to do any better in handling/solving/curing the problems.

To illustrate a "too poorly cross-joined family" and its interaction with a "too poorly cross-joined child care system," one specific case collected in a follow-up study (see Schwartzman et al., 1981) will be described. This was a study designed to examine the pathways taken by specific children into and out of a children's ward in a state mental hospital.

MARK

Mark is an 11-year-old white male with a long history of problems. He is currently in the state department of corrections largest detention facility for juveniles. Mark's pathway to this facility is revealing of both family and service system dynamics. Mark's mother is solely responsible for her children, as the husband abandoned the family (mother, Mark. and one older sibling) when Mark was 6 months old Mark's mother reports that she began experiencing problems with him very early (age 2) as he was disobedient and hard to control. Over the years these problems seemed to escalate from disobedience to fighting, truancy, curfew violations, shoplifting, fire setting, running away, threatening with weapons, drug overdoses, and major theft. Mark's mother responded in one of two ways to this behavior. She would first try to argue, threaten, make deals, and/or conjole Mark. If this did not work, she would then lose her temper and attempt to involve some outside person/authority (e.g., call a caseworker, therapist, or the police). Mark's mother also took parent effectiveness training classes on several occasions, but she claimed that they did not work.

Mark's school and most subsequent service system interventions followed a similar intervention strategy to Mark's mother, although often using more sophisticated techniques and jargon. As is evident in Figure 5-1, Mark's behavior and family dynamics produced a string of involvements with various service system personnel, including special education classrooms, police, court, medical and mental hospitals, family welfare agencies, residential treatment facilities, and correctional institutions. Mark's behavior produced/provoked responses similar to that which he encountered at home. This pattern has been described as centrifugal or expelling by Stierlin (1974), and this characterizes Mark's journey through the system. In school he was placed in a special education class for behaviorally disordered children. When this program, a form of behavior modification (i.e., equivalent to mother's deals and threats), did not work, he was given detention. Mother became more and more exasperated with his behavior and took him out of this school and placed him in a military school, but he was expelled from this school for allegedly starting a fire. Mark returned to his original school, but began to exhibit increased truancy and incorrigible behavior. He also threatened to stab his girlfriend's mother (this charge was dropped) and received numerous station adjustments by the police. (These station adjustments are basically threats with little or no consequences attached to them.) At this point Mark's mother filed a Minor in Need of Supervision petition (MINS petition) in court for both of her children, but no consequences followed this declaration.

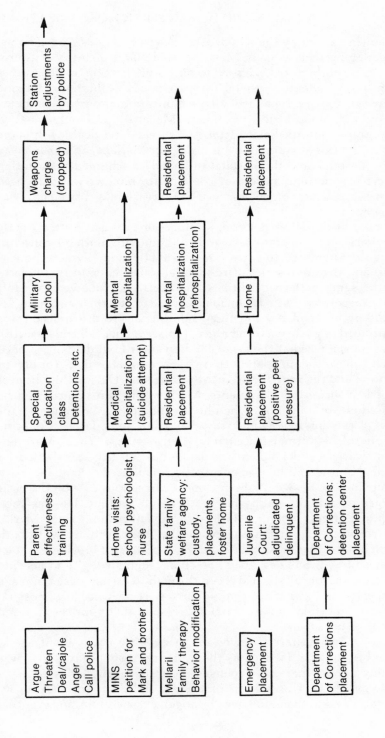

Fig. 5-1. *Family and system interventions for Mark.*

99

Following a visit by the school psychologist and nurse to his home, investigating his whereabouts, Mark ingested a large quantity of aspirin and had to be hospitalized. This led to his hospitalization on a children's ward in a state mental hospital for psychiatric evaluation. Here he encountered a more rigid behavior modification program combined with psychopharmacological treatment (Mellaril) and family therapy. This program continued the pattern of threats and deals with some success in the closed system of the ward, but Mark began to run away from the hospital; and the hospital ultimately discharged him, stating that there was nothing more they could do for him. He was diagnosed "adjustment reaction of adolescence" and residential placement was recommended.

Because of the MINS petition, Mark became a "case" with the state child welfare agency who took custody of him (with mother's consent). This agency attempted to place him in a foster home (where he was rejected) and then in a series of residential placements. In these placements the same pattern of threats and deals was followed. As staff became exasperated with his inability to adapt to their program (as evidenced by his tendency to run away), the pattern of expulsion was also continued (e.g., he was discharged, replaced, rejected, and so forth). He was rehospitalized at the same children's ward but discharged once again with the recommendation that no more could be done for him in this context and residential placement was needed. During this phase of continued unsuccessful placements, Mark would run home when he was placed out of home; but when he was home (e.g., a home visit, or between placements), he would run away from home (at least once he ran to one of his former placements). During these "runs" Mark engaged in a variety of delinquent and dangerous acts (e.g., car theft, drug and alcohol abuse) and he was eventually adjudicated delinquent. With charges piling up, he eventually became a corrections case on the basis of charges of assault against his mother and brother. He was then placed in the largest detention facility for juveniles in his state. Mark's mother reported that during this phase she "broke contact" with both her sons. In fact, Mark's mother exhibited a pattern of breaking contact with her children. She described herself as "high strung" and needing time to recover from all she had "been through." During these times she fully expected and demanded that public service agencies (e.g., hospital staff, court, and child welfare staff) take responsibility for the care and treatment of her children.

Mark's child welfare caseworker, in his case notes about Mark, sums up his personal (as well as the system's) response to Mark. It is interesting to note that this response is very similar to Mark's mother's response to Mark. The pattern of threats and deals with no consequences attached to them, followed by anger, exasperation, and eventual expulsion is evident in these notes which describe one specific interaction with Mark.

> Mark remained at Placement A until January 1980 when I picked him up for a train trip to Center City to face the bench on charges of car theft. Finally arriving at the depot, Mark refused to go to court (walk one mile or less) unless I called a cab. For financial and other reasons, I refused and told him to come along or I would probably call the police. He still smugly refused, so I took his wool hat to use it as "the carrot before the donkey." He hit me a number of times at which time I decided to do or say anything I wanted with no regard for his feelings. I was truly angered and, as reported in court, when I went back to the station where he retreated, I grabbed a stick and raised it above him, telling him that he was going to get moving on the path to the court and there would be no cab. I threw down the stick and grabbed his arm to lead him down the street—he started again to kick and hit me with dirty shoes and fists. Then he followed me down the street as I shouted at him and told him how detestible he was and what a beggar and worthless child he was—he continued to follow and shout obscenities and periodically hit me in the back and threatened he was going to "break my neck." At about half way down the road, he picked up a yellow three foot three-by-four and said he was going to hit me with it. I was then leery of being in front of him. He ultimately disposed of the item down the walk. Finally, we were in the Justice Center where he admitted to car theft and was detained for one week.

The caseworker informed us in an interview that after this incident he was "so disgusted" with Mark that he charged him with "aggravated battery."

Mark is a case on the move (on the run) in a too poorly cross-joined system. His family and the service system he encountered illustrate an expelling, centrifugal, and exclusionary pattern in their attempts to deal with his behavior, and these attempts invariably led to his movement to another place (presumably for treatment). Because he was constantly on the move (and his behavior produced and perpetuated these moves), he became involved with a great variety of social service personnel (approximately 80), although never in any organized fashion. Each of these service providers believed that they had something new and different in the way of treatment or help to offer to Mark; and when this service did not work or they became exasperated with his behavior (or he with theirs), then Mark either ran from the placement or was expelled, excluded, discharged, replaced, and so forth. It was impossible for the helpers to observe how their behavior paralleled that of mother and all other service providers because each helper has a much greater investment in viewing their service as different and distinctive. This allowed Mark and his family to maintain a variety of connections with multiple service providers, but the service providers themselves had few connections with each other and were therefore unable to observe and reflect on how their interaction with this "case" reproduced the pathology of the family. In this system Mark was able to change placements constantly without ever having to change his behavior.

Normal Systems

It is difficult to generalize about the characteristics of a normal service system for children, and it is also difficult to find one. The literature is crowded with ideas about how child and adolescent service systems *should* be organized (i.e., they should be coordinated, they should provide continuity of care, they should be accessible, etc.). Unfortunately, there are very few research studies available that describe how, in fact, a "normal" system actually works. In this chapter it will be argued that a normal system works in ways similar to that of a normal family. These ways, however, are very difficult to describe because they are very context dependent. In general, it is possible to suggest that a normal service system is flexible and able to adapt quickly to changes in its environment. The normal system also establishes clear boundaries and hierarchical relationships among participants so that triangling, conflictual relationships and overinvolvement of parties in the system is avoided. These boundaries are established structurally (e.g., in intra- and interorganizational relationships) and also culturally (e.g., they appear in participants' beliefs and actions).

To illustrate a normal service system at work with a particular child and family, one case collected in the Schwartzman *et al.* (1981) follow-up study mentioned earlier will be used.

SHARON

Sharon is a 9-year-old black female who did not start out in a normal system. Sharon's original family was a white, middle-class family who adopted her and another child (Bill, now age 10) when they were infants. Unfortunately when her adoptive parents had their own child, Sharon and Bill became dispensible children. In this case Sharon's family adopted a rejecting and expelling pattern but fortunately both children were expelled into a functioning service system that was able to help and not hinder their development. The system was able to do this for several reasons to be discussed below.

In the first place, the children elicited a great deal of sympathy from all service providers, who believed that the parents were at fault because they were rejecting their children. There were also reports of harsh and prolonged punishment, including isolation in their rooms, deprivation of food and water, and beatings. These reports were investigated, and it was decided that psychological (although probably not physical) abuse was present in the home. The parents also requested that the children be removed from their home. These events motivated child welfare and mental hospital staff to act quickly; and when the parents brought Sharon and Bill to the children's ward of the state mental hospital, they were immediately admitted for evaluation to aid in placement planning.

From the beginning, the parents portrayed Sharon as a hopeless case, whereas the helpers defined her as a hopeful case. This definition of the problem was crucial for mobilizing personnel and resources in the system. Unlike many hospitalization experiences for children, this particular hospitalization appeared to be well planned and well timed. It was felt that a foster family experience would not be useful because both children were coming from a very difficult family experience. Helpers believed that the children would benefit from a positive experience with adults (e.g., hospital staff) that was not in a family context. This would then facilitate their placement in a new home or homes. Fortunately, hospital staff liked Sharon and she was able to experience positive relations with adults in this context.

In this case the ultimate goal of helping personnel was to move Sharon *out* of the system by finding another potential adoptive family.[3] Sharon's behavior was defined as relatively normal for a child her age, given her "environment." This was very important as workers began to search for a new family for her. The child welfare office that handled her case was able to find a family for foster placement (and eventual adoption) that shared this definition of her behavior.

This office was located in a rural–suburban area, and staff were quite cohesive as a work group. Staff had also developed longstanding relationships with a variety of foster families as well as therapists in the area that were familiar with placement problems for foster/adoptive children. This office was also able to control and coordinate the variety of helpers involved in the placement of children. Clear lines of authority and responsibility between helpers had already been established because of past history, so there was less possibility for conflict and triangling to occur among service providers. The therapist involved with Sharon assembled the variety of family members (new foster family, Sharon's original family, and Sharon's brother's new foster family) and helpers (therapist, child welfare workers, and sometimes teachers) involved with this case to meetings and therapy sessions (especially in the beginning phase of placement). Following this, therapy sessions with the new family (including father, mother, three adopted children, and

3. This is in contrast to cases such as Mark, discussed earlier, where helpers appeared to believe (or were resigned to the idea) that the child could only move around *in* the system.

Sharon) were held in the family's home and periodic sessions with Sharon and her brother were held in the therapist's office.

When the final follow-up interview for the Schwartzman *et al.* (1981) study was conducted it was found that Sharon was adapting well to her new family. This family had initiated adoption proceedings, and it was anticipated that this would proceed smoothly.

There are many factors that explain what we see as the successful handling of this case by the service system. These include: (1) a flexible and fairly rapid response to the troubles of Sharon, her brother Bill, and their original family; (2) appropriate use of the hospital and a positive hospital experience from the viewpoint of the children; (3) a reframing by helpers and the new family of Sharon's presumed negative/patho-logical behavior as normal for her age and circumstances; (4) a desire to move Sharon *out* of the helping system; (5) existence of a relatively small working group of helpers with well-established lines of authority and responsibility; and (6) opportunities created for all family members and helpers involved with the case to meet each other and also to discuss aspects of the case. All of these factors appear to have contributed to the successful handling of this case, and it is possible to suggest that they may be characteristic of a normal service system. As suggested earlier, many of these features are also characteristic of normal family functioning as discussed in the literature.

Summary and Clinical Implications

In this chapter we have suggested an analogy between normal and abnormal family systems and normal and abnormal social service sys-tems. Three types of family and helper interaction patterns have been identified: (1) the too richly cross-joined system, (2) the too poorly cross-joined system, and (3) the normal system. There are several clinical implications of recognizing how and when the service system replicates functional and especially dysfunctional family patterns.

The first step toward correcting service system replication of family problems is obviously recognizing that such replications exist. This means that it is crucial for service providers to assess not only the state of the family but also that of the service system treating the family. It is suggested here that too richly cross-joined families should not, in general, be treated by too richly cross-joined systems. The reverse of this is also suggested: that too poorly cross-joined families will not, in general, benefit from treatment and/or services dispensed by a too poorly cross-joined system. The major point to be emphasized here is that family problems will not be resolved by a treatment/service system that repeats these problems at the helping level.

Recognition of the phenomenon of problem replication does not, however, necessarily mean that this replication will disappear. There may, in fact, be many systemic reasons why the problems are repeated at this level. These include the service system's need to maintain itself at all costs and the service providers' need to emphasize their distinctiveness as a treatment or service organization. This need will make it very difficult for service providers to see how their behavior may repeat dysfunctional family patterns. Periodic assessments of family *and service system* functioning in specific cases would appear to be one way to correct this problem.

To avoid the type of problem replication described in this chapter, it is possible to learn something from an examination of a normal service system. This examination has also been undertaken here by describing the case of Sharon. This case suggests that a normal service system functions in a similar fashion to a normal family. A normal service system: (1) is flexible and quick to adapt to changes in its environment; (2) establishes clear boundaries and hierarchical relationships among all parties involved in the treatment or service; and (3) provides opportunities for all parties to meet each other and recognize the part they have to play in both the treatment and/or maintenance of the family's problem.

The characteristics of a normal service system and a normal family are not surprising or difficult to understand, although they may be very difficult to achieve in practice. It is important, however, to recognize both that such systems do exist and that dysfunctional service systems patterned after dysfunctional family systems also exist. We believe that clinicians and all helpers will learn something important about their role in treatment by recognizing the existence of both types of systems.

REFERENCES

Aponte, H. The family–school interview. *Family Process*, 1976, *15*, 303–311. (a)

Aponte, H. Under-organization in the poor family. In P. Guerin (Ed.), *Family therapy: theory and practice*. New York: Gardner Press, 1976. (b)

Ashby, W. R. *Design for a brain*. London: Chapman & Hall, 1960.

Barbera-Stein, L. *Organizational cultures of service and issues of referral*. Institute for Juvenile Research, Research Report, December 1981.

Bateson, G. *Steps to an ecology of mind*. New York: Ballantine, 1972.

Bettelheim, B. *A home for the heart*. New York: Knopf, 1974.

Bettelheim, B., & Sylvester, E. A therapeutic milieu. *American Journal of Orthopsychiatry*, 1948, *18*, 191–206.

Bettelheim, B., & Wright, B. The role of residential treatment for children. *American Journal of Orthopsychiatry*, 1955, *25*, 705–719.

Bowen, M. The family as the unit of study and treatment. *American Journal of Orthopsychiatry*, 1955, *31*, 40–60.

Bowen, M. The use of family theory in clinical practice. *Comparative Psychiatry*, 1966, 7, 345–374.

Bowen, M. *Societal regression as viewed through family systems theory.* Paper presented at Nathan Ackerman Memorial Conference, New York, February 1974.

Bowen, M. Theory in the practice of psychotherapy. In *Family therapy in clinical practice.* New York: Aronson, 1978.

Bradshaw, S., & Burton, P. Naming: A measure of relationships in a ward milieu. *Bulletin of the Menninger Clinic*, 1976, 665–670.

Children's Defense Fund. *Children without homes.* Washington, D.C.: Author, 1978.

Dickson, W. J., & Roethlisberger, F. J. *Counseling in an organization.* Cambridge, Mass.: Harvard University Press, 1966.

Ebner, M. J. Hard hats vs. soft hearts: The conflict between principles and reality in child and adolescent care and treatment programs. *Child Care Quarterly*, 1979, 8, 36–46.

Fleck, S., Cornelison, A. R., Norton, N., & Lidz, T. Interaction between hospital staff and families. *Psychiatry*, 1957, 20, 343–350.

Freud, A., & Burlingham, D. *War and children.* New York: International Universities Press, 1943.

Gustafson, J. P. The pseudomutual small group or institution. In W. G. Lawrence (Ed.), *Exploring individual and organizational boundaries: A Tavistock open systems approach.* Chichester: Wiley, 1979.

Haley, J. The Art of being schizophrenic. In *The power tactics of Jesus Christ.* New York: Avon, 1969.

Haley, J. *Leaving home.* New York: McGraw-Hill, 1980.

Harbin, H. T. Families and hospitals: Collusion or cooperation? *American Journal of Psychiatry*, 1978, 135, 1496–1499.

Henry, J. Types of institutional structure. *Psychiatry*, 1957, 20, 47–60.

Henry, J. The culture of interpersonal relations in a therapeutic institution for emotionally disturbed children. In *On sham and vulnerability and other forms of self-destruction.* New York: Vintage Books, 1973.

Hirschhorn, L., & Gilmore, T. The application of family therapy concepts to influencing organizational behavior. *Administrative Science Quarterly*, 1980, 25, 18–37.

Hoffman, L. *Foundations of family therapy.* New York: Basic Books, 1981.

Kaplan, M. Problems between a referring source and a child guidance clinic. In S. A. Szurek & I. N. Berlin (Eds.), *The antisocial child: His family and his community.* Palo Alto, Calif.: Science & Behavior Books, 1952.

Kerr, M. E. *Bridge over troubled waters: A work system experience.* Paper presented at Georgetown University Symposium on Family Psychotherapy, Washington, D.C., November 1973.

Krause, M. K. Personal communication, 1982.

Litwak, E., & Meyer, H. J. A balance theory of coordination between bureaucratic organizations and community primary groups. *Administrative Science Quarterly*, 1966, 2, 31–58.

Minard, S. Family systems model in organizational consultation: Vignettes of consultation to a day care center. *Family Process*, 1976, 15, 313–320.

Minuchin, S. *Families and family therapy.* Boston: Harvard University Press, 1974.

Montalvo, B., & Pavlin, S. Faulty staff communications in a residential treatment center. *American Journal of Orthopsychiatry*, 1966, 36, 706–711.

Olson, D. H., Sprenkle, D. H., & Russell, C. S. Circumplex model of marital and family systems: I. Cohesion and adaptability dimensions, family types and clinical applications. *Family Process*, 1979, 18, 3–28.

Parsons, T. *The structure of social action.* Glencoe, Ill.: Free Press, 1949.

Piliavin, I. Conflict between cottage parents and caseworkers. In A. Kadushin (Ed.), *Child welfare services: A sourcebook.* London: Macmillan, 1970.

Reiss, D. Varieties of consensual experience: I. A theory for relating family interaction to individual thinking. *Family Process*, 1971, *10*, 1–27. (a)

Reiss, D. Varieties of consensual experience: II. Dimensions of a family's experience of its environment. *Family Process*, 1971, *10*, 28–35. (b)

Roethlisberger, F. J., & Dickson, W. J. *Management and the worker.* Cambridge, Mass.: Harvard University Press, 1939.

Scheinfeld, D. *Banter in staff–patient interactions: Illustrating a psychosocial approach to understanding the actions of caretakers on a children's mental ward.* Institute for Juvenile Research, Research Report, Chicago, December, 1981.

Scheinfeld, D. Personal communication, 1982.

Schwartzman, H. B., Kneifel, A. W., Barbera-Stein, L., & Gaviria, E. *Children, families and mental health service organizations: Cultures in conflict.* Paper presented at the 28th Annual Meeting of the American Academy of Child Psychiatry, Dallas, October 14–18, 1981.

Schwartzman, J., & Bokos, P. Methadone maintenance: The addict's family re-created. *International Journal of Family Therapy*, 1979, *1*, 338–355.

Steinfeld, G. J. Parallels between the pathological family and the mental hospital: A search for a process. Psychiatry, 1970, *33*, 36–55.

Stierlin, H. *Separating parents and adolescents.* New York: Quadrangle, 1974.

Sullivan, H. S. Socio-psychiatric research: Its implications for the schizophrenia problem and for mental hygiene. *Psychiatry*, 1931, *10*, 977–991.

Szurek, S. A. The family and the staff in hospital psychiatric therapy of children. *American Journal of Orthopsychiatry.* 1951, *21*, 597–611.

Toennies, F. *Fundamental concepts of sociology.* New York: American Books, 1940.

Walsh, F. (Ed.). *Normal family processes.* New York: Guilford Press, 1982.

Weber, G. H. Conflicts between professional and non-professional persons in institutional delinquency treatment. *Journal of Criminal Law, Criminology and Police Science*, 1950, *48*, 26–43.

White, W. L. *Incest in the organizational family: The unspoken issue in staff and program burn-out.* Paper presented at the National Drug Abuse Conference, Seattle, April 3–8, 1978.

Wynne, L., Ryckoff, I. M., Day, J., & Hirsch, S. I. Pseudo-mutuality in the family relations of schizophrenics. *Psychiatry*, 1958, *21*, 205–220.

6

The family and the psychiatric hospital

HENRY T. HARBIN
University of Maryland Medical School and
Maryland Mental Hygiene Administration

Introduction

This chapter will focus on how families of psychiatric patients can be helped and managed more effectively during the hospital phase of treatment. This will include a discussion of specific engagement and treatment techniques for families of inpatients, a unique family-oriented inpatient ward, some outcome studies, and special problems of families of chronic patients (Harbin, 1978, 1979, 1980, 1982a, 1982b; Krajewski & Harbin, 1982). I will also describe some of the transactional processes that occur between hospitals and families as organizational entities, as well as briefly delineate the different structures and functions of bureaucracies like hospitals and primary support groups like families. Finally there will be a brief focus upon families' abilities to influence, both in a positive and negative sense, the functions of psychiatric hospitals. The primary goal of this chapter is, however, a clinical one: to inform mental health professionals of various strategies and options available to them when they involve the family in a systematic, planned way during the treatment of a hospitalized psychiatric patient.

As a clinician begins to observe and alter the transactions that occur between himself as a part of the staff of a psychiatric hospital and the family of the mental patient, it can be enlightening to be aware of both the broader, sociological functions that institutions/hospitals and families serve, as well as the developmental history of how psychiatric hospitals and families have been intertwined in the past. Sussman, Litwak, and others have conceptualized the linkage between bureaucratic organizations such as hospitals and primary support groups such as families as an accommodating, complementary one (Dobrof & Litwak, 1977; Sussman, 1982). They view this model as more accurate than earlier theories that described bureaucracies as either incompatible with, or needing to be isolated from, families. Simply put, families and bureaucracies need each other, as they are interdependent; but they also have different missions, strengths, and functions. This particular sociological framework seems to be a helpful one for clinicians, as it can assist in the difficult process of

(1) understanding the sometimes confusing and contradictory behaviors of families as they interact with psychiatric hospitals as organizations, (2) becoming aware of the conflicts inevitably present in the transactions of large formal organizations with primary informal support groups, which may not be the result of an internal dysfunction of either systemic entity, and (3) enabling hospitals to fully assist families to maximize their potential as curative, rehabilitative agents for themselves and their patient/family members.

Families, as small informal primary groups in society, have a number of properties that are distinct. They function primarily as an emotional system designed to produce a supportive, caring milieu for individuals, both young and old. Individuals are members for life and families seem best able to handle the simple tasks of society, like preparing food and cleaning, as well as the more complex mandates of transmitting the values of society throughout the generations. Individual members may carry out multiple roles at once and tend not to specialize. Generally there is a hierarchy present, but it is more flexible than the chain of command in large organizations. Additionally, families can handle unusual, idiosyncratic events more flexibly and easily than can a bureaucratic organization (Dobrof & Litwak, 1977).

Bureaucracies, such as hospitals, tend toward a great deal of specialization of roles for individual workers, as well as requiring the existence of well-delineated and fairly rigid hierarchies. Psychiatric hospitals, as one type of bureaucracy, use multiple specialists to accomplish various caretaking responsibilities like cooking, cleaning, and dispensing of medication, which might be handled by one or two family members. Individuals are not present for emotional support but are involved in instrumental tasks geared towards the accomplishment of the organization's objectives. Bureaucracies handle routines best and do not cope well with unusual behaviors or events. Reward, advancement, and inclusion are based more on merit than in families; and, of course, individuals can and do leave bureaucracies, either willingly or unwillingly.

The interactions between families with a mentally ill member and psychiatric hospitals can be better understood when one views them as subsystems of the broader macrosystem of families as primary informal groups in society and hospitals as a type of formal bureaucracy. The above discussion helps orient the clinician to certain conflicts and potential solutions that are embedded in the roles that families play in society and the interaction of these roles with the organizational behaviors of the hospital.

A clinical example can help illustrate the necessity for understanding the influence of these formal properties upon families when they deal with the psychiatric hospital and with the constraints upon clinicians when they try to intervene in such family–bureaucratic linkage transitions. One of the more common conflicts that families with a mentally ill relative have with hospitals is the arbitrariness and restrictiveness of visiting hours. Family-oriented clinicians who try to actively engage families in inpatient treatment are aware that the design of visiting hours can be crucial to the success or failure of the engagement of a particular family or of the whole program. Usually the visiting hours are set by the nursing staff or the hospital administration. At first glance they might seem arbitrary and even anti-family. Yet as we refer back to the discussion of the typical functions of a large bureaucracy, routine handling of tasks is a necessary and integral part of an effectively functioning organization. We can also see that this is not necessarily so for families. Although they need to maintain their own rituals and patterns, they have a greater tolerance and allowance for spontaneity and emotional responsiveness. It would not be helpful or effective for a family to rigidly plan all visits with each other. To ask a hospital to arrange visiting hours only for the convenience of families might lead to considerable inefficiency for nursing staff and others. Their routine tasks, for example, dispensing medication, arranging lab tests, would be disrupted by having to divert their attention to family members at any time. Planning for the accomplishment of non-family-oriented activities may become impossible, thereby leading to the minimization of other therapeutic goals for patients. On the other side, very rigid and restrictive visiting hours, such as are present in many psychiatric hospitals, will decrease family–patient contact, may encourage more negative feelings by the family members toward the patient because of the increased inconvenience, and may undermine the treatment goals of intimately involving the family in clinical decision making and planning. The therapist desiring to better accommodate a particular family and a specific psychiatric hospital/bureaucracy needs to be aware of the systemic constraints and rewards on both sides. If visiting hours are redesigned, critical if one wants to involve family members, then the nursing staff and administrators will need to be part of the planning so that the necessary disruption of hospital routine can be minimized and the organizational integrity of the hospital maintained.

As clinicians take into account these family–bureaucratic transactions, they must also be aware of the ability of their own psychiatric hospital to operate as an effective organizational instrument of change. The Mental health professionals will be focusing upon the strengths and weaknesses of the family system as they plan treatment strategy for patients. The goals will usually include stabilizing the structure of a family, increasing the quality of communication to alleviate the stress of the patient, and educating the family about how to cope with the patient's problem. Yet the clinicians must also attend to their own organizational/professional milieu as the stability and consistency of the hospital as a system will inevitably affect the quality of the therapeutic effort for some families.

In the previous discussion, I briefly delineated some of the properties of a viable bureaucracy. This baseline information becomes crucial as one tries to assess when a large organization is not functioning effectively. The hierarchy of authority in a psychiatric hospital may be split or unclear, thus leading to indecision and poor management. The family and/or clinician can easily be caught in this intraorganizational difficulty when he or she begins to try to change a family system. Family members may respond by allying with one part of the hospital against the primary therapist, thereby leading to a therapeutic impasse. Some detailed clinical consequences of these administrative maneuvers by families have been discussed in previous papers by the author (Harbin, 1978; Krajewski & Harbin, 1982). I want to draw the reader's attention to the relationship of this reaction on the family's part to the organizational stability or lack thereof of the psychiatric hospital. Basically, the less efficient the hospital as a bureaucratic organization, the more likely the family–patient treatment will derail in this manner. Again, awareness of how families and bureaucracies should optimally function as individual systems, the type of the macrosystem that they form when interacting, and how they are in fact affecting each other in a particular instance is crucial knowledge for the clinician as he or she designs either an individual treatment plan for a family–patient or a family-oriented program on an inpatient unit.

Clinical Approaches

This part of the chapter will explicitly focus upon treatment issues for the family. I realize, however, that this will highlight only one part of the family/hospital transactional sequence, the hospital staff's attempt to change family/patient and not the reverse. My experience in this area comes from a variety of sources. As a psychiatric resident, I engaged a number of families to help with the treatment of inpatients, usually without a clear therapeutic rationale or consistent support from my educational and administrative supervisors (with the exception of the social worker on the ward). Later, working with outpatients and their families, I received a great deal of family therapy supervision. When I took over an acute admitting inpatient unit of a univeristy hospital in 1975 as a ward administrator, I decided to develop the whole treatment program with a family orientation and to conceptualize the process and try to identify unique treatment strategies for this type of family work. I was told by a few experts in the field that this was an impossible task, as one could not change a family while the patient was hospitalized. As some of the results indicate, this was not an accurate prediction. Changing the therapeutic orientation of an inpatient unit was much easier from the position of being a physician–administrator, but it is possible to create similar alterations from other staff roles and positions. Later I will describe in more detail how this particular ward developed.

The ideas and conclusions generated on this family-oriented unit were later applied to a variety of other psychiatric settings by myself, as well as students and residents who rotated through the ward. These other settings included state hospitals, both acute and chronic units; nonuniversity general hospital wards; special private psychiatric hospitals; adolescent units; and children's residential centers. The concepts presented in this chapter are drawn from these multiple applications, the professional literature, as well as from the author's experience as an outpatient psychiatrist who has admitted patients to the hospital and has attempted to make this a therapeutic event for both the family and the patient.

Literature Review

There is a scanty and not particularly increasing professional literature on the subject of the family's involvement with the psychiatric inpatient. This is, of course, markedly different from the trend in the professional literature with outpatient family work. There have been a number of clinical articles which point out the value of involving families during the hospital phase of treatment (Burks & Serrano, 1965; Gralnick, 1963, 1969; Laqueur & LaBurt, 1964; Norton, Detre, & Jarecki, 1963; Fleck, Cornelison, Norton, & Lidz, 1957; Rabiner, Molinski, & Gralnick, 1962; Schween & Gralnick, 1966). Usually these articles do not develop in any great detail the exact family therapeutic strategy. There have been several early interesting papers on hospitalization of whole families or couples, and this information is quite useful to clinicians (Abroms, Fellner, Whitaker, 1971; Bowen, 1965; White & Molnar, 1972; Grunebaum, Weiss, Gallant, et al., 1971; Main, 1958; Steinglass, Davis, & Berenson, 1977).

None of this work is still going on, to my knowledge, and there has been nothing in the literature on this recently. Apparently this is a phase that never developed fully, unlike the involvement of families when one member was hospitalized. The reasons for this are quite evident: (1) cost of hospitalization for more than one person, (2) the trend away from hospitalizing anyone, (3) brief hospital stays, and (4) the very questionable rationale of hospitalizing a family member who is not actively symptomatic and/or experiencing a diagnosed mental illness. It is interesting that a community mental health center in Maryland that was planned during the 1960s had a ward designed and built for the admission of whole families. When the unit was finally opened in 1980, it was renovated so that only individuals could be admitted.

With the exception of recent articles by Lansky (1977) and Anderson (1977), much of the clinical literature in this area usually emphasizes the following: (1) family involvement only for selected patients, (2) conjoint family therapy usually does not start at the beginning of the hospitalization, (3) there is often no systematic involvement of the family in all phases of the hospital treatment, (4) the family/therapist's role is split from the primary therapist or physician, (5) family therapy is often a secondary consideration and may only be initiated after a crisis has occurred. Both Lansky and Anderson have published articles that describe wards somewhat similar to the ones at the University of Maryland in which the whole inpatient treatment program has been geared towards involving and engaging the family. In addition to these clinical articles is the important work done by John Bell (1982) in his survey of how families are involved in other countries in both medical and psychiatric hospitals. He found that many developing countries rely heavily on families as a support system for the patients while they are in the hospital and that this worked rather well.

There have been a few outcome studies that have attempted to measure both the impact of family involvement as well as treatment during hospitalization. The reader is referred to Glick and Clarkin (1982) for a more detailed review. The results are mixed at this stage, which one might expect with such a complex research design and with so few studies. Nevertheless, some researchers do show a definite positive effect both for family presence and treatment. As with all psychotherapeutic outcome research, data are missing in terms of who will benefit from what approach and how much and what kind they need. It is interesting, however, that most clinicians who have attempted to involve and change patients with their families during the hospital phase have felt that it usually but not always offers clear advantages over noninvolvement of the family.

University of Maryland Family Ward

In 1975 I became director of a 15-bed acute inpatient ward, which was a major teaching unit for the Institute of Psychiatry and Human Behavior, University of Maryland Medical School. As I mentioned, this ward was gradually changed so that a family orientation was adopted for almost all inpatients during all phases of treatment. My leadership of this ward lasted 3 years, and during this time, the families of over 80% of the patients were engaged in at least two or more family treatment sessions. During the 3rd year, over 90% of the families were involved; and the psychiatric residents, who were usually the primary therapists (this role also incorporated that of the family therapist), would conduct somewhere between 180 to 220 conjoint family sessions in a year. Clearly these statistics show that engagement was a success even though outcome studies were not systematically conducted. All families, if present, were evaluated—and this might include any important person in the social network, not only biological relatives. Anyone living with the patient who helped either financially or socially was seen as a priority. The families were included in a number of ways in this particular unit: "(1) family admission interviews, (2) conjoint family therapy sessions, (3) multifamily groups, (4) family-oriented therapeutic leave of absences, (5) the constant review, via staff meetings and conferences, as to how the family is effecting the hospitalized patient's behavior and vice versa, and (6) administrative policies that encouraged the inclusion of families into the ward life" (Harbin, 1979).

While the implementation of a family orientation in a psychiatric hospital would clearly vary depending upon the type or mission of the institution, there are a number of generally applicable principles. Family treatment techniques with inpatients need to be symptom oriented, flexible, pragmatic, usually short-term, applicable to the severely ill patient, seen as one phase of the treatment, and must be integrated with other treatment modalities. We no longer live in an age when hospital psychiatric treatment is seen as either an appropriate beginning or end phase of treatment; even if this sometimes happens by default. Consequently, family involvement has to be seen as complying with this phase-specific perspective. It is less and less often that one sees a mildly disturbed patient in the hospital, as these people are usually treated in outpatient settings. Therefore, one must use family techniques that are applicable for the severely ill patient like chronic schizophrenics and their parents or patients with severe effective disorders and their spouses. One cannot successfully carry out family therapy on an inpatient ward without integrating other treatment methods like group treatment, medications, individual psychotherapy. There are almost no research data that supports family therapy alone, excluding medications and other interventions, with severely ill patients, and my own clinical experience does not support this with these patients, who are the ones that predominantly reside in psychiatric hospitals.

Stages of Treatment

This next session will describe the general phases of family treatment during the hospital stay as well as discuss some special problem areas related to this.

Admission, Engagement, and Problem Identification

The admission of the psychiatric patient is almost always perceived as a crisis by the family even if they are somewhat estranged from the patient. If a patient has been living at home, then most likely there have been a series of disturbing interpersonal and intrapersonal incidents that have necessitated some kind of institutional intervention. The staff of the traditional psychiatric hospital will usually try to interview the family upon arrival or within the first few days. The focus will probably be on acquiring historical information and on looking at the family's desires for future support of the patient. It is likely that the patient will not be present during the interview. Sometimes the family may be given detailed information about the hospital, sometimes not. It is unlikely that the family will be formally reinvolved until discharge is near.

If one wants to fully utilize the strengths of the family during the hospital phase of treatment, then these traditional procedures are insufficient. Ideally the family will be notified at the preadmission stage that their presence is necessary on the first day of hospitalization. If engagement is to be maximally effective, the family should be involved from the beginning and during all phases. Preferably all adult family members living with the patient should be interviewed on the first day, both with and without the patient. The focus of the first interview should not be only upon historical gathering of facts but on a clear description of the patient's problem as each family member perceives it and some observations of how family members deal with each other.

In addition to clinical techniques specific for the family, which I will amplify shortly, there are a number of programmatic/administrative procedures available that will enhance engagement. All staff, from the clerical staff to the physicians, should be aware of the importance of involvement of the family and of their role in this process. If the staff nurses give the impression to a family that they are in the way during the admission procedure, while the primary therapist is telling them they are crucial to success, problems will ensue. Consistency of communications by all staff will become paramount to successful treatment. This can be very difficult to achieve given the rampant ideological splits that are often present among mental health professionals. Each person will want to emphasize his or her own area of expertise and implicitly minimize either the importance or the necessity of other treatment systems. The ward director needs to constantly attend to the staff perceptions of their roles with the family, no matter how peripheral. A special danger arises if a family orientation is being introduced as a new treatment. The clinician with the family therapy expertise may oversell the approach and thereby increase resistance. Special care must be taken during the early stages to present the family orientation as one additional modality; it does not necessarily replace the others. Later when all staff members are comfortable in their understanding of family treatment techniques and have seen that it can be a powerful force, more frank discussions of the relative merits vis-à-vis other treatment strategies may take place. This may be particularly hard for family therapists with outpatient experience, as they are accustomed to more complete and autonomous control over therapeutic decision making. This type of control and independence is much harder to achieve in an inpatient unit.

Each staff member should receive some education about family dynamics and treatment, and the more involved they become, the easier this is to accomplish. The importance of the admission staff cannot be emphasized enough. Sometimes the admitting officer or fiscal clerk may introduce confusion about how to handle a family. This happened in one hospital when a particular secretary encouraged all adolescents to sign in voluntarily, even though this was not necessary or helpful in some cases with the parents. At the University of Maryland, we designed a routine admissions procedure for families. They were always included in the tour of the unit given to the parents, were interveiwed extensively, were invited to multifamily group meetings, were told that their involvement was of utmost importance, and were given a letter written by the ward director for families. This letter tried to briefly explain why families were involved in the hospital in this particular way and requested their presence at certain meetings. For several reasons not every patient was told that conjoint family therapy was indicated. It was not felt that all families needed this, and this decision was left up to the primary therapist. The primary therapist was not always able to do the admissions interview even though this was desirable. These various interventions by the ward director were partly responsible for the high degree of engagement at the University of Maryland ward.

Many hospitals split the role of primary therapist from that of the family therapist. A number of reasonable explanations are given for this; sometimes, however, the split sometimes disguises the fact that the primary therapist is really not working closely with the patient; and the only therapy going on is with the family by another therapist. However, in my view, this is an unwieldy situation for the treatment of most families. Generally families want relevant information from the therapist of the individual patient and should have access to this. The primary therapist can use this time to assess and try to guide the family in more effective ways to interact with the patient/family member. The purpose of the inpatient family treatment is to help those living with the patient to deal with him or her in a different manner, if necessary. To split off the patient and his or her therapist from this process only reduces the leverage of the hospital staff. A primary therapist who is going to truly understand and manage all aspects of the individual patient's situation will need to know and guide the family as well as the individual. This does not mean that individual therapy sessions will be eliminated. Further, the family therapist, if different from that of the primary therapist, may become ineffective if he or she does not have control or input into key treatment decisions like discharge date and leave of absences. Imagine working with the family on a certain set of crucial issues only to find that the individual therapist or physician has made a unilateral decision to send the patient home.

GUILT VERSUS RESPONSIBILITY

Involvement of families in either inpatient or outpatient settings carries some real risk. The primary one is an increase in the family's sense of guilt about the patient. This is particularly true of parents of seriously disturbed offspring but can become a major point of contention for spouses also. Unfortunately some psychiatrists and other mental health professionals have communicated to families that they are somehow to blame for certain mental problems in children. Family therapists have unwittingly contributed even further to this problem when they have tried to explain to families that there are communication patterns that create symptoms. The lack of clarity in the field about the etiology of the major mental illnesses has exacerbated the guilt of families, and clinicians need to be particularly sensitive to this when they involve families during the evaluation phase of treatment.

When families are asked to participate during the hospital stay, they are often being told explicitly that they should assume some responsibility for the management of the illness of their family member. Of course, some families will choose not to resume further responsibility for their relative, and this choice must be respected. The clinician should carefully differentiate this management responsibility from any implication that the family caused or is to blame for the creation of the illness (Weinstein, 1982). Even if the family does not raise the issue of guilt, it should be addressed explicity, as it is almost a universal phenomena. The mental health professional can communicate to the family that a supportive, consistent social network will be helpful in the rehabilitation of any illness, physical or mental. Further, some families can be told that they may have to change various aspects of how they deal with the patient, not necessarily because there is anything inherently wrong with their present style but because of the particular problem or circumstances of the patient. Some patients will benefit from a different approach by the family. For example, parents of an acting-out teenager may be requested to spend more time discussing how they can be more consistent in their limit setting. The parents may ask why this is necessary, as they did not have to do this with their other children, and are the therapists implying that they are abnormal somehow? The therapist can clearly state that if they did not have a teenager who was not able to control him- or herself, and was not so sensitive to inconsistency, then the change in their style would not be necessary.

CASE EXAMPLE[1]

The following case discussion is presented to demonstrate a variety of issues: (1) how a family member's sense of guilt can be destructive to the treatment, (2) how the engagement process can be handled, and (3) some factors relevant to the hospital and family treatment of chronic patients. The patient was a 55-year-old white female, Jane, admitted for the fifth time to a psychiatric hospital in Maryland. She had been in and out of psychiatric hospitals over a 15-year period and carried a diagnosis of chronic paranoid schizophrenia. She was committed to the hospital this time for delusions, hallucinations, loose associations, bizarre behavior, autistic behavior, and aggressive acting out. She had gone off her medications several months prior to hospitalization and had stopped outpatient treatment.

Jane was married and had three children, all but one of whom had moved out. The pattern in the marriage was one of increased estrangement, with the husband becoming more and more of a caretaker for his invalid, disabled wife. She alternately fought and eagerly pursued this kind of paternalistic attention from her husband. Her periods of assertion with him were usually marked by irrational outbursts that invalidated her attempts at autonomy. She was very hostile on admission; but with the reinstatement of her medications and a stabilizing milieu, she calmed rapidly. The husband was interviewed separately on the first day and then with his wife during the first week. He was told that it was desired that he would attend weekly conjoint family therapy sessions with his wife and occasionally the children would be included. He had previously stated that he wanted to continue living with his wife. The purpose of the sessions were explained, that is, to help him better support his wife, to find ways to cope with her disturbing behavior, and to seek strategies to improve the relationship. The husband agreed reluctantly but did not express any feelings of guilt or blame. He did state that he didn't think that the family sessions were necessary, as he had been through this kind of treatment before when she was an

1. The primary therapist for this patient and family was Dr. Sunday Morgan, a psychiatric resident at the University of Maryland who was managing the patient at Springfield Hospital Center, a state hospital in Maryland.

outpatient and that his wife's problems would not be solved by anything he did or didn't do. He stated that the major problem was her non-compliance with medications and that all he needed help with was finding a way for the clinic or hospital staff to force his wife to be compliant with outpatient treatment. The family therapist, an experienced psychiatric resident who was also the primary clinician, stated that these were indeed serious problems and that the hospital would try to help him with his situation. She, the therapist, did not try to argue with the husband that he did not understand family dynamics and that if he was changed in some way, that his wife's illness would disappear. Instead, the therapist went on to elicit what past steps the husband had taken to try to deal with his wife's major symptomatology, for example, bizarre behavior, writing on walls, withdrawal, yelling. This was done in front of the wife, but the language used by the therapist was neutral and nonblaming and attempted to explain her symptoms in behavioral terms that could be observed and segmented into discrete entities. For example, when the husband was asked about her delusions, he would state that she was irrational and thought that everyone was after her. The therapist then asked what the husband did when she acted on these fears and to describe what both his actions were as well as his wife's. This lead away from a preoccupation with motivation and affects of the wife to observable behavior around which a plan of action could be established for the husband. The husband responded well to these questions by the therapist, but the wife became somewhat agitated at the rehashing of these previous episodes of her loss of control. The therapist stated that if she got too restless, she could leave for a few minutes and then return and that the rationale of the sessions was not to blame her but to help her. The option of sending patients out of the room when they become too agitated shows the advantage of having an office on the ward, which gives more structure and control to acutely psychotic patients.

The first conjoint family session ended with a general plan and the husband's restating his pessimism about his wife's condition. The therapist, in attempting to ally with the husband, agreed that his wife's situation was chronic but injected a cautious note of optimism based on a number of factors. The wife was trying a new medication. She had many supporters and assets, particularly her family. Although she might not be "cured," she had a lot of room for improvement and for reaching a higher level of functioning than she had for the past several years. The therapist took this stance with the husband because of the chronicity of the situation and because the husband probably would not have listened to her if she had been overly optimistic. With psychotic patients who are not chronic, a more optimistic approach would have been appropriate.

The husband engaged well in this family session; and as his wife improved, he became more and more hopeful. Part of the family treatment included having the couple spend more time together in social and recreational activities on weekends. After approximately 6 weeks, the wife reported that they had begun sleeping in the same bedroom for the first time in several years. Due to her previous bizarre behavior and poor grooming, the husband had moved into another bedroom of their house.

The therapist attempted to help the husband with his worries about noncompliance in two ways: (1) by encouraging more assertion on his part in weekend tasks and (2) by putting the patient on an extended convalescent leave that would allow for rapid readmission to the hospital if she began to decompensate. Additionally, the husband and wife were assigned the task one weekend (after she had reached symptomatic stability for several weeks) of having her practice having a return of some symptoms and pretending to refuse help or return to the hospital. This pretend situation required the husband to call his oldest son (who had been involved in these scenes before), and the two of them were to escort the wife back to the hospital to practice forcing her into a structured setting when she was out of control. This was carried out on a Sunday, a day when she was planning on returning to the hospital anyway. It took several weeks of practice before the husband and wife would comply fully with the task, but they eventually accomplished it in their own manner. It was felt that this increased the husband's confidence to confront his wife and demonstrated to her that she could be pushed more forcibly by him when she was out of control. While this intervention may have had an impact because of its paradoxical nature, the primary rationale was a behavioral rehearsal of how to handle a feared situation.

In the final family session prior to transfer to an outpatient therapist, the husband was moderately optimistic and was very grateful to the hospital therapist, admitting that his initial skepticism of the family approach was not totally correct. He also voiced for the first time his longstanding fears that he was and had been blamed for "causing" his wife's illness by being a "bad" husband in the past. Naturally, the therapist reassured him that this was not the case, but it was interesting that the sense of guilt was there anyway. Again, it was pointed out that helping him to better cope with his wife's problem did not imply that he caused it. The wife had improved considerably after approximately eight weeks of hospitalization and had done well on a month-long leave of absence. The quality of the marriage had also changed dramatically and for the first time in years, the husband and wife were acting more as a couple and the husband was beginning to see his wife as an asset rather than a liability.

Problem Identification and Therapeutic Orientation

This clinical vignette elucidates several points. One is the importance of engaging the patient and family where they are and not trying to radically change their perception of the situation immediately. Another is the necessity of being very specific and problem-oriented with the family. Inpatient family treatment usually needs to be problem/symptom oriented with a behavioral focus. There are many models of family therapy, and only a minority seem to emphasize a behavioral approach (Madanes & Haley, 1977; Hoffman, 1981). It is hard to imagine how a nondirective, explorative family treatment will be helpful with most inpatients and their families. Yet, as I consult and supervise with other professionals doing this work, this seems to be the more common orientation. Many family therapists, having been trained to work with less severe problems in outpatient settings, try to (1) accomplish too much in the hospital with families, (2) encourage too much interaction and affective interchanges, (3) explore sensitive issues too quickly, and (4) focus primarily on clarifying and opening up communications. These strategies can lead to trouble with hospital patients and their families and often increases resistance. The therapist should focus on very concrete, specific problems that can be translated into behavioral and/or cognitive goals.

The presenting problem of the patient that necessitated hospitalization is the area for most of the therapeutic attention. Change of long-term patterns can rarely be attempted during the hospital phase. If the patient has come in because of a suicide attempt, the family treatment efforts need to be directed to preventing another self-destructive episode. If the chief complaint is depression, then only those behaviors or cognitive difficulties related to the depression that necessitated hospitalization are targeted during the hospital treatment. Of course, the family will often have to change its structure and/or communicational patterns when it responds differently to the patient, but these alterations will be centered around the major symptomatology of the patient. The family clinician needs to be aware of pertinent family dynamics and structures, as these familial interactions may serve at worst a symptom-maintaining function or at best are just not optimally supportive of positive growth. Basically, the hospital therapist does not attempt to "descapegoat" the patient but keeps the focus on the patient. This orientation will also help alleviate the family member's guilt about being somehow to blame for the mental illness.

A great deal of the skill involved in this type of work comes into play in defining or relabeling the problem of the patient and the family. Once this is done, useful treatment strategies can be designed that will change the patient as well as the context in which the patient resides.

This focus is maintained even though the therapist is aware of the theoretical assumption that it is the interpersonal nexus that is a part of the problem of the patient. The change in the patient's behavior is, of course, in part related to altering the family context, but one tries to use the symptoms as the lever for this realignment. The patient and the family are not coming to the hospital overtly for treatment of their interactions but to ameliorate some problem in an individual. In fact, it is often a disadvantage to use the term *family therapy* with some patients and their families as this terminology can imply that the problem to be changed is the family and not the patient. It sometimes is more useful to use words like "family involvement in treatment" or "helping the family cope better."

Middle Phase of Treatment

Once the therapeutic alliance has been established, the problems have been identified, and the family has been oriented to the rationale and type of treatment, then the family therapist may shift to another stage. These steps may take one session or more, depending on the particular situation. The second phase of treatment encompasses the direct planning and implementation of change strategies. By now the therapist has decided what needs to be done and will begin to move the family into a particular direction. Naturally, the specific type of treatment strategy will vary with the individual and family dynamics, but some general principles will be outlined.

It is often helpful to divide and classify symptomatology of the more severe problems into ones that are actively out of control and, therefore, require methods of suppression by the family or behaviors that are more related to withdrawal and passivity and, therefore, are in need of strategies of activation and/or motivation by the family. The various subtypes of depression and the negative symptoms of schizophrenic, extremely anxious, phobic persons are representative of the latter classification. Some examples of the disruptive, out-of-control symptoms are violent behavior, severe agitation and manic symptoms, and delusions and hallucinations that lead to overt, bizarre, and obnoxious behaviors. These two types of symptomatic groups are often interwoven and can occur with the same patient during the same day.

With the out-of-control, disruptive behaviors, the family will need to be supported by the therapist to regain some sense of authority and mastery over the patient. The hospital staff can be either very helpful or very destructive in this process. If the hospital staff attempts to gradually shift the control of the patient to the family, then the family may begin to reassert their authority. If the hospital staff, as often happens, excludes the family and does not help them exert leverage with the disruptive symptomatology, then these behaviors may escalate whenever the patient goes home. The exact techniques for making this transition to control by the family will vary depending upon the family structure and the idiosyncratic situation of the patient. If the patient is a violent husband and the wife needs help in learning how to protect herself and to set limits on her husband, then one type of intervention will be warranted. If the patient is a teenager with schizophrenia who is paranoid and agitated, then the parents will be encouraged to use a different type of control and structure.

The first step in helping the family reestablish control is during the problem-definition stage, which almost always involves some confrontation with the patient about his disturbing behavior. Then the patient, whether psychotic or not, will attempt to deny or minimize the destructive consequences of his or her behavior. The family will often collude with this denial. The therapist must help describe and label these acting-out behaviors as just that and to clearly communicate the expectation that the symptomatic actions will cease. When accomplished skillfully, this first session can be extremely powerful in helping the family feel confident about their management of the patient.

CASE EXAMPLE

This case vignette is a composite of a number of typical situations handled on most inpatient units. The patient is an adolescent or young adult with either a severe conduct disorder or borderline personality and some aggressive behaviors. The patient is living at home but (1) is not following rules, (2) is disruptive (perhaps violent), (3) is not working or going to school, and (4) is possibly abusing drugs or alcohol. During the initial interview, the parents minimize the seriousness of the problem, and it is only with some pushing from the therapist that accurate information is elicited as to how serious the out-of-control behavior is. The therapist attempts to reestablish a clear and consistent hierarchy of authority with both parents being in charge. Naturally, this goal is complicated by the patient being in the hospital where the staff is in charge. Further, the parents seem to disagree about how to handle the patient's dysfunctional behaviors. The crucial test periods occur on the weekend leave of absence during which clear directives are given to the parents. They are asked to focus on a specific set of behaviors, in this instance, violent symptoms, to define it, and to plan on what they will do if it occurs over the weekend. If the young adult is getting drunk on the weekend and breaking up furniture, then the parents should design a series of action steps for what to do. This may include taking away any alcohol, talking to the patient, physical restraints, or calling the police and having the patient brought back to the hospital. Naturally, if the patient's behavior reaches a dangerous level, either self- or other-directed, while on leave of absence, then return to the hospital is indicated. However, it is important not to plan this alternative as a first choice, as it may encourage too much dependency on the hospital. Having the hospital available as a backup to the patient and family is a tremendous support. This will encourage the family to find new techniques to reestablishing a stable home situation.

Once the patient has been able to set limits on himself for several weekend leave of absences and the parents feel confident that they are on top of things, then discharge can be considered. Even though the family therapy has been patient/symptom oriented, the family has had to make changes in its organization and communication patterns. The parents have had to talk with each other more and in a clear and specific fashion. They have had to exert authority as an executive team without undermining each other. Even though the therapist does not focus explicitly on these patterns, in the session, he is aware of numerous disagreements between the parents prior to the hospitalization about the seriousness of the youngster's behavior and how they should deal with it. The therapy, however, helps the family change these communication patterns in order to reestablish a different way of dealing with the patient's symptoms, not because their disagreements themselves are seen as a problem. The parents have changed while they have been attending to the patient's behavior. This brief composite case example outlines the importance of the weekend leave of absence and of changing the structure of the family utilizing the patient's dysfunctional behavior as a lever.

EXPECTATIONS

When the therapist helps the family attempt to either regain control over or activate the patient (naturally, he is also trying to help the patient do this for himself), then discussion of how much is reasonable to expect of the patient will inevitably ensue. Hatfield (1978) and others have identified that it is in this area of what to expect from the patient that families most need help (and rarely receive it!). This is indeed a difficult issue and unfortunately, the professional field seems split, particularly in how to deal with schizophrenia. Some psychiatrists sincerely believe that schizophrenic symptoms are totally related to biological changes and, therefore, the patient cannot be expected to exert any control or discipline over him- or herself. The family may be told that if the medications don't work, then there is not much else that can be done besides hospitalization. On the other extreme, there are those therapists who believe that the social context is totally responsible for the symptom and that only in this area is change needed (Haley, 1982). Therefore, the family and the patient are held accountable for all actions, and the parents may be put fully in charge of changing the patient without any other assistance, either from medications or the hospital. I, and many others, certainly see a middle ground but sometimes the actual translation of what to advise family members to expect and when can be extremely complicated. In general, I suggest to families that patients are responsible to some degree for their behavior no matter what the etiology or type of illness. This does not mean that patients are merely being manipulative or consciously deceitful when they acts in a disturbing way. Yet it is important to explain that patients usually have some degree of self-control and that the most important goal is to help them expand this area of this personal mastery of self. I explain that what is therapeutic is the expectation by the families to the patients than they can and should exert more self-accountability. The family is asked to match these expectations to the present level of functioning of the patient but to always be one step ahead. If the patient has not been to work in 3 years, it would be unreasonable to expect full employment in 2 months. Yet asking the patient to do one chore a day in the house no matter what his or her symptomatic status would be beneficial and reasonable. To suggest to families and patients that there is nothing they can do to help themselves except through medication or hospitalization is an extremely demoralizing message. On the other side, it is also important not to unrealistically inflate the family's expectations of what is possible, as this can be just as self-defeating.

PASSIVE/WITHDRAWN BEHAVIORS

Although violent, overtly bizarre behaviors can be very difficult to manage, the quiet, unmotivated patient, who is always acting and talking in a self-deprecating manner, can be maddening to the family. Often the family will have long dialogues about why the patient isn't doing more, whereas the patient states that he or she is sick and helpless. Sometimes one parent will agree with the patient while another family member will berate him or her as a lazy, useless creature. The therapist will (hopefully) help the family find the middle ground. Withdrawing types of behavior rarely, in and of themselves, lead to hospitalization unless suicide or total neglect has happened. Consequently, the family therapist in the hospital will usually focus initially on establishing controls for the more disruptive, acting-out types of behaviors. It is common for many schizophrenics to develop deficit-type symptoms when controlled on medication, and this behavior may begin to develop within a week or so after hospital admission. At this point, the therapist will need to shift attention to strategies for remotivating the patient to establish more appropriate social and prevocational skills. Some caution should be raised, however, as some clinicians feel that rapidly pushing treatment-resistant, chronic schizophrenics to active lifestyles will provoke relapse (Anderson & Reiss, 1982). This is an important issue, and the answers are not always clear-cut. The more longer term, drawn-out approach for reactivation may well be the best for those chronic schizophrenics who have been treatment failures when rapidly pushed. However, unless these failures have happened, it would probably be best initially to try and actively push the patient to be more functional, socially and vocationally. The clinician will need to individualize the strategy for a particular family, but my own recommendation is that one should err on the side of being slightly higher with expectations with schizophrenic patients that have only had a few psychotic breaks and are not clearly treatment failures. The danger of not pushing is that the patient may have more potential for vocational and social success but is positively rewarded by the therapist and family for not achieving this by being encouraged to stay home. The family is particularly sensitive to the attitudes of the therapist in this area, partly because of their own confusion as to what to do and partly because there are no clear professional guidelines. The therapist, by encouraging a long recuperation period, may be teaching the family that the patient is hopeless and more disabled than he or she actually is.

Specific strategies that can be used by the family to motivate the patient are (1) taking the patient out for walks within the hospital complex itself if the patient is very regressed, (2) very brief leaves of absence in which some potential pleasurable activity is accomplished, (3) joining with the staff to demand that the patient attend all ward activities, and (4) planning and implementing a leave of absence in which the patient is expected to accomplish a number of concrete specific tasks like cooking dinner, cleaning rooms, and going out to dinner with family. Often the family will complain that the patient does not seem interested or actively resists these plans. They need to be reassured that initially this is to be expected and that an important goal of the family is to create a supportive structure in which normal behaviors are expected even if not achieved and positive support and caring are demonstrated. It may take weeks for the patient to respond to these interventions of the family, and patience is required. The hospital staff can play a pivotal role in helping patient motivation if they form a positive, consistent alliance with the family, so that both of these subsystems have the same goal. There is, however, a natural limitation of the hospital, given that it is a culturally abnormal setting for the patient. The patient will only be able to achieve a certain amount because of rewards for remaining dependent. This is not a criticism of the hospital, as it is their mandate to take care of sick, dependent people, but there is an inevitable conflict that will occur when the patient begins to progress to a certain level of functioning.

WEEKEND LEAVES OF ABSENCE

Within a few days or weeks after admission, the hospital team will need to consider planning a family-oriented leave of absence. If the patient is single or without a natural support system, the leave of absence may be designed to help him or her begin to establish such a network. As mentioned above, the hospital has certain limits on its ability to help the patient be independent and to simulate actual conditions outside the hospital. Additionally, the family treatment will be limited as long as the patient is not living with the family as a functioning member. This is, of course, what clearly differentiates family approaches in the inpatient setting from that of the outpatient sector. When the patient is at home, there is more anxiety and consequently, some increased motivation for the family to solve problems because there is no one else to share the burden. In the hospital the staff, as they should, take on the responsibility of management. The weekend leave of absence is a mechanism by which the hospital as an organization begins to delegate and shift its responsibility for the patient back to the family. Naturally, this will be a time of high anxiety, mistrust, and potential miscommunication between hospital and family.

The family therapist will spend most of the second phase of treatment planning weekend leave of absences; and as the patient progresses, more demands will be placed on the patient and his or her family. The ward family sessions will usually consist of a review of how the family accomplished their assigned tasks from the previous weekend and detailed planning for the next. More and more of the hospital staff's focus during this phase should be on how to reinforce the goals laid out by the family for the weekend. This will be in contrast to the earlier phases of the hospitalization when it may be the family helping the hospital staff with its goals for the patient's behavior on the ward. For example, if the patient is supposed to be looking for a job on the weekend with family supervision, then the milieu interventions should mirror this and encourage practice job interviews, and so forth. This hospital–family alliance will maximize the success rate.

Some, if not most, hospitals use the hospital leave of absences as a reward or punishment to the patient for cooperative behavior on the ward. This can become a serious problem when therapeutic work is going on with the family. The patient may not want to deal with his family on weekends and consequently act up during the week to remain restricted. More importantly, this is the only time in which the family has to try to change the way they manage the patient. If this time is curtailed, thère will be less improvement in the patient–family system and consequently greater likelihood of relapse after discharge. It is often necessary to restrict the patient from going on a weekend pass if he or she is acting dangerously, but the difficulty arises when these restrictions are made part of the routine behavior management program on the ward. This practice seems to be more for the convenience of the staff than for achieving the goal of having the patient change behavior in the setting which counts: home or community. It is easy for the hospital staff to forget that the primary goal of the patient is not to get along better with other patients and staff but to improve his or her situation in the natural context to which he or she will inevitably return.

Discharge

Discharge planning ideally begins when the patient is admitted to the hospital. The previously described family interventions were all directed at how to prepare the patient for discharge. This can be both a time of pride and/or anxiety for the family and patient. A very structured and well-planned discharge will help alleviate some of the stress and increase the chances for success. Naturally, the family should be fully involved both in the decisions on when to discharge as well as on how the plans should be implemented. The typical discharge decision in most psychiatric hospitals today is accomplished without full involvement of the natural support system. It is rare for a family to be put in charge of the decision and not often are they even asked their preference for timing. Yet it is the family who will shoulder the major burden and responsibility. Even the best planning can be complicated by some external constraints such as limited insurance coverage. But even with these financial limitations, if the family is fully involved from the beginning, they will be able to exert some control over the timing and type of discharge plans. My own experience has shown that if the inpatient therapists have worked closely with the family during the hopitalization, then the hospital staff and the family and the patient will be in general agreement on the goals and timing of discharge.

Sometimes the patient will want to leave the hospital prematurely or even against medical advice. If the patient is going to return to the family, then they should have a major voice in this decision. It is not unusual for a family to feel guilty about the decision to put the patient in the hospital, and consequently, they may feel that they will have to take the patient back whenever he or she demands it. The patient may actually be bullying the family into compliance with threats. This can be a crucial time for change in what may be a chronically conflictive situation. The therapist should use the authority of the hospital to ally with the family to make the decision for the patient. If the therapist strongly feels that the patient should not leave the hospital, and the family feels the same, then the family should be supported to not take the patient home unless he or she complies with the treatment. This is a weighty decision for both therapist and family and should not be taken lightly and only after having tried more straightforward interventions. Naturally, if the patient is dangerous and in need of further hospitalization, then the therapist may have to make the decision for involuntary commitment. However, this can sometimes be delayed until work with the family encourages them to make and implement this recommendation for continued hospitalization against the patient's will. This may indeed be a practice run for a situation very likely to arise after hospitalization. These decisions particularly come up with adolescents and young adults, and it seems to be the practice of many hospitals that the adolescent is given an inordinate amount of authority in deciding when he or she should leave. However, I recommend strongly that the parents, if they are going to be legally and emotionally responsible for the adolescent or young adult, have a major say in these important decisions.

One of the most difficult parts of inpatient family work is trying to find an outpatient family therapist to refer to on discharge. Many family therapists do not want to work with severely disturbed patients and their families. Most psychiatrists who do work with chronic patients do not work with families. A further limitation is the orientation of the family therapist. It is often difficult to find a family or marital therapist who works in a directive, problem-oriented fashion with the goal of symptom reduction. As previously discussed, I and others have found this type of family work most effective with seriously disturbed patients and to transfer a patient to a therapist with a different methodology can be upsetting.

Family Interventions with the Hospital

In an initial section of this chapter, I presented the model of the hospital as a large formal organization interacting with the family as a small primary system. As these two subsystems form a macrosystem, their transactions will inevitably affect and alter both. The major thrust of this chapter has been to describe how the hospital can change and alter the family and the individuals in it. Yet we should not ignore families powerful impact on the functions and structures of hospitals (Krajewski

& Harbin, 1982; Harbin, 1978). The role that families play in changing a psychiatric hospital can be very constructive or misdirected or somewhere in between. I am restricting my comments here to families that have or have had one of their members as a patient in the psychiatric hospital that they are trying to affect. The families may take a major interest in mental illness after the experience of having one of their members hospitalized. They may work with the mental health association or serve on the advisory board of the hospital. Problems can arise when the family members do this while the patient/family member is in the hospital and especially when they are in conflict with the hospital staff over the management of the patient. This can lead the family to intervene at various levels of the hospital hierarchy to change the practices of the primary treatment team. Unfortunately, many families may be upset when the ward therapist attempts to involve or change them in some way that upsets their previous balance. If the family is too upset and does not feel listened to by the primary therapist, then they can go over the head of the treatment team. Sometimes the family does not present, and they may not know what is really bothering them; but they focus on an issue that will elicit the interest of the hospital administration; for example, the patient is being neglected, overmedicated, or restricted too often. Of course, the administrators need to review all cases to assure that the primary therapist is following acceptable standards of care. At times the treatment may indeed be substandard and the family's intervention will be helpful for the patient. I have seen a few cases in which the family uses these complaints to ally with the hospital administration in order to block some of the demands that are being made for change within the family–patient system. If they are successful, the family treatment may be undermined and a therapeutic stalemate will result. If the hospital staff at all levels are aware of these maneuvers, they can learn to look for and prevent these strategies and use the opportunity to further educate the family (and hospital administration) about the goals and purposes of the treatment.

Conclusion

I have attempted to give an overview of some of the clinical and programmatic options available to hospital staff when they chose to work closely with the families of psychiatric inpatients. As can be seen from the discussion, this orientation can require different modalities of intervention distinct from outpatient family therapies. Further, the hospital family therapy must constantly be aware of the broader macrosystem that the hospital and family forms in order to better understand and implement changes in the latter.

REFERENCES

Abroms, G., Fellner, C., & Whitaker, C. Admission of whole families. *American Journal of Psychiatry*, 1971, *127*, 1363–1369.

Anderson, C. M. Family intervention with severely disturbed inpatients. *Archives of General Psychiatry*, 1977, *34*, 697–702.

Anderson, C. M., & Reiss, D. J. Family treatment of patients with chronic schizophrenia: The inpatient phase. In H. Harbin (Ed.), *The psychiatric hospital and the family*. New York: Spectrum, 1982.

Bell, J. E. The family in the hospital: Experiences in other countries. In H. Harbin (Ed.), *The psychiatric hospital and the family*. New York: Spectrum, 1982.

Bowen, M. Family psychotherapy with schizophrenia in the hospital and in private practice. In I. Boszormenyi-Nagy & J. L. Framo (Eds.), *Intensive family therapy*. New York: Harper & Row, 1965.

Burks, H., & Serrano, A. The uses of family therapy and brief hospitalization. *Diseases of the Nervous System*, 1965, *26*, 804–806.

Dobrof, R., & Litwak, E. *Maintenance of family ties of long-term care patients: Theory and guide to practice* (U.S. Department of Health, Education and Welfare Publication, ADM 77-400). Washington, D.C.: U.S. Government Printing Office, 1977.

Fleck, S., Cornelison, A. R., Norton, N., & Lidz, T. Interaction between hospital staff and families. *Psychiatry*, 1957, *20*, 343–350.

Glick, I. E., & Clarkin, J. F. The effects of family presence and brief family intervention for hospitalized schizophrenic patients: A review. In H. Harbin (Ed.), *The psychiatric hospital and the family*. New York: Spectrum, 1982.

Gralnick, A. Conjoint family therapy: Its role in rehabilitation of the inpatient and family. *Journal of Nervous and Mental Disease*, 1963, *136*, 500–506.

Gralnick, A. Family psychotherapy: General and specific considerations. In *The psychiatric hospital as a therapeutic instrument*. New York: Brunner/Mazel, 1969.

Grunebaum, H. U., Weiss, J. L., Gallant, D., *et al.* Mentally ill mothers: In the hospital and at home. In G. Abroms & N. Greenfield (Eds.), *The new hospital psychiatry*. New York: Academic Press, 1971.

Haley, J. Alternative views of "schizophrenia" and their consequences for therapy. In H. Harbin (Ed.), *The psychiatric hospital and the family*. New York: Spectrum, 1982.

Harbin, H. T. Hospitals and families: Collusion or cooperation? *American Journal of Psychiatry*, 1978, *135*, 1496–1499.

Harbin, H. T. A family oriented psychiatric inpatient unit. *Family Process*, 1979, *18*, 281–292.

Harbin, H. T. Family therapy training for psychiatric residents. *American Journal of Psychiatry*, 1980, *137*, 1595–1598.

Harbin, H. T. Family treatment of the psychiatric inpatient. In H. Harbin (Ed.), *The psychiatric hospital and the family*. New York: Spectrum, 1982. (a)

Harbin, H. T. (Ed.) *The psychiatric hospital and the family*. New York: Spectrum, 1982. (b)

Hatfield, A. B. Psychological costs of schizophrenia to the family. *Social Work*, 1978, *23*(5).

Hoffman, L. *Foundations of family therapy*, New York: Basic Books, 1981.

Krajewski, T. F., & Harbin, H. T. The family changes the hospital. In H. Harbin (Ed.), *The psychiatric hospital and the family*. New York: Spectrum, 1982.

Lansky, M. Establishing a family oriented inpatient unit. *Journal of Operational Psychiatry*, 1977, *8*, 66–74.

Laqueur, H. P., & LaBurt, H. A. Family organization on a modern state hospital ward. *Mental Hygiene*, 1964, *48*, 544–551.

Madanes, C., & Haley, J. Dimensions of family therapy. *Journal of Nervous and Mental Disease*, 1977, *165*, 88–98.

Main, T. F. Mothers with children in a psychiatric hospital. *Lancet*, 1978, *2*, 845–847.

Norton, N. M., Detre, T. P., & Jarecki, H. G. Psychiatric services in general hospitals: A family oriented redefinition. *Journal of Nervous and Mental Disease*, 1963, *136*, 475–484.

Rabiner, E. L., Molinski, H., & Gralnick, A. Conjoint family therapy in the inpatient setting. *American Journal of Psychiatry*, 1962, *16*, 618–631.

Schween, P. H., & Gralnick, A. Factors affecting family therapy in the hospital setting. *Community Psychiatry*, 1966, *7*, 424–431.

Steinglass, P., Davis, D. I., & Berenson, D. Observations of conjointly hospitalized "alcoholic couples" during sobriety and intoxication: Implications for theory and therapy. *Family Process*, 1977, *16*, 1–16.

Sussman, M. B. Family-organizational linkages. In H. Harbin (Ed.), *The psychiatric hospital and the family*. New York: Spectrum, 1982.

Weinstein, S. E. The family of the chronic mentally ill patient: Ally or adversary? In H. Harbin (Ed.), *The psychiatric hospital and the family*. New York: Spectrum, 1982.

White, N., & Molnar, G. Admissions of married couples. *Canadian Psychiatry Journal*, 1972, *17*, 449–454.

7

Acting out and staying in:
Juvenile probation and the family

JOHN SCHWARTZMAN
Center for Family Studies/The Family Institute of Chicago
Institute of Psychiatry
Northwestern Memorial Hospital and
Northwestern University Medical School

ROBERT J. RESTIVO
Former Chief Probation Officer, Du Page County, Illinois

Introduction

This chapter utilizes a cybernetic metaphor to better understand the functioning of the system created by juvenile probationers and those with whom they interact.[1] The social system created to treat them, their families of origin, the world view of the probationers, and their symptoms can all be viewed as metaphors for one another, creating and maintaining a hologram—that is, a self-regulating system characterized by similar structure and basic premises at different levels of organization and abstraction in which each part contains the whole. This can best be described by adopting a cybernetic metaphor.

A cybernetic metaphor assumes the psychosocial world to have both cybernetic and metaphoric characteristics. It combines aspects of the model of self-maintaining circular processes guided by information characteristic of cybernetics, with metaphor: Understanding is always the perception of something from the point of view of something else. Therefore, all knowledge is metaphoric. Additionally, rather than an objective reality, the metaphoric frame, or basic premises of the observing system, creates that system's reality to some degree. A cybernetic metaphor provides a model to describe the functioning of purposeful adaptive systems, individuals, families, neighborhoods, and so forth, that includes the experienced reality of its members.

---

1. This chapter is based on 2 years of consultation with a juvenile probation department and 10 years' experience working with acting-out adolescents and their families—both those families that became involved with the probation department and those that did not, a total of 60 families.

All adaptive systems must have some means of maintaining their structure within contexts characterized by brief temporary variations and long-term permanent changes. "Adaptation" as defined by Rappaport (1979) refers to "the process through which living systems maintain homeostasis in the face of both short-term environmental fluctuations and by transformations in their own structures through long-term, non-reversing changes in their environments as well" (p. 145). Therefore, in environments universally characterized by change, both elements are necessary for successful adaptation.

In the process of self-regulation, adaptive systems use the results of past behavior to guide future behavior. In this way they function to eliminate the differences between their expected and their actual states, in their internal structure as well as their relationship to context. This enables systems to respond to rapidly changing fluctuations in their immediate contexts. At the same time, they must be able to self-organize and change their own structure and basic premises to respond to more pervasive, long-standing changes in their environments.

Consequently, adaptive systems demonstrate Romer's Rule (see Hockett & Ascher, 1964) named after the paleontologist Robert Romer. The rule states that successful evolutionary change is initially conservative attempts to remain the same under changed circumstances. Change at one level in a system can be understood as maintaining other more basic aspects of the system unchanged: Change at one level is self-regulating at a more inclusive level. Novelty, which is initially "selected for," is what allows the system to maintain itself at a more inclusive level of organization and/or at a higher level of abstraction. As Hockett and Ascher (1964) stated, "The initial survival value of favorable innovation . . . renders possible the maintenance of a traditional way of life in the face of changed circumstances" (p. 50). Consequently, a cybernetic metaphor utilizing Romer's Rule indicates the necessity of considering multiple levels of organization and abstraction in the external environment and internal structure of adaptive systems.

A cybernetic metaphor includes another basic characteristic. As Simon has argued, organized complexity (Weaver, 1948) characteristic of biological and social systems is by necessity organized into a hierarchy of levels that is the most adaptive structure at any level of organization. He states that "nature is organized in levels because hierarchic structures . . . provide the most viable form of any system of even moderate complexity" (Simon, 1973, p. 27). Hierarchy in terms of levels of abstraction is also an omnipresent aspect of the information (or novelty) that any self-correcting system must use as feedback to compare actual and expected states and behave accordingly to maintain their structure and achieve other goals and purposes. The exchange of information with any social context can be described as multileveled discourse. It contains not only messages but also messages about messages and messages about messages about messages, and so forth. The fundamental properties of discourse are created by the relationship among its various levels of abstraction. Those of higher levels of abstraction are "meta" to other messages and frame these messages as to mode, for example, "this is information; this is a joke, a dream, a fantasy, a metaphor, and so forth." The meaning of any message is always a function of the relationship of these levels of abstraction. Because the theory argues that a discontinuity between varying levels of abstraction must be observed, "it is assumed that the distinction between a class and its members is an ordering principle in the behavioral phenomena which we study" (Bateson, 1972, p. 252). When violated, this creates the possibility of paradox that has many important effects on the discourse of which it is a part. This makes self-reflexive communication possible in which statements "comment" on themselves *and* the messages these comments frame. These become truly paradoxical when the metacommunication disqualifies itself; for example, "This is a lie." These self-disqualifying communications become a core characteristic of several communicative modes including play, fiction, psychotherapy (Haley, 1963), and ritual. Especially in play it can be seen how the frame communicates its own disqualification; for example, "This is play," including this (playful) statement, so that if it is play, then it is not play and vice versa. As a result, a number of the most complex communicative modes are based on self-reflexive paradoxes. Consequently, it can be assumed that adaptive systems are not only hierarchical in internal organization but also must be able to orient themselves within contexts characterized by hierarchy, both in terms of levels of organization and levels of abstraction.

The multileveled nature of the biosocial world requires multileveled learning by adaptive systems to understand and maintain internal and external hierarchical organization. Limits on the amount of information systems can store and use necessitates hierarchical "habits of thought" (Bateson, 1972) within the "mind" of the system so that certain basic premises about the nature of the system's relationship to its context are automatically assumed to be true without critical examination or testing by trial and error.

As a result, learning in the broadest sense, at any level of organization—for example, an individual, a family, or an entire social system—must be multileveled. The reception of information is always accompanied by more abstract metainformation, rules for the structure or contingencies of that context of learning. An adaptive system, to survive, must "learn from experience" implicit rules about "what to expect" or "where to look," which are so basic that they are generally unquestioned and out of awareness. Bateson has termed this level of learning, deutero-learning or learning II, coded as the system's basic metaphor. Systems must classify information by means of some metaphor more abstract than the information itself. This determines what will be perceived as information or, in Bateson's (1972) terms, the "difference which makes a difference," which reintroduces purpose into psychosocial reality so that any system can be understood as purposeful if it has some means of matching its actual state against its expected state and the ability to alter its behavior to reduce the difference, that is, that it be self-regulating. However, information, as generally used, is borrowed from the mathematical theory of communication and is a measure of improbability. It does not include meaning. Metaphor fills this gap.

Metaphor is created by linking elements from different domains by describing one domain in terms of another. This results in a more inclusive domain containing the now-transformed aspects of both. In this process the metaphor emphasizes certain aspects of the principle subject and suppresses others by communications about it that normally apply to the subsidiary subject (Black, 1962). For example, "George is a rock" emphasizes his rock-like qualities and ignores others. Another basic characteristic of metaphor is (semantic) paradox because the speaker or writer is, in some sense, *not* asserting the statement he or she makes. Beardsley (1958) defines metaphor as a linguistic expression which is "either indirectly self contradictory or obviously false in context" (p. 142).

Any self-maintaining system's functioning, whether an individual's, a family's, or a sociocultural system's, can be assumed to be the result of deutero-learning the basic premises of earlier contexts and internalizing these as a metaphor for contingencies in current contexts. The most probable contingencies encountered in early contexts of learning are coded at some level somewhere within the system and become what Powers (1973) has termed "reference conditions," that is, the system's relationship to its context that demands no response because it matches expectations. This is generally so abstract and unquestioned that it is out of awareness. Purposeful social systems maintain particular patterns of interaction and a set of beliefs about the relationship of the system and its social context that maintain these contingencies so that the patterns and the beliefs are mutually validating. As will be described in this chapter, the inappropriate behavior of the delinquent, the contingencies of family interaction in which members attempt to "help," and the treatment of the inappropriate behavior by therapists and/or probation officers are all metaphors for one another, that is, all are talking about the "same thing" in terms of something else and all function to maintain the problem they intend to change.

Family Functioning: The Social Context of Delinquent Behavior

As has been frequently stated in the family therapy literature (Haley, 1980; Satir, 1971), a recurring characteristic of the family of origin of symptomatic children and adolescents is "dissonances" between their parents in terms of irreconcilable differences about some core aspect of their relationship. This dissonance is often metaphorized in their expectations and perceptions of their children and their behavior. If it is assumed that the child must learn to validate the contingencies of his or her parents' deutero-learned premises, and these are contradictory, "inappropriate" behavior by the child is probable because what is an appropriate response for one parent is inappropriate for the other.

These contradictory expectations are often exacerbated during those periods in the life cycle when changes in behavior and relationships are culturally appropriate, for example, late adolescence. The "solution" that transcends the contradictory injunctions are often that type of paradoxical behaviors termed "symptomatic," in which the adolescent acts in a particular way and at the same time indicates that this behavior is "just happening," that is, out of his or her control (Haley, 1963).

Symptoms often appear as an appropriate response to contradictory injunctions especially about a core aspect of individual development: dependency and autonomy (Sluzki & Veron, 1971). To be successfully resolved, a context providing a delicate balance between stability and nurturance is required and, concurrently, a positive response to change especially for increasingly autonomous behavior and its accompanying differentiation and separation from the family.

In families with symptomatic children, often after some period of inappropriate behavior the child is defined as not responsible for the behavior because of his or her problems or "illness" and by this is able to transcend incongruent expectations or contingencies. In this process the symptomatic response to paradoxical or contradictory injunctions links the dissonances and becomes a metaphor for them. Symptomatic behavior can often be understood as a metaphoric link of contradictory expectations for functioning both as an autonomous individual and as a part of the family or other social system. At the same time, at a more inclusive level of organization, the appearance or perception of symptoms functions to regulate the symptomatic individual's parents' marriage by appearing "spontaneously" when change threatens this relationship. The symptomatic behavior demands parental attention and defocuses from their problems but produces inevitable disagreement about how to respond to the problem, which generally exacerbates the marital dissonance and maintains the problem (Jackson, 1957; Weakland,

1960; Schwartzman, 1975). The dissonance previously located in the marital dyad is now transformed into the child's symptomatic behavior and his or her parents' attempt to "treat" it. Parental attempts to "help" or cope with the problem alter the structure of the marriage, which becomes more inclusive and hierarchical, adding the symptomatic child as an integral part, a social metaphor maintained by the symptom, itself a metaphor for the paradoxical contingencies. This then interferes with appropriate changes in the family's and the juvenile's life cycle. The adolescent may have been involved in his or her parents' marriage from birth. By becoming symptomatic or behaving in culturally inappropriate ways, the adolescent maintains this arrangement.

At another level of abstraction, as in the creation of any metaphor, a new gestalt is created in which the individuals are linked by this novel contiguity. This transforms the process of separation and differentiation (Bowen, 1960) necessary for normal development into one characterized by the self-maintenance of the whole family. The symptomatic individual and his or her parents create their novel contiguities; the symptomatic adolescent's communication of a need for help and parents' attempt to help, maintaining a relationship characteristic of a particular stage in the life cycle which does not change, whatever the actual chronological ages of family members. This becomes the chronological template by which relationships appropriate at this stage of the life cycle for the adolescent and the parent continue to be the standard by which the appropriateness of the relationship is measured.

The symptomatic behavior functions as a homeostat by its definition as "out of control" and the unquestioned attempts to "treat" it by significant others (and therapists) that are contingent on individual changes that maintain the structure and basic premises of the whole system. Consequently, Romer's Rule is acted out in these families with an adolescent who becomes symptomatic or behaves inappropriately because change at one level maintains the system unchanged at a more inclusive level. For symptomatic children and adolescents, the core dilemma often is a "pull" to separate and become more autonomous in relationship to the family of origin and contradictory "tugs" to stay and maintain an inappropriate relationship with a parent legitimated by the symptom. Symptomatic behavior is a metaphoric response to those contradictory injunctions to change and concurrently stay the same. As a result, symptomatic individuals and those in their social context utilize change as a metaphor for staying the same. The appearance of symptomatic behavior changes the individual so that the family is maintained unchanged. The onset of symptomatic behavior is a change in the individual that legitimates a lack of culturally appropriate change at the level of the family and the extrafamilial context.

The inappropriate behaviors of juvenile probationers can be understood as paradoxical metacommunications in which they act in a variety of culturally inappropriate ways and define these behaviors as "out of their control" (Haley, 1963). This is a metaphor for the contingencies of interaction in their families of origin characterized by long-term conflicting or inconsistent expectations and a lack of consequences for their inappropriate behavior. As a result, these juveniles learn as an out-of-awareness basic premise (and code as a reference condition) that there are no actual constraints in their families and generalize this to the social world beyond their families. At the same time, these interactional contingencies are metaphorically transformed "inside" the juveniles, who are thus defined as out of control. This transformation and dissonance in the structure and basic premises of the family and between the extrafamilial social world result in the maintenance of the inappropriate behavior.

The onset of culturally inappropriate behavior that results in an adolescent receiving the label *delinquent*, and probation, can be seen as triggered by one of several changes at different levels of abstraction in his or her immediate social context. Most common among these are changes or threatened changes in the adolescent's parents' relationship, either improvement or exacerbation of their core issues. The resolution of conflict or its exacerbation can both function as contextual stimuli for the onset of inappropriate behavior by the adolescent or for the perception of inappropriate behavior by the adolescent by someone in the family. In single-parent families, this behavior can start as a result of a parent's creation of a new relationship or the dissolution of an old one. For example, after the mother of a 15-year-old with school problems ended a 3-year relationship with a man that her son liked (the man had refused to marry the mother), the adolescent stole several hundred dollars from her and took a train trip of several hundred miles, returning home when he ran out of money.

Other important triggers are those periods in the life cycle that demand culturally appropriate changes for the adolescent, especially concerning autonomy and separation from the family of origin. These changes are most obvious in late adolescence, where the most radical changes in the adolescent's relationships must be made. This period itself can be understood as a metaphor for the developmental process characteristic of the entire life cycle around the universal core problem of dependence and autonomy (Sluzki & Veron, 1970). At the conclusion of this process, the adolescent must be transformed from a child in his or her family of origin to young adulthood in which he or she interacts with those outside the family a great deal of the time. The family can help or hinder the adolescent in making the necessary changes during this period of transition. Parents help by setting clear limits, by being supportive during setbacks and failures, tolerating mood swings, and most importantly, reinforcing culturally appropriate autonomy and activities outside the family. They hinder by communication that age-appropriate autonomous behavior is inappropriate and that extrafamilial relationships are disloyal, by the positive reinforcement of inappropriate behavior, and by ambiguous and conflicting expectations.

The separation and concurrent social expectations for autonomy is especially difficult for those families of "protodelinquents" if one or both parents had troubles during their own adolescence that they did not resolve. In these families, the struggle for autonomy is more difficult for both parents and adolescents because the parents were not success-ful in this process themselves and at least partially as a result are currently involved in intense marital conflict. The marital conflict is frequently communicated through the adolescent, interfering with his or her appropriate separation and autonomy.

The marriages of delinquents' parents are often characterized by pervasive dissonances about power, control, family-of-origin loyalties, values, and a number of other issues that are transformed metaphorically into conflicts "about" the adolescent. Often one parent defines the other as weaker than the juvenile and frequently defines this as the cause of the problem. This parent is often defined as out of control because he or she has some obvious problem—for example, obesity, alcoholism, a violent temper—or because of his or her inability to control the adolescent. The adolescent's out-of-control behavior often becomes a metaphor for the parent's behavior in that it is a means of both communicating and not communicating about it at the same time. By this, the adolescent replaces a parent in an analogous pattern of interaction with the other parent. In this process one parent attempts to alter the out-of-control behavior of the spouse, repeatedly fails, and gives up. This is then acted out in this parent's behavior with his or her adolescent.

Often the adolescent's symptom is such that it metaphorically communicates something one parent is unable to communicate to the other. For example, in a family seen by the first author, the son of a high school teacher in an academically oriented family was continually failing and truant from school. This behavior made his father extremely angry, resulting in repeated hostile arguments between them. The adolescent's mother had a number of basic disagreements with her husband about her own abandoned career and her husband's chronic vague illness. This disease was supposedly stress related, so she never felt she was able to become overtly angry at him. However, she metaphorically expressed these conflicts by supporting her son against her husband in their arguments, thus making her husband continually angry at her as well, which he seldom communicated directly. Consequently, the adolescent communicated his hostility to his father, whereas his mother was unable to do so directly. The father overtly blamed the mother for not supporting him, and the mother blamed the father for being too critical and hostile to their son. The result was that they never cooperated to set clear limits on their son. At the same time, their son's behavior was a metaphor for parental dissonance and maintained it because they generally disagreed about it.

This process, which results in a lack of constraint by the parents concerning their children's behavior, is often characterized as one parent's attempt to set some limits on the adolescent that fails when he or she doesn't "listen to reason." The other parent often overtly or covertly criticizes the attempt, but also does not enforce clear consequences for the inappropriate behavior. In addition, marital problems are generally exacerbated because the parents undercut one another.

For example, the first author saw a family in therapy that clearly exhibited this pattern. The daughter, 15, had been hospitalized several times and was on probation for truancy, running away from home, and taking drugs. The mother, who described herself as "nervous," was defined as "inadequate" by her now-divorced husband, who was a logical, critical, engineer. A typical pattern of interaction was that the daughter, Debbie, would begin to get into trouble (e.g., stop going to school), her mother would weakly attempt to make her change, fail, and get in touch with her ex-husband. He was angry when involved with his daughter in this way, and blamed his wife for Debbie's problems. She would withdraw while her ex-husband would try to "straighten out" Debbie. He would be successful briefly, withdraw, and then the cycle would repeat as Debbie would begin to misbehave and her mother would fail in her attempts to get her to behave appropriately.

Single parents often fail in their attempts to constrain their symptomatic adolescents, and by this maintain a relationship with their former spouses. If a former spouse is not involved, mental health or legal personnel eventually become involved. These organizations and individuals act as a metaphor for the peripheral parent and are often covertly undercut by the overinvolved parent's permission to the adolescent to continue inappropriate behavior. The adolescent is defined as more powerful than his or her parents because of the symptom that cannot be controlled or ignored. Simultaneously, he or she is defined as less powerful because of the symptom's communication of failure, pathology, and need for help. Consequently, the delinquent behavior can be seen as functioning to confuse or reverse hierarchies within the family (Madanes, 1980).

Often a parent will ask what the adolescent wants in return for changing his or her behavior or under what conditions he or she will not misbehave. A number of parents have told the authors that they never refused their children's requests no matter how outrageous their behavior. At times a parent threatens to leave home as a result of the adolescent's behavior, prior to making any plans for the adolescent to leave home or change. In these families the decision making is controlled by the adolescent's inappropriate or symptomatic behavior.

Moreover, because the peripheral parent consistently failed—or had given up trying to set limits on the adolescent—he or she was defined as less powerful because of the adolescent's coalition with the other parent. In addition, the covert alliance between the overinvolved parent and the adolescent against the peripheral parent makes a clear definition of their relationship impossible. Concurrently, this type of functioning that results in intense family involvement, interferes with appropriate peer interaction, so that if there is any attempted interaction, it is often with other adolescents having analogous problems and from similar family contexts.

This recurring pattern of interaction results in that type of family structure that Haley (1967) termed a "perverse triangle." It can be defined as a covert coalition across generations against another person. This structure has been identified in families and organizations with dysfunctional or symptomatic members. These families communicate more information (positively and negatively) across generations than within them, especially between one parent and the adolescent about the adolescent's problem or about the other parent. One parent directs most of his or her affect and attention toward the adolescent's problem, but does not attempt to actually control it. The parents inevitably disagree between themselves and undercut one another's attempts to set limits. Their expectations are generally different as are their tolerances for the adolescent's discomfort. After years of conflict with his or her spouse, one parent may become peripheral, involved only when there is a crisis. The peripheral parent attempts to alter the adolescent's inappropriate behavior in every way except uniting with his or her spouse to set clear limits with actual consequences.

Thus, the inappropriate behavior can be understood as a metaphor for the parents' marital dissonance. For example, in one family seen by the first author, the parents stated that their 15-year-old daughter was uncontrollable. This behavior consisted primarily of her violating curfew and occasional truancy from school. This couple had a distant relationship and the wife stated that she had "given up" on changing it. The husband was a somewhat passive individual who tried to avoid any conflict with his wife, but covertly allied himself with his daughter against his wife. He talked to their daughter positively and smiled at her often during therapy. He weakly defended her against his wife's accusations and clearly was much less critical of her than his wife. In fact, he was only critical at all if he was strongly encouraged to be so by his wife. At the same time, he was able to state her positive attributes, which his wife was unable or unwilling to do. Instead, she constantly alluded to their daughter's abortion that had taken place the previous year. This situation was especially evident when the daughter's responsible functioning at work was pointed out to the mother. She was, however, extremely interested in but critical of her daughter's social life. She disapproved of her daughter's boyfriends and discussed their sexual intentions but never attempted to limit her daughter's interaction with them. Her husband was either ignored or brought in as ineffective support by this wife in criticizing the daughter and verbalizing negative expectations of her. In this family the daughter's sexuality was crucial to family functioning in that it kept her parents in contact with one another through her problem and was a metaphor for problems in her parents' relationship. The daughter's sexuality, defined as out of control, metaphorically communicated the out-of-control "lack of sexual interest" the parents showed in their marriage; and her implicit need for constraint functioned to reunite her parents around a sexual problem.

Many families with delinquent adolescents are characterized by ambiguous rules and differences within or between parents (contradictory expectations). As a result, the adolescents are often rewarded for their lack of culturally appropriate control and responsibility and not for their attempts to function more autonomously.

For example, in another family seen by the first author, a psychiatrist and his wife, a teacher, had a highly conflictual marriage. The parents acted out one aspect of this conflict in terms of their expectations for their 16-year-old daughter. The father wanted her to go to medical school, whereas the mother wanted her to go to a local school and make her own decisions about a career. The girl would break into her father's medicine cabinet, steal barbiturates, become intoxicated and angry and fight with her father. Her mother would accuse the father of being insensitive or overreacting and come to her daughter's defense. This pattern seemed to be triggered by increased distance in the marriage. When the father was away from home too much, the mother would complain to her daughter and criticize her husband, but she would not confront him. At the same time, she would reinforce her ideas for her daughter's future. Then, her daughter would get high, father would be angry that she used his medicine, and the cycle would be acted out. Both parents defined themselves as unable to keep her out of the medicine cabinet. As a result of this pattern of interaction, the dissonances between the parents were maintained within tolerable limits because they defocused onto the adolescent when their conflict became too intense. At the same time, the out-of-control behavior is maintained because it demands constraints and the parents' cooperation, which inevitably fails and thus maintains their conflicts. Their inability to set limits and directly express anger is metaphorized in the daughter's behavior.

These examples illustrate how the symptom metaphorically comments on a problem in the marriage and in this way functions to regulate the parents' marriage and is regulated by it. The parents' relationship to the adolescent, their conflictual marriage, and the problem all remain unchanged. What is consistent in these families is that the attempts by the parents to constrain the adolescents' "out of control" behavior (e.g., truancy, drug use, fighting, running away) frequently fail. This pattern of interaction, however, is largely ignored. Instead, the creation of a metaphor at another level of organization is used to explain the adolescents' inappropriate behavior. One domain is inside the adolescent consisting of his or her genes, biochemistry, or innate characterological flaws. This is linked to another domain outside the family (e.g., the neighborhood, bad friends, or the "times"). Consequently, that inside the juvenile and the wider context are linked, creating behavior metaphorically defined as "out of control." By linking these domains in the creation of this "being out of control" metaphor, change in the adolescent's behavior is attempted where it cannot be successful. Simultaneously, the contingencies of interaction are transformed "inside" the adolescent and are manifested by his or her behavior so that the contingencies of this behavior are ignored. Neither the adolescent nor his or her parents perceive the connection between their relationship and the inappropriate behavior.

The process of an adolescent's inappropriate behavior creating and created by a social system and maintained by his or her status as "on probation" can be understood as a structural metaphor. It links the dissonant domains of an adolescent struggling with his or her autonomy and the parents' marriage. The family composed of the rule-governed relationships of its members is maintained unchanged by the appearance of improper behavior by the adolescent. In the process of separation and differentiation from his or her parents, the adolescent alters his or her behavior and becomes symptomatic or behaves inappropriately in some way and the parents attempt to correct this behavior in such a way that the relationship and the behavior are maintained. As a consequence, the adolescent does not have to make culturally appropriate changes nor do the parents as they try and fail to alter his or her behavior. In this process one element of the family, the adolescent, changes to maintain the entire family system unchanged, especially the marital conflict and the cross-generational tie between the overinvolved parent and the adolescent. The family is transformed from one in which parents are struggling with their own problems and those in their marriage to one in which they are attempting to "help" with their adolescent's problem. Certain perceptions about the adolescent maintain the family system unchanged by interfering with his or her culturally appropriate behavior, especially that leading to increased extrafamilial autonomy. In this process certain "facts" about the adolescent are emphasized by the parents repeatedly, especially those about his or her inappropriate behavior. If positive behaviors appear, they are ignored or disqualified by the parent(s).

For example, in the family described above with the 15-year-old girl who had had an abortion, the mother was literally unable to recognize that in some ways—for example, concerning her job and her household tasks—her daughter was extremely responsible. When these were mentioned, her mother immediately responded with statements about her pregnancy and other past evidence of her irresponsibility suggesting that she would probably get pregnant again. By this, the family structure was regulated as it was by the ineffective constraints on her social life.

If it is assumed that the adolescent who becomes delinquent is, by necessity, deutero-learning the contingencies repeatedly encountered in early contexts of learning, and metaphorized as his or her reference condition, then it can be seen that lack of constraint in this context is transferred into a concept of self experienced by the adolescent as "out of control." Concurrently, the adolescent learns to control by being out of control as an adaptive strategy for dealing with the social context outside the family. As a result, he or she behaves as if lacking constraints and by this creates a context characterized by a lack of constraint by manipulating adults who attempt to constrain them—analogues to their parents. These adolescents learn to discover dissonances between two people more powerful than themselves that they manipulate so that they are never actually constrained.[2] This validates their basic premises about a social universe characterized by no constraints. Consequently, it can be seen that the adolescent's inappropriate behavior is a metaphor for the contingencies encountered in his or her family of origin in which he or she acts inappropriately and is self-defined and defined by others in their contexts as "spontaneously" out of control. The parents, obviously more powerful, define themselves as unable to constrain their child. These adolescents learn that they themselves and the social systems of which they are a part do not actually have constraints. By his or her

2. This study is based on only one probation department and thus could not be generalized for all juvenile probation departments. Its functioning is probably contingent on a number of demographic variables, especially the socioeconomic status of those being served and the resulting case-load size. Most, but not all, of the experience about which we write has been with white, middle income, suburban delinquents whose parents are not criminals. This does not include delinquents who have been abandoned at an early age, systematically neglected, or physically abused.

"spontaneous" out-of-control behavior, the adolescent both controls and also implicitly communicates the need for help which results in failing attempts at constraints by those who "help." As a consequence, the adolescent is concurrently defined as more *and* less powerful than his or her parents. The adolescent controls by being out of control, but his or her paradoxical definition forces him or her to behave inappropriately in the extrafamilial context, so that the adolescent is in a bind between these levels. At one level the adolescent's parents communicate, "Stay in the family and act like an irresponsible child." Those in the extrafamilial context implicitly communicate, "Grow up and act like a responsible adult."

Inappropriate behavior, defined as bad and/or mad, transcends the necessity of making a choice because the behavior legitimates lack of change. Parents often blame one another for their children's problems which are defined like any symptom (Haley, 1963) as not under individual control, so that they do not have to change. Concurrently, within the family the out of control behavior of the delinquent, which can spontaneously appear at any time, ironically maintains order when change threatens or functions to eliminate the change that has taken place.

At some point, the inappropriate behavior becomes problematic to someone outside the family, for example, the school, police, or neighbors. If the juvenile becomes involved with the legal system because he or she continues to behave inappropriately, the juvenile probation department —the court's social service (and control mechanism)—often at least temporarily stabilizes the family. Frequently, the parents "give up" and say they cannot control their child and place the responsibility on the probation department to do this limit setting. As will be discussed in the following section, this frequently re-creates the family structure at a more inclusive level. At the same time, the dysfunctional family relationships are formalized.

This process begins at an initial meeting with the family and the probation officer. At this time the probation officer will explain the probationer's responsibilities and suggest that the parent(s) take charge of their child's behavior and be firm with him or her. Often they have heard this many times before, so that they weakly agree, and they do not follow through because of their problems in cooperating and/or setting limits with their child. At this level the parent(s) and the delinquent are covertly allied against the probation department, in that they do not actually work to alter their relationship because of the symptom's homeostatic function for the family, or they feel that it is hopeless or pointless to attempt to change after so many failures. Consequently, the family and the probation department do not necessarily have the same goals. In addition, there is a more basic dissonance in the probation system.

The juvenile court articulates contradictory messages in that it unavoidably functions to both blame and not blame delinquents for their inappropriate behavior. Judges, lawyers practicing in the juvenile court, and probation officers do not intend to convey this contradiction; nevertheless, it has been at the heart of juvenile court since its inception.

Juvenile Court: Creation of a System

The Illinois legislature created the juvenile court in 1899 in an effort to humanely control the increasing numbers of children who, it was felt, had fallen victim to the social chaos of the time. During the economic collapse of the 1890s, impoverished farming families gave up the land and came to the industrialized cities looking for work. Instead, they found crowded living conditions and high unemployment, which affected city workers most of all. Adding to the state of disorder, immigration patterns shifted during this period, so that higher percentages of immigrants came from Southern and Eastern Europe, bringing with them language and customs that made their assimilation especially difficult. In the harsh, desperate atmosphere of the cities' slums, the capacity of the family to supervise and provide for its children eroded.

The authorities had few alternatives for handling minors brought to their attention. Wayward children, if their conduct warranted, could appear before the courts and be processed in the same manner as an adult charged with a criminal offense. Or, they could be taken to the reformatory, where "in a combination of prison and school, apart from the world, they might learn through manual labor, religious and academic lessons, the value of hard work and subordination" (Ryerson, 1978, p. 19). Reformatories had been in existence since the middle of the 19th century; however, by the 1890s they had come under attack for their cruel conditions and their inability to make productive citizens of their charges.

Neither of these alternatives could be countenanced by the reformers of the period. The solution some favored consisted of investing judges with the responsibility and authority to take children under their protection and guidance. Behind this solution was the assumption that the parents of these minors could not or would not provide properly for their care. Another crucial, though more subtle, assumption identifies delinquency as a behavior not entirely within the control of the delinquent. This premise was consistent with the prevailing theory of criminality. In contrast to the classical model of criminality, which held that the criminal exercised free moral choice in deciding to disobey the rules of society, the notion of heredity as playing a determining role in criminal conduct was also advanced. It was also suggested that urban chaos and poverty were primarily to blame for crime. In both cases the criminal was perceived as victim as well as victimizer.

Despite its critics this benevolent attitude survived as the juvenile court's moral imperative. In an address to the American Bar Association in 1909, one of the country's first juvenile court judges, Julian W. Mack, reasoned in this way:

> Why isn't it just and proper to treat these juvenile offenders as we deal with neglected children, as a wise and merciful father handles his own child whose errors are not discovered by the authorities? Why isn't it the duty of the State instead of asking merely whether a boy or girl has committed the specific offense, to find out what he is, physically, mentally, morally, and then, if it learns that he is treading the path that leads to criminality, to take him in charge not so much to punish as to reform, not to degrade but to uplift, not to crush, but to develop, not to make him a criminal but a worthy citizen? (Empey, 1979, p. 3)

Some proponents of the juvenile court less inclined to justify its existence through rhetoric turned to a concept in common law, *mens rea*, as a basis for the separate treatment of children. According to this principle, one is accountable for a criminal act only if there is criminal intent. In common law, children under age 7 could not have criminal intent and children between the ages of 7 and 14 were presumed incapable of criminal intent, though a prosecuting authority might prove a specific child capable. The juvenile court's critics argued that, since *mens rea* was already available as a proper defense in criminal court, no new court was needed for its exercise. A child who had committed an offense against the law and who was not shown to be capable of criminal intent was acquitted of all charges and set free. The reasoning proved irrelevant to the concerns of the reformers. As Ellen Ryerson (1978) explains:

> While the reformers did indeed wish to remove children from the ambit of the criminal law, they did not want to let them go. While they said that children were incapable of criminal intent . . . the reason for civil jurisdiction . . . was, like the insanity defense, to authorize the restraint and control of people who, according to the concepts of criminal law, were not guilty of a crime. (p. 79)

To summarize: The initial proponents of the juvenile court concept held in effect that (1) the parents of the delinquent child were unable or unwilling to provide proper care and guidance, so the delinquent was appropriately grouped with dependent and neglected children, and

(2) the child brought to the court's attention as a consequence of his or her conduct needed the court's protection rather than its reproach.

From its beginning, the guarantees of due process were notably lacking in the juvenile court. For decades, the absence of formal procedures was tolerated because of a faith in the good intentions of the court. The judge was permitted considerable latitude to carry out the purpose of the court, which in the case of delinquents, included saving children from lives of crime and profligacy. However, during the 1960s, the Supreme Court found that the juvenile court's benevolent purpose constituted insufficient grounds to deny due process to children alleged to be delinquent. *In re: Gault* (1967) established the right to counsel, the right to confront accusers, and other safeguards guaranteed to adults accused of a crime. Three years later (*In re: Winship*, 1970) the Court determined that the only permissible standard of proof for a delinquency proceeding was proof "beyond a reasonable doubt," the same standard for criminal conviction.

The *Gault* and the *Winship* decisions are paradoxical; in the text of each the Court endorsed the belief that formal intervention into the lives of delinquents is in the best interests of those children while it severely limited the possibility of that intervention. The juvenile court, though "not intended to be adversary in character," began to function like criminal court complete with prosecuting and defense attorneys, trials, and plea bargaining. Yet, despite the criminal court-like procedures, punishing minors for having disobeyed the law continued to be excluded from the purpose of the juvenile court.

The contemporary juvenile court judge hears allegations and evidence presented by the prosecutor that define the respondent minor's conduct as willful and criminal while the youth's attorney seeks to avoid any unfavorable characterization of his or her client. If the minor admits to the prosecutor's allegations or those allegations are proven beyond a reasonable doubt, the court assumes the responsibility for his or her well-being. Hence, at precisely the point that the court finds that the child's conduct has been willfully criminal, it undertakes the role of the child's ultimate protector, his or her parental surrogate. At that point the court will order the probation officer to conduct a social investigation and to prepare a report describing the minor's problems and needs for consideration at a future hearing. At that hearing the court will determine how best to acquit itself of its responsibility: whether to return the child to his or her parents' custody for a period of probation with, perhaps, social, medical, or educational services; whether to place the child in a foster home with or without special services; or any of a number of other dispositions which will "serve the moral, emotional, mental, and physical welfare of the minor and the best interests of the community" (Illinois Juvenile Court Act, Ch. 37

Sec. 701-2). One of the court's options includes sending the minor to the state's Department of Corrections, the current version of the reformatory, which, like its 19th-century predecessor, has a reputation for abuse and ineffectiveness. However, most juvenile statutes clearly imply that committing a minor to the state's correction institution is to be considered a last resort. In recent years, changes in juvenile codes have permitted the ordering of restitution and public service work; nevertheless, the imposition of penalties for delinquent conduct remains foreign to the purpose of the proceedings.

And so the Juvenile Court continues to convey the same ambivalence toward its delinquent children that the culture has for its mentally ill: "conflicting wishes to exculpate and to blame; to sanction and not to sanction; to degrade and to elevate; to stigmatize and not to stigmatize; to care for and to reject; to treat and to mistreat; to protect and destroy" (Katz & Goldstein, 1971, p. 419). The delinquent standing before the juvenile court judge is an identified wrongdoer and an identified patient. By his or her conduct he or she is the subject of proceedings and his or her well-being is their object. By his or her conduct, he or she is responsible for his or her presence before the court, but by virtue of age, is not to be held accountable for his or her crime.

Therefore, there is a basic dissonance built into the juvenile probation system's ideology.[3] The system was created to provide proper care for juveniles who had parents who were unwilling or unable to care for them. The juveniles were seen as needing the court's protection, not punishment for their misbehavior. As a consequence due process of law was ignored until the 1960s because of the initial, generally unquestioned faith in the court's good intentions. Over time this changed and the courts became more and more like a criminal court in which proof was demanded for a juvenile's alleged misdeeds. However, if the juvenile is found guilty or admits his or her misdeeds, the court as defined in its original mandate, becomes the juvenile's surrogate parent(s), so that the parents are undercut by the legal system. At the same time, the imposition of penalties is foreign to the proceedings of the juvenile court. As a result, there is little sanction for punishment or constraint for the juveniles by the courts.

As stated earlier, there is evidence that the juvenile's inappropriate behavior is at least partially an adaptive response to the lack of constraints and confused generational hierarchy in the family. Both of these are reinforced by the juvenile court system that further weakens

3. The division consisted of 10 probation officers, 1 supervising probation officer, an assistant supervising probation officer, and 2 secretaries. The unit was responsible for handling the minors in need of supervision and delinquent youth who came under the jurisdiction of the juvenile court. Neither the supervisor nor his assistant carried case loads. Their primary duties consisted of overall division management and case consultation respectively.

the parents, but does not provide constraints for the juvenile's inappropriate behavior, so that the problem is reinforced at this more abstract level. In addition, this creates a context for a number of conflicting views about the juvenile's relationship to his or her inappropriate behavior and contradictory means to alter it. Because of dissonances at various levels of abstraction in the social system created to treat them, the juveniles have an implicitly contradictory relationship to their inappropriate behavior, particularly to what degree it is under their conscious control. Most basically, in their relationship to the legal system, they are defined as both blamed and at the same time not blamed for their inappropriate behavior. Each juvenile in his or her interaction with the department of probation acquires a "book" or reputation as to whether they are "bad" or just "troubled," which helps to determine whether they are to be blamed or not blamed for their problems or inappropriate behavior. This begins in the courtroom where the prosecuting attorney argues how *bad* the juvenile is and the defense attorney argues for treatment or "help," implicitly communicating that the adolescent is not responsible for the inappropriate behavior.

Depending on the ideology, the juvenile's behavior is explained as the result of "badness" or as a result of his or her emotional problems or "illness." This creates a relationship based on conflicting contingencies. If it assumed that the juvenile has "problems," then the treatment consists of attempts to establish a trusting relationship with the juvenile and thereby help him or her to achieve insight into his or her problems that will eventually result in a change in behavior. The juvenile's acceptance of the officer's explanation of the problem is viewed as evidence of improvement. If it is assumed that the juvenile is bad, then the relationship is more likely to be based on punishment for inappropriate behavior. The basic dissonance in the "mad" versus "bad" ideology often is manifest in the relationship between the juvenile court judge and individual probation officers. One assumes a mad or bad ideology toward a particular juvenile which conflicts with the other. They will then view one another as either overprotective or punitive, which will result in lack of constraint, an unchanged social system, and unchanged behavior.

This same conflict can also be acted out within the probation department. Some assume that creating a relationship with the juvenile and providing some guidance and understanding will lead to change. At the same time, for some officers there is an expectation that particular juveniles are bad and act inappropriately in a willful way because they enjoy breaking the law and acting inappropriately or think that these behaviors might escape detection. This definition of the problem results in the probation officer's attempts to constrain the juvenile to make him act appropriately by various kinds of negative reinforcement. Neither of these expectations are clearly articulated by probation officers, but they are continually acted out in their relationships. The ambiguous differences in belief about the problems and how to solve them was particularly important because the juveniles were experts in manipulating dissonances within and/or between adults, learned and acted out in their families of origin. The re-creation of this type of function became even more likely as a result of the shift in the basic structure of the probation department.[4] After a number of years using an individual case-load model, in 1976 the Juvenile Probation Division adopted a team approach.

The division's transition into teaming brought with it important alterations in functioning that went beyond redeployment of staff. Prior to the implementation of the teaming model, each probation officer carried a separate case load and functioned autonomously within the boundaries of policy and statute. Historically the division had been comprised mainly of young, energetic staff members less interested in the classical concerns of corrections (e.g., retribution, proportionality, deterrence) than in providing comprehensive youth services. The probation officer's role, like that of the juvenile court, was vaguely defined and included any and all activity which would effectuate the best interests of the minor and the community.

Crisis intervention tended to be the predominant mode of intervention exercised by the probation officer. This reflected, in part, the policy requirement for the probation officer to make himself available after hours to respond to his clients on an as-needed basis. Probation officers themselves favored this approach. Intervening, for instance, in a family crisis afforded the officer opportunity to easily identify the parent–child conflicts and to negotiate an at least temporary resolution. The interaction seemed cathartic; the probation officer felt a sense of accomplishment, and often peace (however uneasy) was restored. However, efforts to sustain intervention with a given family were overwhelmed by the endless series of apparent crises cropping up elsewhere on the case load while new cases received scant attention until and unless they attained a critical status.

Exhaustion and a pervasive sense of futility eventually would become typical of the probation officers' experience. Though relatively autonomous and influential (over 90% of their recommendations to court would be enacted), the probation officers found themselves in a state of perpetual disorganization, harassed by rather than managing their case loads. In addition, because deviant behavior by the juvenile tended to be the stimulus for crisis, their attentions were repeatedly and unavoidably drawn to circumstances indicative of their failure. And while failure could be well documented, the broad, unfocused, best-interest mandate made the identification of successful intervention a

4. This was reported to the first author on several occasions by a number of staff members and by several probation officers who had some knowledge of its functioning.

matter of conjecture that was not backed by any formal sanction or clear evidence. Conscientious probation officers, aware that no one in the system including their supervisors or the courts could have suffi- cient knowledge of their cases to assess their performance, were es- sentially alone and without standards or concrete data in evaluating the success of their work.

These and related problems were identified, and one proposal in which several probation officers jointly were responsible for a case load was greeted with general approval. Because teaming offered the op- portunity to share cases with colleagues, the probation officer could expect support from team members in dealing with difficult and un- willing clients. In addition, teaming potentially would be the source of fresh perspectives and new ideas. Though no final commitment to the concept was made at that point the Juvenile Probation Division, by consensus, gave the task group the job of developing a model for team functioning. This task was accomplished over the ensuing months.

The plan for teaming was designed to address the futility of crisis management as a predominating style of intervention. In addition, the locus for intervention would become the family, whereas the child's or adolescent's deviant behavior would be perceived as a signal of family dysfunction. The goal for the team's intervention would be set for each case early in its tenure and a plan comprising a number of discrete steps toward meeting the goal would be developed. Cases would receive maximum attention when they were new to the case load; as casework goals were met, the team's involvement would diminish. To help insure follow-through, teams would meet often to review newly developed case plans, to discuss the previous day's activities, and to identify tasks to be completed and assigned to each team member. In addition, the task group proposed that training be secured in family assessment and intervention.

The model ultimately adopted by the division consisted of three teams, each composed of three members. Each team had responsibility for a case load, and team members were encouraged to share the work load associated with each of the team's cases to the extent that such sharing was practical. If the team delegated primary responsibility for work with a given case to one of its members, all members of the team remained, nevertheless, equally accountable for the case. All major decisions, including matters concerning the team's scheduling, the formation of case plans, and the recommendations to be made to the court, were to be arrived at by team consensus.

The division assumed that teaming would produce a variety of desirable outcomes. Joint accountability for work flow would help assure that case planning and follow-through would be consistently under- taken. Discussion with colleagues occasioned by shared decision making enhanced the probation officer's opportunity for professional growth.

The family focus would prove more effective than child advocacy in maintaining minors in their own homes and reducing the rate of recidivism. In an effort to assess the efficacy of teaming, a number of evaluative criteria including recidivism and placement rates were identified. Unfortunately, the areas to be measured could not be compared to past performance due to a lack of data; instead, ideal standards for each criterion were fixed. Most importantly, the mere establishment of evaluative criteria served to provide the probation officer with clear goals and a means of measuring performance.

Finally, teams were formed through a process of selection involving both supervisors and all the probation officers. Because it provided maximum flexibility for each team, diversity was the primary consideration. Teams were composed of officers who differed in gender, lengths of service, and professional strengths. As an aid in completing team formation, the supervisors conducted an all-day workshop devoted to team building exercises.

Several months later in 1976, teams became operational with an average case load of 90. The most pressing business for probation officers entailed their becoming familiar with 60 additional cases while handling a tripled rate of intake. Because of multiple responsibilities, the probation officers initially channelled most of their energies toward those cases they had brought to the team load, and joint meetings with new families tended to be impractical. The court, police, and school communities responded favorably to the division's move. Each perceived an increased responsiveness, probably because an appropriate officer was three times as likely to be available for telephone calls or other forms of contact.

Within a few months, the most difficult problems associated with teams began to emerge. Some probation officers found the movement from entrepreneurial autonomy to a state of interdependence particularly difficult. Teaming brought with it a sense of increased accountability and routinization requiring officers to conform their schedules as well as their work to the will of the team. As a consequence, in some instances competition for control of the team arose, and covert alliances developed, creating and maintaining resentments that would have a continually disruptive influence on the team's functioning. On such a team, a small mistake or an oversight would become a major incident. Supervisors would intervene when a team's functioning became disrupted. Usually, this intervention involved meeting with the team in an effort to identify the source of conflict. The team members were encouraged to work out compromise solutions; and when they proved impossible, the supervisor would determine the team's course of action.

Data gathered throughout the first year were examined and teaming met or exceeded each of the previously established standards. Yet, during the first 18 months of the team experience, seven of the original nine team probation officers left the division. None cited teaming as a determining factor in their decision to leave; some, however, indicated that they had felt stifled by the team and preferred their experience of operating independently.

In addition, there was some covert disagreement between the director and associate director on the efficacy of this structure for their staff or what to do if there were problems among team members. Another problem was that the staff had mixed feelings about one another's competence and the efficacy of the team approach itself. Unresolved conflict was manifest on each of the teams about their relationships with clients, that is, whether each probation officer has an equal role in the treatment of each client or whether it was actually a team effort in which treatment strategy was a joint decision. The lack of resolution about this issue made cooperation difficult with the teams, especially because of some divergent personalities on the probation staff. For some this was a function of the stage in the life cycle in the individual probation officer. The younger staff members often identified with the juveniles and saw their parents as blameworthy for their problems, whereas the older probation officers, with children of their own, often identified with the parents of the juveniles and saw the juveniles as blameworthy for their own problems. In other words, the mad versus bad dichotomy was acted out on the teams as well, which exacerbated the covert conflict and dissonance that was already present within the staff. In this process the staff divides into "nurturers" and "cops." The "nurturers," those staff members who see their role primarily as that of therapist and whose personal relationship is seen as the primary motivator for change for the juveniles whom they believe have psychological problems, are pushed to be even more supportive and protective of the juveniles because of what is viewed as the arbitrary authoritarianism of their fellow team members. This in turn, pushes those staff members who define their role as a constraining one, as cops, who see the juveniles as bad, into attempting to be even more punitive because of what they view as the lack of enforcement of appropriate constraints by their team members. This makes cooperation and the agreement on clear goals for treatment even more difficult to establish because they are forced into joint decision making about each juvenile.

These dissonances make it possible for the juvenile—as long as he or she continues to act inappropriately—to create an analogue to the family of origin in which unclear constraints are established by a team which are manipulated by the juvenile, so that there are again no clear negative consequences for inappropriate behavior. This process is maintained by the conflicting basic premises of the probation officers, which often function to create differences in constraints, so that the juveniles are never actually constrained—just as in their families of origin. For example, a planning session with a probation officer, her fellow team members, and the first author was held to set up a treatment plan for a juvenile who was a chronic runaway and her family. A therapeutic strategy was developed so that the parents of the juvenile were to be given a number of tasks to help them cooperate in establishing clear limits for their daughter acting as a unit, that is by providing concrete consequences if she did not behave as agreed. As soon as the family sessions began, the probation officer began directing all of her attention to the girl, disregarded the strategy previously discussed, and ignored the parental assignment completely. After the session the probation officer then explained that the girl was "relating" to her for the first time, and she wanted to establish a "good relationship" with her. The girl successfully manipulated both her parents and the probation officer so that she was not even encouraged to change her behavior, recreating her family structure at a more inclusive level in which her parents together became the "peripheral parent" and the probation officer became the over-involved but nonconstraining parent.

Concurrently this behavior increased the conflict on the team. The other members felt that the probation officer described above was not competent and could not be trusted to function as a team member. She said that they were insensitive and could not relate to the adolescent's problems. Consequently, as in her family of origin, the adolescent's behavior maintained conflict in the system, so that the adults with whom she interacted were never able to cooperate in altering her behavior.[5]

---

5. This was acted out at another level of organization in the probation department also: the youth facility. The Youth Home is a detention facility that temporarily holds some juveniles involved with the court. This facility operates on a behavior-modification system: Appropriate behavior is a means by which juveniles earn privileges by the demonstration of increased responsibility. Misbehavior results in the loss of these privileges. However, there was often covert conflict between the shifts, who disparaged of each other for their constraints on the juveniles' misbehavior. The more lenient night shift defined the more rigid day shift as "insensitive," who in turn termed the night shift members as lazy or easily manipulated. This was expressed to the authors at various times in terms of who was incompetent, shirking their job responsibilities, and the like, on the other shift. Some juveniles were able to manipulate the differences in flexibility around certain rules, for example, whether they could make extra telephone calls, by making a relationship with a staff member contingent on these extra privileges. The covert message was "Bend the rules for my cooperation" or as evidence of your competence (and unlike staff on the other shift). By this certain of the most manipulative juveniles created covert coalitions with staff members against others. The mutual negative perceptions of each shift's competence made continuity and cooperation between the shifts even more difficult. The result was that confused constraints again re-created another analogue to the functioning that these juveniles experienced in their families of origin.

Because of such situations, a recurring metaphor is created, maintained, and recreated throughout the juvenile probation system. The adolescent described above as "out of control" in that she could not or would not make herself go to school or stay at home, was beginning to create a covert coalition with one probation officer against her fellow team members. This family was characterized by an analogous structure in that the daughter was covertly encouraged to act out by her mother and ineffectively constrained by her seductive father and by this regulated and was regulated by her parents' marital conflict, which was similar to many other families seen by the authors and described in the literature (Ferreira, 1960).

At the same time, at another level of organization, conflict in this team maintained the dissonance between the director and assistant director about the efficacy of the team concept. Consequently, the dissonance at a number of levels of organization is created and maintained by the "problem"—the inappropriate behavior of juveniles—that the system is set up to treat. The "mad" or "bad" juveniles who act in inappropriate ways and define this behavior as out of their control can be seen as a metaphor for the contingencies they encountered in their families of origin and that they created and recreated in those social systems with which they became involved because of their behavior.

The juveniles on probation eventually discover that level of organization with the most dissonance and thus the least able to constrain them and against it they act out.[6]

At a more inclusive level, the human services system of which the juvenile probation department is a part also influences its functioning in such a way that it makes the setting and following through of a treatment plan difficult. One of the factors that interfered with their functioning was a longstanding conflict with the mental health department in which both were originally involved in treating a number of the same juveniles and/or their families. At least one perspective suggests that the conflict between the Juvenile Probation Division and the mental health department began because mental health workers did not like to work with involuntary clients, which formed the bulk of those composing the juvenile probation department's case load. As a consequence, the Juvenile Probation Division referred few clients to them and instead tended to rely on other agencies and private practitioners. This resulted in minimal contact and virtually eliminated cooperation between them. This again created a more inclusive analogue to the family functioning of many of the juveniles, in which dissonance at a more inclusive level made the setting of clear limits and the manifestation of clear con-

6. Kaplan (1952) and others (Howe, Howe, Ellison, & Rackley, 1976) have noted this manipulation of two or more adults or organizations by delinquent juveniles.

straints, an important aspect of the solution to the problem being "treated," impossible.

Conclusion

The most basic assumption utilizing a cybernetic perspective is that of self-regulating systems that orient themselves by the exchange of information. At the level of the entire juvenile probation macrosystem, the most important information or novelty transmitted is the clients themselves. They can be "heard" especially clearly when exchanged among the parts of the social system created by the need to constrain or treat their inappropriate behavior. What is implicitly communicated by the client each time a client enters a new relationship with someone in this social system is that previous "help"—the courts, therapists, lawyers, or probation officers—all failed to alter his or her inappropriate behavior. This creates a context where the individual in the new relationship will try harder to "relate" and thus not threaten the relationship by constraining the juvenile or give up because of numerous previous failures with this adolescent. In neither case would the inappropriate behavior be constrained, validating for all that the problem was "inside" the juvenile. At the same time, as discussed earlier, the client must act inappropriately to maintain his or her homeostatic function within the family. That paradoxical behavior by which the adolescent acts and this action is defined as out of his or her control remains an essential aspect of the social system. It allows the client to go through the treatment/probation system always maintaining the implicit, contradictory definition of blamed/not blamed for his or her inappropriate behavior. The clients' inappropriate behavior links family members with one another and the family to the court, to the probation department, to therapists; often implicitly communicating, They failed, you try to help me. The adolescent must continue to lack control/ understanding in order to maintain the system. Dissonances at various levels in the system described above make this more likely.

It has been suggested by a number of theorists and therapists that the paradoxical nature of symptoms "spontaneously" appearing and limiting change in a system threatened by change can often only be altered by paradoxical interventions. A number of systems-oriented family therapists, especially Haley (1963, 1976) and Hoffman (1971), have utilized paradox and at the same time been aware of the nested hierarchy in dysfunctional social systems in which, at different levels of organization, there are contradictory pulls and tugs, some of which are deviation amplifying whereas others are self-regulating. Few, however, have included the varying levels of organization in social systems when describing the process of therapeutic change (see Watzlawick, Weakland, & Fisch, 1974). Romer's Rule linked with metaphor suggests a more inclusive context for understanding this process.

A successful general strategy for change would be to utilize the hierarchical nature of the social world and human discourse by the creation of novel contiguities that overtly or covertly metaphorically communicate that the continuation of the problem and/or the response to it will cause the system to change at some fundamental level. Consequently, what must be communicated is that the system must change, and change as a metaphor for staying the same would be utilized as the general therapeutic strategy to intervene in the juvenile probation system.

As described earlier, the process of achieving the status of juvenile probation has become more and more similar to getting convicted of a crime or admitting guilt for a crime in adult criminal court. However, instead of a criminal conviction, the court becomes a surrogate parent for the juvenile whose problems are implicitly "caused" by his or her parents' shortcomings and failures as parents. By this, it further legitimates the confused or reversed hierarchies in the families of juveniles. The parents are blamed for the problem because of their failure as parents and their remaining power is undermined.

There is another aspect of the system that must be considered to change it. The court has no sanction to punish, constrain, or even set limits on these juveniles. As discussed earlier, this appears to be an important aspect of the etiology of the problem. At the same time, the juvenile probation system no longer has as its primary function to provide protection for poverty-stricken, immigrant children whose parents are overwhelmed by their social and economic problems creating a chaotic family context (at least in this country). Instead, these juveniles are often from families that are in some sense, too well organized and rigid. Neither the families nor their juvenile members make culturally appropriate changes in their relationships. Instead, as described earlier, their inappropriate behavior and their parents' attempts to stop or cope with these behaviors function to maintain the juvenile's relationship to his or her family unchanged. As a result of this type of functioning, the family hierarchy remains confused or reversed, so that the parents often define themselves as equal or less than equal to their children in terms of power and responsibility. Their children often control them by being out of control. Consequently, the court, which by legal precedent functions as a surrogate parent for juvenile probationers, still has an appropriate role as a surrogate parent because the parents are often not doing an adequate job of parenting as manifest in their children who are behaving inappropriately. These parents had often been overtly and covertly blamed for their children's problems by numerous human service personnel. As a result, they often state that they cannot control their children and that the court should do it. However, due to changed circumstances, for example, different etiology, different family structure, larger case loads, and longer, slower, more complex routinized procedures, the freedom of the court and the probation department is limited. Consequently, the most useful function of the court system as surrogate parent under these changed circumstances is to use its power to put the parents back in charge of the parenting.

The court must also validate the probation department in the same fashion, as surrogate "grandparents," perhaps (at least as an analogy) who because they only have time for short-term involvement and in crises, can also fulfill their roles best by using their expertise to support the parents in terms of their children, especially by using clear expectations for appropriate conduct with clear consistent negative consequences for their inappropriate behavior and coaching in supporting appropriate behavior. Consequently, both judges and the probation officers should be encouraged to continue to do what they have traditionally done, act as surrogate kin by using their power and expertise to support the juveniles' actual parents or foster parents. There is little value in concentrating on the past in insight-oriented therapy—or blame. Both often interferes with getting parents to take charge of their children in the present. During crises, when parents are the most stressed, probation officers should be most available as advisors and support for the parents and ultimately as a metaconstraint for the parents and the juveniles.

At the same time, by defining the court's and the juvenile probation department's role as surrogate kin, whose primary interaction is to support the parent(s), they may be more able to circumvent their ideological dissonances by defocusing to another level of abstraction where this is not a conflictual issue. For example, the etiology of the problem could be ignored and the court could be overtly defined as aiding the family's long-term planning, while probation could be defined as helping the parents in terms of more immediate, concrete decision-making crises.

Another important change would be to reestablish contact and communication with the department of mental health so that they could coordinate their services provided for each family with a juvenile on probation. Similar goals for treatment are essential for adolescents whose primary problem is a lack of constraint. This might be done by defining the mental health workers who become involved with families. and juveniles on probation, as consultants whose expertise could be used for particularly difficult families rather than only for "motivated" clients. Another possibility is to make personal contact with particular mental health personnel who have a special expertise or interest in working with these types of families, in other words, to utilize informal personal relationships.

An additional step might be to create a more formal network of like-minded therapists to which the probation department might provide referrals and consultation who would also make the central goal of the therapy to help put the parents in charge of their children and setting clear limits on their behaviors. Within the probation department itself, the team concept might be altered slightly. The director and assistant director must resolve their disagreements about its functioning and clarify the relationships of the individual staff members and the entire team to each juvenile on their case load. There must also be an efficient means of resolving differences between and among staff members at the level of director rather than acted out through the clients and their families.

The social system created by the probation department, the juveniles with which they interact, and the other human services organizations of which they are all a part, can be seen as a hologram. All have similar structure and basic premises at each level of organization, from the personality or worldview of the delinquents to the contingencies of family interaction, the families' relationships to the probation department, and its relationship to the rest of the human services system. All can be seen as metaphors for each other in which unresolvable dissonances at various levels of abstraction and organization result in ambiguous constraints, rules, and consequences. At the same time, the problem creates more and more inclusive systems as additional organizations and individuals are called in to "help" or control the problem.

REFERENCES

Bateson, G. *Steps to an ecology of mind*. New York: Ballantine Books, 1972.

Beardsley, M. *Aesthetics: Problems in the philosophy of criticism*. New York: Harcourt Brace & World, 1958.

Black, M. *Models and metaphors*. Ithaca, New York: Cornell University Press, 1962.

Bowen, M. A family concept of schizophrenia. In D. Jackson (Ed.), *The etiology of schizophrenia*. New York: Basic Books, 1960.

Empey, L. The progressive legacy and the concept of childhood. In L. T. Empey (Ed.), *Juvenile justice: The progressive legacy and current reforms*. Charlottesville: University of Virginia Press, 1979.

Ferreira, A. The double-bind and delinquent behavior. *Archives of General Psychiatry*, 1960, *3*, 359–367.

Haley, J. *Strategies of psychotherapy*. New York: Grune & Stratton, 1963.

Haley, J. Toward a theory of pathological systems. In G. Zuk & I. Boszormenyi-Nagy (Eds.), *Family therapy and disturbed families*. Palo Alto, Calif.: Science & Behavior Books, 1967.

Haley, J. *Problem-solving therapy*. San Francisco: Jossey-Bass, 1976.

Haley, J. *Leaving home*. New York: McGraw Hill, 1980.

Hockett, C. F., & Ascher, R. The human revolution. *Current Anthropology*, 1964, *5*, 135–168.

Hoffman, L. Deviation-amplifying processes in natural groups. In J. Haley (Ed.), *Changing families*. New York: Grune & Stratton, 1971.

Howe, B., Howe, S., Ellison, K., & Rackley, M. The therapist and parole/probation officer as co-therapists with involuntary patients. *Family Therapy*, 1978, *3*(1), 35–45.

Illinois Juvenile Court Act, Smith–Hurd Ann. Stat., Ch. 37 Sec. 701-2.

Jackson, D. The question of family homeostasis. *Psychiatric Quarterly Supplement*, 1975, *31*(1), 79–90.

Kaplan, M. Problems between a referring source and a child guidance clinic. *Quarterly Journal of Child Behavior*, 1952, *4*, 80–96.

Katz, J., & Goldstein, J. Abolish the "insanity defense"—Why not? In A. Goldstein & J. Goldstein (Eds.), *Crime, law, and society*. New York: Free Press, 1971.

Madanes, C. *Strategic family therapy*. San Francisco: Jossey-Bass, 1980.

Powers, W. *Behavior: The control of perception*. Chicago: Aldine, 1973.

Rappaport, R. A. *Ecology, meaning, and religion*. Richmond, Calif.: North Atlantic Books, 1979.

Ryerson, E. *The best-laid plans: America's juvenile court experiment*. New York: Hill & Wang, 1978.

Satir, V. Symptomatology: A family production. In J. Howells (Ed.), *Theory and practice of family psychiatry*. New York: Brunner/Mazel, 1971.

Schwartzman, J. The addict, abstinence, and the family. *American Journal of Psychiatry*, 1975, *132*, 84–87.

Simon, H. A. The organization of complex systems. In H. H. Patlee (Ed.), *Hierarchy theory*. New York: George Braziller, 1973.

Sluzki, C., & Veron, E. The double-bind as a universal pathogenic situation. *Family Process*, 1971, *10*, 397–410.

Watzlawick, P., Weakland, J., & Fisch, R. *Change: Principles of problem formation and problem resolution*. New York: Norton, 1974.

Weakland, J. The double-bind hypothesis of schizophrenia and three-party interaction. In D. Jackson (Ed.), *The etiology of schizophrenia*. New York: Basic Books, 1960.

Weaver, W. Science and complexity. *American Scientist*, 1948, *36*, 468–471.

8

Family therapy and methadone treatment of opiate addiction

PETER J. BOKOS
Interventions, Chicago, Illinois

JOHN SCHWARTZMAN
Center for Family Studies/The Family Institute of Chicago
Institute of Psychiatry
Northwestern Memorial Hospital and
Northwestern University Medical School

Introduction

The need for macrosystemic perspective for the understanding and treatment of mental illness and deviant behavior has been made increasingly clear in the last 20 years by what has been described as a revolution in psychiatry (Haley, 1971) in the development of ecological systems approaches to the understanding and treatment of psychosocial problems. In this paradigm shift (Kuhn, 1960), the locus of the problem has been transferred from inside the individual into an aspect of and comment on the social context of which he or she is a part. This can be seen most clearly in the development of family-interaction research and theory.

Although there are some exceptions, the context under consideration generally stops at the level of the family or the institution, such as a hospital, which treats the symptomatic individual. Seldom are more inclusive systems considered.

Haley (1967) has demonstrated how the family of the schizophrenic and the ward staff resemble one another in their treatment of the individual, described by Bloch (1964) as "psychosocial replication." Harbin (1978) has discussed the means by which families alter the functioning of the hospital and maintain their own structure by forming coalitions with various staff members to split the treatment teams. This becomes possible because of conflicting ideologies at several levels: between the administration and that of the medical personnel, between differing ideologies at the level of the treatment team or medical personnel, and between differing ideologies among psychiatric personnel.

This chapter describes part of a methadone treatment system and is based on observations of more than 100 families, each with an addicted member. It suggests that the chronicity of a number of problems generally considered to be extremely difficult to treat, particularly schizophrenia, alcoholism, and drug addiction, can be understood as maintained by the flow of the clients among the institutions treating them. Often in conflict, these institutions function in such a way that the macrosystem reinforces and maintains a problem while attempting to reduce it. A study of the functioning of a part of a methadone treatment system of a large urban area demonstrates this.

Heroin "addiction" is described along with the social structure and culture created and maintained by the behavior of the addict within his family of origin, as a member of a marital dyad, and as a client at a series of methadone clinics. "Addiction" is defined as *a paradoxical communicational response to this social system, which concurrently maintains it*, rather than as a disease. The functioning of the institutions that treat addiction and their relation to the addict's family and the social system created by the addict's inability to remain abstinent are interpreted with reference to this definition. The social system is maintained by certain myths about addiction, by rituals to "treat" it, and by the addict's "out-of-control" behavior, which contains certain other pervasive dissonances within tolerable limits.

The functioning of several methadone clinics, institutions with which a large number of addicts are intensely involved, is described. Particular emphasis is given to dissonances in basic premises between professionals and paraprofessionals about "treatment"; the relative status and expertise of these professionals and paraprofessionals; and how their differences, coupled with the implicit conception of addiction as a disease, maintain staff conflict and elicit behavior that is defined as a manifestation of the addict's pathology, the inability to remain abstinent.

The addict's family of origin is also described, both as a most important context of socialization where the addict learns basic premises and a worldview and as an integral part of the social system with which he or she remains intensely involved, often for life.

A description of addicts' oscillation between, and functioning within, their families of origin and the institutions that treat them demonstrates how the cultural construct "addiction," a reification of the responses to the injunction "Be out of control," creates and maintains a more inclusive social system and legitimates and maintains that behavior most characteristic of the addict, addiction.

Addiction in Perspective

Definition of Addiction

In 1967 two researchers (Dole & Nyswander, 1967),[1] basing their approach on the assumption that heroin addiction was the result of a metabolic disease or biochemical deficit (either preexisting or the result of chronic drug use), had developed a treatment that they claimed was successful in helping addicts to stop using illegal opiates, allowing them a crime-free, more productive lifestyle. The basis of the treatment was the use of methadone, a synthetic opiate developed by the Germans in World War II. Methadone is cross-tolerant to heroin and creates a blockage that limits the euphoric effects of heroin and the "craving" for it or other opiates. Using methadone enabled the addict to feel normal in contrast to experiencing the peaks and valleys—"sick, cop, nod, sick" (Ramer, 1971)—typically experienced by urban addicts.

Goldstein (1972), a psychiatrist who has conducted extensive research on methadone, suggests that there is more evidence for explaining addiction in terms of conditioning theory than on the basis of biochemical need (see also Wikler, 1968, 1972). He believes that heroin-using behavior can be extinguished by a lack of reinforcement. Stabilizing the addict's dependence on methadone, thus blocking the euphoric effects of heroin, eliminates reinforcement for heroin use. A motivated addict, then, who wishes to give up heroin is able to do so; and he can later gradually reduce his dependence on methadone.

Regardless of the nature of opiate addiction, almost all of the large-scale drug treatment programs, including those on which this study is based, have utilized methadone. Even in programs emphasizing abstinence as the goal of treatment, methadone is used as the "carrot" to establish an initial relationship with the addicts so that they will stay in treatment. However, at different levels in the system, methadone treatment is hindered by dissonances that almost inevitably interfere with achievement of abstinence or changes in lifestyle or worldview.

The most basic dissonance in the methadone treatment system is the definition of the phenomenon "addiction" itself, which Jaffe (1970) gave as "compulsive drug use." However, as Mello (1975) has argued for alcoholism, but which is equally true for drug addiction, the concepts *need* and *craving*, which are used as primary diagnostic criteria for

---

1. Vincent P. Dole and Marie Nyswander developed *methadone maintenance*, a treatment method now used in approximately 700 drug rehabilitation centers in the United States. They started their research on methadone in 1964 with the New York Health Research Council.

alcoholism or addiction, are defined by the behavior they are supposed to explain, making the definition a simple tautology.

Preble and Casey have found that, often, hospitalized narcotics addicts deprived of drugs give no evidence of physiological withdrawal.

> The activities the individuals engage in and the relationships they have in the course of their quest for heroin are far more important than the minimal analgesic and euphoric effects of the small amount of heroin available to them. If they can be said to be addicted, it is not so much to heroin as to the entire career of a heroin user. (1969, p. 116)

In addition, there is more recent evidence that large numbers of individuals use heroin irregularly for years and never become addicted or involved with law enforcement or mental health personnel (Bourne, Hunt, & Vogt, 1975; Hunt & Chambers, 1976). The research mentioned above suggests that the phenomenon of addiction cannot be reduced to a chemical problem but is always related to the social context of the addict. If the purposeful behavior of the addict, a constant quest for a largely unobtainable drug, has a covert goal of maintaining a particular lifestyle rather than satisfying a craving, then the definition of addiction as compulsive drug use is not satisfactory. Therefore, taking cognizance of Preble and Casey's (1969) observations of the importance of the lifestyle rather than the chemical effects of the drug, addiction will be assumed to be a class of paradoxical messages communicated by addicts to those in their context, by which they absolve themselves from responsibility for much of their behavior.

"Addiction," defined as *a craving or a compulsion*, is an example of what Haley (1963) believes to be an essential characteristic of any symptomatic behavior in which an individual acts in a particular fashion and frames this behavior as "just happening," out of his or her control. Bateson, Jackson, Haley, and Weakland (1956), Haley (1963), Sluzki and Veron (1971), and others have suggested that such symptomatic behavior is a paradoxical attempt to respond to incongruent, paradoxical messages from the social context of which the individual is a part.[2] As Wilden (1974) suggests, all messages are also "comments" on their context.[3] Consequently addiction, as an example of the paradoxical communication characteristic of any symptomatic behavior, must be examined in

2. For example, the incongruence between the verbal and nonverbal in the speech of schizophrenics has been explained as the result of their attempts to orient themselves in contexts in which they were given only the "illusion of alternatives" (Weakland & Jackson, 1958) or punished for being right (Bateson, 1976).

3. He states, "No matter what it is about it itself, any theory—or any statement or message whatsoever, as it happens—is also a communication about the context in which it arose and from which it cannot in fact be isolated" (1974, p. 279).

the context where it occurs, because it is assumed that this behavior is in some sense appropriate or adaptive in this context.

The Family of the Addict

One significant context for most addicts is their natal family, in which it could be hypothesized that addicts find it adaptive to act as if they are not actually responsible for their behavior but instead it is the result of an uncontrollable craving for narcotics. As has been stated in the literature (Ganger & Shugart, 1969; Schwartzman, 1975, 1977; Schwartzman & Bokos, 1979), there are several characteristics that seem to be particularly important in understanding the relationship between the addict's perception and experience of his social context and those behaviors that are collectively the evidence for his addiction and his experience of it.

Often in the family of origin of the addict there is a pervasive, long-standing dissonance between the addict's parents, manifested either in constant conflict or a distant, covertly hostile, denigrating relationship. Frequently one parent—often but not always the mother—is extremely overprotective and intrusive in her relationship with the addict, in contrast to her relationship with her spouse, which is distant and hostile.[4] This family structure, termed a perverse triangle (Haley, 1967), is characteristic of families with a variety of symptomatic members (Haley, 1973).

In families of substance abusers, the content of communication is metaphorically about loss of control. These families are often characterized by various other types of out-of-control behavior—particularly alcoholism, gambling, and obesity—by family members (Rosenberg, 1969, 1971) and myths about loss of control in the past, so that lack of control appears to be a core concern. In addition, the parents are unable to tolerate actually constraining the addict so that he is not actually ever frustrated (Vaillant, 1975).

This lack of control is manifested most pervasively by the addict's inability to assume responsibility for his own behavior and his parents' inability to constrain him, particularly—but not exclusively—in regard to drug use, so that concern but unsuccessful constraint is elicited by the addict's behavior.

Very often the parents undercut one another's attempts at setting limits on the addict, both as a metaphor for their covert conflict and a covert means to avoid frustrating him. The addict learning to "punctu-

---

4. In this study a majority of the addicts were male, so each will be referred to as *he* in the text. A majority of the "overinvolved" parents were their mothers, so the overinvolved parent will be referred to as *she* in the text.

ate" (Watzlawick, Beavin, & Jackson, 1967) and understand his social context by the transformation of messages exchanged within it to the expectations of these messages, hears again and again that he is "out of control," covertly communicated by the intrusiveness of the overinvolved parent in that parent's constant attempts to constrain him. Yet behavior of the parent who sets only "pseudolimits" communicates both the addict's need for constraint and its impossibility. The addict, by communicating an inability to control himself, generally is rewarded. This pattern of interaction is redefined by the parents so that their inability to constrain him is defined as the addict's inability to be constrained. His discomfort reinforces this definition. The message "Be out of control" is communicated to the addict at several levels, and as a *demand* for spontaneity this injunction is paradoxical. The addict's "spontaneous" out-of-control behavior is an appropriate response to a context in which the addict pervasively receives the injunction "Be out of control."

The adaptive response to this paradoxical injunction is to control by being out of control and to need constraints but not be able to be constrained. The addict remains overinvolved with a parent and is able to separate only briefly by means of his craving for drugs, which often results in an exacerbation of drug-induced crises and in his rescue and return home or incarceration. Often the addict oscillates between his family of origin and somewhat brittle marital or other types of dyadic relations.[5] These often remain less emotionally intense than the relationship with the overinvolved parent. Living arrangements were often a metaphoric comment on the impermanence of the relationship: motels, cheap hotels, parents' homes, or apartments without leases. During the addict's crises, each partner frequently returned to his or her natal family. Separations and divorces were frequent. Many couples spent as much time living with their respective parents as they did with one another.

Addiction, analogous to many other symptoms (Haley, 1963; Jackson, 1957), promotes homeostasis for the system of which it is a part, in this case the family of origin of the addict. The addict's frequent crises and demands prevent the parents from attempting to solve their own marital problems. In addition, the parents' pervasive dissonances, including differences in their tolerance to the addict's experienced discomfort caused by his inability to tolerate constraints or frustration, are inevitably exacerbated when the parents are forced to respond to the various crises in which the addict finds himself. At the same time, the parents create contexts in which out-of-control behavior such as that characterized by addiction is an "appropriate" response. For example,

---

5. Addicts describe their relationships in the drug subculture as nonintimate and manipulative.

after many months a 20-year-old heroin addict had stopped using heroin and had been "detoxed" from methadone. Both his parents verbalized their desire that he "do something"—either get a job or go to school. He announced that he was going to get a job in a music store. His father said he thought that was a good idea, but his mother raised many objections to this kind of work, for example, poor pay and no future. He then spent several more weeks at home, getting high occasionally and not looking for a job. Finally he said that as a temporary measure he had obtained a license to drive a cab. His mother was enthusiastic about this job; his father, however, was opposed to it, stating that all cab drivers were involved in illegal activities, particularly drug dealing, and that he would no doubt become reinvolved with drugs if he took the job. When the addict increasingly expressed anger, his father began to wonder whether he might have suffered permanent brain damage as a result of his drug use. The addict remained at home, not working and "chipping" occasionally, while his parents disagreed often as to whether he was using drugs and what to do about it.

The addict's experience in interacting in this type of context in which others' expectation is that he is "out of control" is "deutero-learned" (Bateson, 1972) and generalized to other contexts.[6] For example, after several months of conflict, an addict's wife, who was not sympathetic to his drug problems, left him. He quickly formed a relationship with another woman who was much more tolerant of his drug use. Several times he stated in discussing her virtues that "Mexican women expect their men to mess up."

The addict's purposeful, goal-directed behavior, which he defines and which is defined by others as compulsive drug use or craving, can be understood as a response to the injunction that the addict be out of control. But as Bateson suggests, "To act or be one end of a pattern of interaction is to propose the other end. A context is set for a certain class of response" (1972, p. 275). The addict, by his addiction, communicates a paradoxical response to a paradoxical injunction. He maintains contexts characterized by dissonances between two people whom he manipulates so that he is not constrained.

Responses to the paradoxical communications of the addict's addiction in other contexts, particularly attempts to constrain or persuade him to control himself, are frequently such that structural analogues to his family are created. Often the addict communicates his need for constraints by establishing a relationship with a "nurturer" who will respond to this need and who also has a covertly conflictual relationship

---

6. Bateson (1972) suggested that all learning is a multileveled process in which not only is specific content learned but the contextual contingencies are also learned. Initially Bateson termed this contextual level "deutero-learning," but he later altered the terminology, referring to it as "learning II."

with someone else involved with the addict. The addict then indicates his inability to be constrained and demands the assistance of the "nurturing other." Each success the addict experiences using this type of manipulation validates the expectation that he is out of control owing to the power of his craving for heroin and defocuses from the contingencies in the social context that make this type of interaction adaptive for the addict and for those who interact with him.

At some point after the dissonance in the family has been exacerbated beyond the level of effective self-regulation, the addict, often with extrafamilial legal pressures to get treatment, becomes a client in a methadone clinic. However, methadone clinics are often characterized by structural dissonances analogous to those experienced in the addict's family of origin to which his inability to remain abstinent was an adaptive response.

The Methadone Maintenance System

A Description

The methadone treatment system in this state was created in response to the criminal justice system. It was realized that if the heroin addict did not need a "fix," he would be less likely to commit criminal offenses. Initial treatment often consisted of hospitalization and detoxification from narcotics, which when completed led to a rapid termination of any therapeutic relationship and a return of the addict to the same "junkie" lifestyle centered around the acquisition of narcotics by whatever means possible. After repeated failures it was discovered that a group of ex-addicts were able to "relate" to the addicts much more successfully than the professional staff, to engage them in therapy (generally confrontation groups) for much longer periods, and in some cases to prevent their return to the use of narcotics if they were currently abstinent. Because of the professionals' treatment failures, paraprofessional ex-addicts were seen by professionals at the most rational choice of staff in the creation of a system for the treatment of heroin addiction.

The state methadone treatment system was composed of about 40 facilities. A few of these were inpatient facilities (generally therapeutic communities modeled after Synanon and Daytop Village), but most of them were outpatient methadone maintenance clinics. Some were operated directly by the state, whereas others had a contractual relationship in which the state paid a fee for a limited number of clients to whom the clinic provided methadone (in the methadone clinics) and varied medical, vocational, and psychotherapeutic services. There were also a number of private facilities whose only relationship with the state system was that they were occasionally monitored by state officials to insure their compliance with state and federal protocols for methadone programs. These private facilities charged their clients fees for their methadone (either on a sliding scale or about $30 per week).

All the clinics had the same formal structure: a director and assistant director in charge of staff, clinical issues, record keeping, and relations with the state and federal regulatory agencies that determine treatment protocols for methadone clinics. At each clinic a medical director was responsible for all medication, and a nurse was in charge of the daily dispensing of the methadone.

Each clinic had from 2 to 10 paraprofessional counselors, often but not always ex-addicts who had been clients at a methadone program or therapeutic community and had become and remained abstinent. The counselor's degree of therapeutic sophistication and orientation was related to the institution or clinic where he had previously been a client. The state drug treatment system provided periodic training programs for counselors on various aspects of drug treatment and counseling techniques.

Generally the counselors provided most of the therapeutic input with the clients: individual or group therapy, casual interaction, urine monitoring to detect drug use, and occasional social activities outside the clinic.

Initially clients are required to come to the facility once a day to get their dose of methadone[7] and once a week to give a urine sample to be tested for its drug content as a check on drug use. Some facilities also require attendance at a certain number of individual, family, or group therapy sessions each week. Often after several months of good behavior, particularly maintaining abstinence from heroin and having no arrests, clients are given several days' dosage of methadone at a time, eliminating the need to come to the clinic every day.

At all the clinics, clients were encouraged to be law-abiding; to stop using illegal drugs; to seek employment, vocational training, or education; to stop associating with other addicts; and, in general, to alter their lifestyle toward more middle-class values, including having a steady job and developing stable interpersonal relationships. The means by which this transformation was thought to occur was determined by the ideology of the particular clinic, as was the wide variation in the degree

---

7. Methadone is given to the clinics in wafers, which are then dissolved in orange drink in dosages from 1 to 100 milligrams depending on the client. The methadone does not dissolve completely, so that it is somewhat "grainy" and cannot be injected. Most clients know their dose by its relative "graininess."

to which the maximum goals were encouraged and the minimum tolerated.

Dissonances in the Methadone Treatment System

Observations of the functioning of several methadone clinics revealed that despite efforts to create a rational treatment system for drug abusers, certain dissonances built into the structure were almost inevitably transformed into deviation-amplifying processes (Maruyama, 1963). The dissonances were related to treatment ideology, the relationshop between paraprofessionals and professionals,[8] and the definition of the "addiction" itself.

The original psychiatrists in the methadone treatment system decreed, as a result of their own failures and evidence of the ex-addicts' success, that paraprofessionals were competent to treat addicts. This created a paradox of self-reference of the form "I, who am incompetent, define you as competent," so that the definition of competence is questionable at a higher level of abstraction by the incompetence of those defining it, creating a paradoxical definition. This is of more than merely logical interest, because there were few unambiguous measures of competence in the treatment of drug abuse. It put the paraprofessionals into the bind of having to continually demonstrate their competence by "relating" to the clients, which was emotionally demanding and frustrating. At the same time, many of the paraprofessional ex-addicts who had been abstinent for only relatively brief periods also had never been more than marginally employed for more than brief periods, so their success as counselors was extremely significant for them.

In addition, there was a great deal of difficulty in getting for paraprofessional ex-addicts the same advantages as other employees in the state mental health system, including civil service status; for a time they could be retained only on "patient–employee status" (Glasscote, Sussex, Jaffe, Ball, & Brill, 1972). This status emphasized their paradoxical position in the state drug treatment system. As "addiction specialists" they were never able to get status equivalent to that of other paraprofessionals in the state mental health program.

Several other aspects of the paraprofessional position made their successful functioning even more difficult, particularly the almost con-

8. At the same time, however, the definition of "professional" or "paraprofessional" was context dependent. At one clinic a bachelor's degree qualified one to be defined as professional. At another clinic an ex-addict with a bachelor's degree and nearly a master's was a paraprofessional. One clinic director was defined and defined himself as a paraprofessional despite having a master's degree.

stant, pervasive, covert conflict with professionals regarding one another's competence, perhaps an inevitable result of the paradoxical
definition of the paraprofessional's position.[9] The professionals often
felt that paraprofessionals were unprofessional; and more basically,
because the primary skill of the paraprofessionals was the ability to
relate to addicts, *they* were implicitly defined as addicts by the professionals.

This conflict was exacerbated by several other factors. First, the
paraprofessionals generally had received their jobs as counselors because
they were good *clients* at a methadone clinic or therapeutic community.
Staff in these facilities had liked them and they had become abstinent.
However, they had no particular therapeutic skills except perhaps as a
role model. The only measure of their skill was that they were popular
and abstinent. Clients are extremely demanding and needy in terms of
support, advice, and time, so the counselor is pushed into providing
these on demand because his primary therapeutic skill is his ability to
maintain positive relationships to clients. This, coupled with the frequent difficulty in setting limits (as a result of the counselor's own
experience in his family of origin), creates an extremely emotionally
demanding relationship for paraprofessionals in which they are constantly required to demonstrate their therapeutic skills by their ability
to relate to the clients.[10] This often was contingent on their being
understanding and making no demands on the clients.

However, attempts to respond to clients' needs and frustrations,
which were described as extremely draining by both counselors (former
clients) and clients, often gradually led to an "overinvolved" (Haley,
1973) relationship. This was due to the counselors' (and clients') inability to tolerate the clients' frustration, their constant crises, and
recurrent demands for assistance. Frequently this situation induced
what has been termed the "burn-out syndrome" (Freudenberger, 1975)
because little was given in return by the clients for the exhausting
effort put into the therapeutic relationship by many counselors, except
more demands and failure after failure. Several ex-counselors stated
how their effort, coupled with the lack of cooperation on the part of
their peers, was such a demoralizing experience that it resulted in their
becoming readdicted. At one clinic, during a period of particularly intense

9. There is evidence from other fields of mental health that frequently there are identity
crises and rivalry over authority when a responsible role for paraprofessionals is created
in a traditionally professional setting (Chappel, Charnett, & Norris, 1975, p. 298; Minuchin,
1969).

10. This was also a problem for a number of professionals, particularly the director of one
clinic studied. There can be a problem as long as there is a difference among staff members
in tolerance for the clients' frustration.

conflict, four paraprofessionals became readdicted within 3 months of one another, although two had been abstinent for more than 3 years. When these were replaced by other paraprofessionals who "knew their place"—that is, who accepted their status as subordinate and their skills as inferior to those of the professionals and who felt that for most clients there was no need for "real therapeutic" input and instead just provided occasional counseling—conflict decreased significantly according to both professional and paraprofessional staff members.[11]

In addition, the increased bureaucratization and formalization of procedures resulted in withdrawal of the professionals and original paraprofessional leaders from clinical positions and their induction into administrative positions. This eliminated much of their contact with clients and consequently increased the client pressures on the paraprofessionals for favors and services (and perhaps increased hostility of paraprofessionals toward professionals working under less pressure for much more pay). The pressure was exaggerated because paraprofessionals were seldom able to leave the field because of their lack of marketable skills. Only 18% of those ex-addicts who worked in the state methadone system ever had worked *anywhere* else (Rhodes, White, & Kohler, 1974). However, another adaptation was available for many paraprofessionals who were "burnt out"—a reduction of contact with the clients. This became possible with the increase of documentation and paperwork required by the state authority, so that time spent doing paperwork legitimated decreased time with clients. Familiarity with the new bureaucratic procedures became a new means of demonstrating competence.[12]

Consequently, the structure of the methadone maintenance system provided the paraprofessionals with alternatives in the treatment of heroin addicts. They could attempt to respond to their clients' endless needs until they were physically or emotionally exhausted or they could withdraw and reduce their contact with clients to a minimum. Either alternative almost inevitably effectively eliminated the possibility of therapeutic change. Dissonances in treatment ideology also hindered attempts to alter clients' drug use and lifestyle.

---

11. A counselor at this clinic stated that after several months of constant conflict about the therapeutic responsibilities of paraprofessionals, he took a friend's advice and decided, "It's not worth fighting about. I'm just going to do my job. I'll do counseling and the professionals can do therapy. I'm just not going to get so upset about it." After this relabeling, perhaps the paradoxical status of paraprofessionals was eliminated at this clinic.

12. In drug abuse, as in other areas of the mental health bureaucracy, therapeutic skill is generally "rewarded" by the therapist's rising in the bureaucracy as an administrator, eliminating contact with clients.

Treatment Ideology

> The State methadone system has as stated goals: . . . all compulsive nar-
> cotic users become law-abiding productive, drug-free and emotionally
> mature members of society, who are given no additional medical or social
> support to maintain this ideal status. (Glasscote *et al.*, 1972, p. 131)

However, one psychiatrist involved in creating the system stated: "We
do not realistically expect very many patients to reach this set of goals.
The minimum goal was that all clients become law-abiding citizens"
(Jaffe in Glasscote *et al.*, 1972, p. 131).

From the beginning of the state methadone treatment program, the
first objective was keeping the clients in treatment (Jaffe in Glasscote
et al., 1972, p. 131). Beyond this, however, there was a wide variation in
philosophy among staff members and clinics concerning goals, particularly regarding methadone maintenance as contrasted with abstinence. In addition, there was a dissonance in implicit assumptions about
the process of treatment and the means to change the client's behavior.
The ideology that predominated seemed to be determined by the relative power of professionals and paraprofessionals at a particular clinic.

A Methadone Maintenance Clinic

Westend in Context

After 8 years of operation, a state drug treatment system was re-
organized in 1976 so that all its methadone treatment facilities, rather
than being run by the state, became independent. Each facility or group
of facilities entered into a contract with the state to provide services for
a certain number of clients in return for a fee. The following is a
description of Westend, a former state facility, shortly after the reorganization.

Westend Clinic was located in a large midwestern city in a densely
populated neighborhood with a large number of deviants including drug
abusers, homosexuals, alcoholics, and prostitutes and the businesses
that catered to them, such as fast-food restaurants, bars, night clubs,
cheap hotels, and liquor stores. The clinic was several blocks from the
edge of a Latino neighborhood, primarily Puerto Rican.

The clinic itself was dirty and dark, occupying no more than
2000 square feet of space on the second floor of a two-story building
located in the middle of a commercial block. The aluminum door, marked
by the clinic's identifying initials, opened onto a flight of narrow, steep
stairs at the top of which was a hall painted an institutional green. At

one end was a small room where the clinic's clerk–typist had his desk. Behind it was the office of the director; and next to it a room shared by the medical director, the other staff physician, and the part-time teacher. Halfway back, the hall opened onto another office with three desks and a couch, for five counselors. Beyond this office was the "dayroom," where the clients waited for their methadone and socialized. This area contained a pool table, Ping-Pong table, a television, and stereo. There was a rule that nonclients were not allowed in the dayroom, but the counselors had difficulty enforcing this rule. Often friends and "old ladies" of clients stayed to talk and play pool. In addition, many of the clients brought their babies and young children, who increased the noise and confusion. A core group of perhaps 20 clients spent several hours almost every day talking and eating in the dayroom. Built into the far end of the dayroom was the methadone station, separated by a Dutch door. Here the clients were given their methadone diluted in orange drink. Clients and nonmedical staff were never allowed in the methadone station.

Before receiving their methadone, clients had to go to the clerk's office and check in. The clerk would inform the counselor when a client arrived or the counselor would see the client and get his methadone card. The client then either had to go into the bathroom and give a urine specimen[13] for his counselor or just get his card signed and present it to the nurse, who gave him his methadone. At times the counselor engaged in more prolonged interaction with the client, at his desk or in the dayroom. The lack of adequate office space and privacy made any type of formal therapeutic interaction difficult, and there was very little such interaction.

The Clients

Drug abusers either came voluntarily or were sent as a condition of probation or parole to become clients at Westend. All clients were given a screening physical examination, and a brief social history was taken at the central intake facility, primarily to ascertain whether they were over eighteen, had a 2-year history of drug addiction, or had made two unsuccessful attempts at detoxification.[14] From the intake facility, clients

13. This means counselors had to go into the bathroom with clients and watch them urinate into a cup. The urine was to be checked to see if the clients were using illegal drugs. They had to be accompanied by a counselor in order to make sure they did not try to exchange their own urine, in case they had used drugs, for a "clean" urine sample.

14. Because state contracts provide funds for a certain number of "slots" for clients, it is in some sense adaptive to discourage therapeutic change, particularly abstinence, for there is no "reward" for successful detoxification of clients; and it requires the additional work of processing new clients to fill the available slots.

were sent to clinics that had openings. If an opening was available, Westend infrequently refused clients—in contrast to other clinics that were much more selective.

There were 127 clients at Westend, of whom 68% were male, 60% white, 18% Latino (primarily Puerto Rican), and 22% black. About one-third were over 30 and the rest were in their 20s. Many had been terminated from other methadone programs. Others had voluntarily transferred because of conflicts with staff. Few were employed and many of those that were, worked for relatives at menial and sporadic jobs as mechanics, painters, laborers, domestics, salespeople, or as employees in other similarly low-paying transient jobs. About half were on welfare.

For many clients their interaction at Westend served as a major portion of their social life. Many clients socialized only with members of their families or other clients, with whom they spent hours at the clinic or nearby restaurants and coffee shops. Many of their interactions with these same individuals revolved around drugs, away from the clinic. These clients came from the same neighborhoods, had grown up together, socialized together, and dealt drugs to one another. Many clients had relatively little experience with nondrug users and were often uncomfortable even in casual interaction with "straights," so that if they became abstinent and lost most of their peer network that revolved around drugs, they would retreat back into their family of origin as their primary social context. However, their relationships with family members were often conflictual or anxiety producing, so they got very little satisfaction from any interpersonal interaction. Although they were uncomfortable within their families of origin, their families continued to be crucial in the clients' social system and affected their functioning and clients at Westend.

The Clinic Staff

The staff at Westend was composed of a director, assistant director, six to eight paraprofessional counselors, a part-time medical director, a part-time physician, a registered nurse, a practical nurse, a part-time teacher, a part-time psychologist, and clerk–typist. Each position will be briefly described.

The director of Westend was responsible for the overall functioning of the clinic, particularly staff performance, and increasingly for the staff's written documentation and completion of the federal and state bureaucratic forms. He met biweekly with the executive director and the assistant director of the corporation of which Westend was one of several clinics, and with the other clinic directors. He had grown up in the neighborhood in which the clinic was located and lived several blocks away. Many times he had turned down offers of the directorship of clinics in other cities where he would have been paid a much higher salary, as he did not want to leave the neighborhood.

At one time this director had been in prison. He had become a client at one of the state methadone facilities shortly after his release, had successfully withdrawn from methadone, and had been a counselor at one of the state methadone facilities.

He became director of Westend several years prior to the reorganization. At the start he felt it was important that much effort be spent in reorganizing the clinic's record keeping and other paperwork. Its disorder had put the clinic in danger of being closed by the state drug authority. In his office was a large sign which read, "If it isn't documented, it isn't done." This was his basic concern in terms of staff functioning.

He was respected by staff members at Westend, at least the senior staff, but was not intimate with them, ate lunch alone, and infrequently socialized with them. At the same time, he said, "My door is always open," which was literally true. He was the only person through which his staff members could communicate with the executive staff of the corporation of which Westend was a part. He attempted to know everything that took place at Westend, including what was said in counselor's casual interaction with their clients and with one another. As a result he was the only person at Westend who had access both to information about Westend from a higher level in the corporation and to Westend's internal communication.

The counselors at Westend Clinic had three ranks: for the first 6 months to a year, they were trainees; then they became counselors; and some went on to become senior counselors.

The primary job of the counselors was to document the clients' attendance at the clinic and to monitor clients giving a urine sample when they came for their methadone. Counselors were also supposed to confront those clients who continued to use illegal drugs or exhibited other antisocial or irresponsible behavior. In addition, they were responsible for completing monthly forms on each of the clients in their case load. Four of the five senior counselors were black male long-time heroin addicts who had served time in prison for narcotics offenses. The other was younger, a black woman who had not used narcotics. Most had not engaged in illegal activities for years and had little contact with drug users away from the clinic except, in the words of one counselor, "at funerals."

When research at Westend first began, there were two junior counselors, who were white and much younger than the senior staff members. One was the only "professional" on the counseling staff with a MA in alcoholism counseling. He was fired several months after research at this clinic began. The other was a former addict who had been a client at another clinic. After 8 months, four new junior counselors were hired. Two were staff members from another methadone clinic: one a black, long-time former addict, and the other a Mexican-American ex-addict. The other two were white college graduates: one was a former addict (but never on methadone) and the other had never used narcotics.

The lowest ranking staff member, the clerk–typist, was a middle-class white man in his early 20s who was only a few credits away from a college degree. He was the only staff member who had complete knowledge of all the necessary bureaucratic procedures required by the director and the state. He corrected the mistakes of the counselors, reminded them to get their forms in on time, and answered their questions. In addition, he wrote or corrected much of the formal correspondence such as letters to other agencies, and grant proposals.

The medical staff consisted of two medical doctors, one a general practitioner and the other a retired surgeon; a registered nurse; and a practical nurse. The doctors were responsible for all changes in methadone dosage for the clients, for prescribing any additional medication, and for making any medical decisions. Neither had had any psychiatric training.

The medical director, one of the doctors mentioned, was a rather authoritarian individual who often made decisions independently of any other staff. His judgment was frequently questioned by nurses, counselors, and the director, out of his presence—also by most of the clients.

The nurses were responsible for dispensing methadone to the clients, keeping medical records up-to-date, and carrying out physicians' orders in their absence. They also did a good deal of informal counseling of the clients and in fact had more contact with some clients than other staff members, particularly those clients who had problems with their counselors or were unable to see them as frequently as they wished. In addition, a clinical psychologist with a great deal of experience in drug abuse provided case consultation for the staff for several hours a week. A teacher conducted general education development classes for clients in the late afternoons.

The roles, status hierarchy, and job requirements for staff were clearly defined at Westend to meet the requirements of the state system. At the same time, various conflicts in interpersonal relationships, coupled with contradictory beliefs about the nature of addiction, made most treatment a function of staff interaction rather than a function of any therapeutic consideration.

The Functioning of the Clinic:
An Analogue to the Pathogenic Family

Ideally, clients were referred from the central intake facility, assigned a counselor, and given a high enough dose of methadone that after several days they began to "feel normal" without other narcotics or illegal drugs. After several months of being "clean"—not using illegal drugs—clients were given "pickups," 1 or 2 days' supply of methadone at one time so they did not have to come to the clinic daily. At this point they could be trusted not to sell their methadone on the street or use it all at once.

After the counselor had established a relationship with the client and the client had remained abstinent for some period of time, gained "insight" into his problems, and made significant changes in his attitude and lifestyle, both client and counselor agreed to begin the client's detoxification from methadone. Detoxification was a gradual process that could take weeks or months (unless it was a punitive "detox," which occurred very infrequently at Westend), involving decrease of a few milligrams each week. It could be stopped (and frequently was) if the client became too uncomfortable or started using illegal drugs. Detoxification from methadone, analogous to withdrawal from any narcotic, is accompanied by physical discomfort, even when done gradually. In addition, many addicts appear to be very sensitive to pain. Some clients said withdrawal was incredibly painful, others that it was no worse than flu. At some other clinics, a mild tranquilizer was supplied to help clients with the transition from methadone to abstinence. Many clients sedated themselves with tranquilizers from the street, with alcohol, or other drugs. According to clients it was harder to withdraw from methadone than heroin or morphine. They insisted that it "gets in your bones." Because of frequent failures and their beliefs about themselves and narcotics, clients were very skeptical about the possibility of successful withdrawal and abstinence as, in fact, were many staff members. A large number of long-term clients remained on extremely low dosages of methadone, one to 5 milligrams, for years but seemingly were unable to achieve abstinence. One client, who had lost a son and a brother to a narcotic overdose and had another son who lost his legs in a barbiturate-related accident, was on a dose of 4 milligrams of methadone. Every spring he tried detoxification, but always had to have his dose raised as soon after it was decreased because he began to return to heroin use.

As is the case in any institution, the functioning of Westend Clinic was contingent on a large number of variables that were not included in a description of its formal procedures. Perhaps most noticeable were the pervasive conflicts at various levels of the organization involving differences in personality, ideology, status, sex, race, and goals. These dissonances, coupled with the clients' perception of themselves and their social context, resulted in the creation of a functional analogue to many of the clients' families. Specific similarities include the pseudoconstraints placed on the clients and the pervasive transmission of the message "Be out of control" at many levels of abstraction and organization.

The lack of constraint in the clinic was the result of pervasive conflicts between staff members which were transformed into their inability to actually set limits on clients' irresponsible behavior. The staff talked *about* the setting of limits and threatened it but took no action to do it. The situation in the clinic was similar to that situation in the client's family of origin where discussing the reason for addiction or the means to stop it generally interfered with the actual setting of behavioral limits by the parents. Consequently, communications "about" his drug use were probably learned by the addict as an implicit message that abstinence would *not* be demanded of him unless it "spontaneously" appeared. In fact, nothing was demanded as long as he defined himself as "addicted," which legitimated almost all his behavior.

At Westend the etiology of the conflict originated from many sources. It could be found at various levels: that of the individual, the structure of the clinic, ideology, and professional–paraprofessional relationships.

The director's style and beliefs about treatment amplified the conflict between himself and his senior staff members. Their relationship was described most clearly by the clerk–typist, who stated that the director "intruded on their apathy." His intrusiveness, his "open door," which he defined as evidence for open communication at the clinic but which several staff members perceived as his "always breathing down your neck," exacerbated the distance between the senior staff and the clients. This distance was legitimated by the staff's increased paperwork, which in turn increased the director's intrusiveness. At the same time, the director discouraged the staff from doing therapy because they were not trained to do it. He stated on several occasions that "they all have family problems," which he considered to be another reason why they should not do therapy. Often what he defined as staff members' inappropriate behavior (generally anger directed at him) he explained as the result of their "family problems."

New staff quickly became frustrated and discouraged because they were not encouraged to actually provide treatment at Westend. The director discouraged the placing of any constraints on the clients by his staff or actual therapeutic intervention to encourage change.

The director put an end to group therapy (which had almost

stopped anyway) when he became director because he thought it was "negative" and his staff did not have the skills to do it, despite the courses on interviewing techniques, counseling, various types of therapy, psychopharmacology, women's roles, and other subjects, provided by the state drug program in which they had been involved. He did not encourage his staff to have any therapeutic interactions with the clients. He told two new staff members that some of their most important therapeutic interactions would take place when they were getting a urine sample from their clients.

If a client continued to use drugs for several months, he was confronted by his counselor or by the director. The confrontation generally involved telling the client to stop using drugs, listening to his explanations of why he was using them and to assurances that he would stop. The client might request that he be given an increase in methadone dosage so that he could stop using illegal drugs. Frequently this request was granted.

At times a formal contract was drawn up between counselor and client in which the client agreed to stop using drugs within a short period or submit to a decrease in his dosage each time his urine screen indicated he was still using them. Sometimes he was given an increase in his methadone. This had to be approved by the director. If the client's drug use continued, the client was transferred to another clinic. A "swap" might be arranged if there was no space in the other clinic, in which he was exchanged for a client who wanted to be transferred to Westend.

The director might be directly involved in these interactions or he might tell the counselor to confront the client; but he was always aware of exactly what took place and would change the contract if he did not like it. In most instances he provided the initial impetus that something be done about the client's behavior. His need to be involved in everything at Westend made any type of directive therapy impossible because the counselor could not actually implement any treatment without his permission at each step, which greatly reduced the counselor's influence with the client and motivation to attempt change. By his intrusiveness and discouragement of counselors from attempting any type of direct intervention with clients, the director constantly affirmed that the counselors needed his supervision and lacked the competence to do actual therapy. He tolerated an extremely low level of functioning by his staff in that they were discouraged from direct attempts at change except when the clients continued to use drugs, and even then the clients were expected to change "spontaneously." His intrusiveness with staff members, rationalized as the result of their lack of skills, and the encouragement of their passivity appear similar to the interaction between an addict and his overinvolved parent in which incompetence is positively reinforced because it creates the "need" for the overinvolved parent's concern, which in turn reinforces the incompetence.

More assertive behavior by counselors was difficult to maintain because the director demanded detailed explanations for the time spent at anything except paperwork. His intrusiveness and constraints on his staff's functioning maintained a low level of therapeutic interaction and low emphasis on change in the clients' behavior.

At the same time, staff members were often indifferent to the clients and did as little as possible to encourage relationships with them beyond what was demanded to complete their paperwork. One staff member stated that it was impossible to be motivated when you could not advance in the system. Senior staff at times told newer members that they should not work so hard. Many clients complained about the negative changes that had taken place since the current director had taken charge of the clinic, particularly the decrease in therapeutic interaction. However, the legitimization of withdrawal of contact with clients by the senior counselors, condoned by the director, perhaps partially explained the low rate of readdiction by counselors at Westend. Only one counselor had become readdicted since this director had taken charge, in contrast to the situation in other clinics where several counselors had returned to drug use. Rumors about paraprofessionals at other clinics who were using and dealing in drugs and about directors of these clinics who were reputed to be drug dealers also validated Westend's "treatment." All clinics had staff members who had "slipped," so the abstinence of counselors at Westend was considered to be at least a sign of minimal success in the clinic's functioning within a context of failure.

As stated previously, at other clinics, counselors, and clients who were former counselors, described how draining the job of counseling was because of the constant crises of their chronically depressed, anxious, and needy clients. Several former counselors blamed the stress on the job for their readdiction. Consequently, the legitimization of withdrawal from interaction with clients reduced their stress and possibly their rate of readdiction.

The patterns of interaction at Westend described above, very similar to those in addicts' families of origin, are manifestations of the family members' problems with separation, the expression of affect, autonomy, and fear of loss of control (Ganger & Shugart, 1969; Schwartzman, 1975; Stanton, Todd, Heard, & Kirschner, 1978). These problems result from the development of patterns of interaction in families in which the addict, discouraged from separating, has been overprotected and then criticized for not being more autonomous and competent. Consequently, structural analogues to the addict's pathogenic family are re-created in the clinic, Westend's director representing the overinvolved parent; the corporation's executive director, the peripheral parent; and the senior staff forming the "symptomatic" third member characterized by indifference to their withdrawal from clients or by involvement with a "special" client that often becomes overinvolvement. Clients in the clinic generally remained unchanged, sometimes for years.

The director's relations with the junior staff were more clearly hostile. All felt he was both cold and intrusive. He scapegoated two of them, particularly the one staff member with a master's degree, whom he described as "coming across like a professional" and "coming out of books." The staff member explained that there was a "personality conflict from the start" and believed that he threatened the director intellectually. The director fired him for incompetence.

The other junior staff member who was scapegoated was described as "not aggressive enough" by the director. She was eager to get a different job, felt that she "had nothing to give," and hoped that none of her clients "wanted anything from me." Her attitude seemed to be a caricature of the attitudes of the rest of the staff.

There were other pervasive conflicts at the clinic also. The junior counselors and the nurses had negative attitudes toward the senior staff members. The two groups almost always ate separately. The junior counselors and nurses criticized the indifference of the senior counselors partially because they had to do and correct much of the work of these counselors. The nurses felt the senior counselors did not provide the clients with any services and were opportunistic, incompetent, and lazy. The senior staff felt that they were not respected by the nurses and younger staff members for their greater experience with drugs and with personal relationships with the clients which sometimes went back many years.

The senior counselors were a close group except for one who was clearly scapegoated by the other senior counselors and the director and was defined as lazy and incompetent by them. Clients on his caseload often heard him criticized by other staff members. One client inquired whether he still worked there and the responses ranged from it was "difficult to tell" to "he never worked here." On a number of occasions the nurses and several other staff members criticized his therapeutic skills. As a group, the senior counselors appeared to be most positive about the clinic and most comfortable with the status quo.

Perhaps the most pervasive conflicts were those between the entire staff, including the nurses, and the medical director. He did not respect the opinions of nonprofessionals nor, for that matter, the other professionals and considered himself to be an expert on drug abuse. At the same time, the staff felt that he was extremely insensitive both to themselves and the clients. The nurses did not respect his medical judgments.

The conflict among staff members described above is perhaps not particularly unusual in any organization. However, it was especially detrimental at Westend because treatment always required the cooperation of several staff members. And because the conflict was constant and pervasive, there was little cooperation among staff. The dissension created a structure analogous to that of the addict's family.

Conflict was exacerbated by any sudden change or desire for change on the part of the clients in their methadone and frequently resulted in the creation of a perverse triangle (Haley, 1968). Clients and counselors created a covert coalition against the medical director, with whom they were almost always in conflict.

Decisions about methadone made by the medical director were often questioned by the staff, who often tried to manipulate around these decisions. On a day when the "more lenient" doctor was on duty, counselors would often try to get increases in methadone dosage for their clients. Neither doctor would prescribe tranquilizers or other types of mood-altering chemicals more than one or two at a time, although it was common knowledge that with a welfare card, clients could get dozens legally prescribed at medical clinics, or they could buy them illegally on the street easily and relatively inexpensively. The counselors condoned this behavior when the clients were particularly anxious or undergoing a crisis, so the counselors were covertly allied with their clients, for whom they frequently had to negotiate against the medical staff. This resulted in minimal communication between counselors and the medical director except that which could be used manipulatively. At the same time, it was very difficult to get any drug-related decisions contingent on client behavior. The counselor had to make suggestions to the medical director (who did not respect counselors' opinions), who then had to interview the client and make his own decision. This procedure diminished the power of the counselor visa-à-vis the client because the doctor based his drug-related decisions almost completely on his own opinions. The result was that no treatment plan was ever really feasible because the covert conflict made cooperation between staff members so difficult. In the patterns of interaction described above, at various levels of organization there is a high probability that any interactions with clients, particularly related to a demand or request, will trigger the overt and covert conflicts that result either in withdrawal from the clients by counselors or the implementation of pseudo-constraints, or rules without consequences, that characterize the families of drug abusers.

In addition, the inability of one or both parents, spouse, or "old lady" to tolerate the client's frustration brought about by the clinic's attempts to constrain him (e.g., by insisting that he show up at the clinic on time, refusing his request for more methadone, or beginning detoxification) often led one of these relatives to undercut the constraints, however limited, by various means. For example, a parent frequently called the clinic requesting or demanding privileges for the client and providing an explanation for the client's continued inappropriate behavior. The maintenance of any constraints by the clinic on the client was generally defined as illegal, unfair, or inappropriate; and if privileges were denied, a family member often undercut the client's success by interfering with appointments and being critical of the manner in which the client was treated by the clinic staff. In one instance the father of a client called the director of the clinic every few days to inquire about his daughter's progress and question the counselor's competence but would never discuss with her counselor ways that they might cooperate to encourage her to become abstinent.

At a more inclusive level, there were recurring deviation-amplifying dissonances in the patterns of interaction between the executive director of the corporation and the staff at Westend, so that a system was created that functioned analogously to that just described and thus was also in many ways a functional analogue to the families of addicts discussed in the literature (Schwartzman, 1975; Ganger & Shugart, 1969). The executive director of the corporation had successfully bid against the director of a "professional" clinic to get the contract for Westend. He had become associated with the state drug program soon after it was started and had directed many training courses for paraprofessionals both for service in the program and for acquiring of credentials (for example, academic credit), creating for them the possibility for career options other than drug abuse (Bokos, 1975). Unlike many other professionals in the field, he personally knew many paraprofessionals working at his facilities and appeared particularly sensitive to their problems in the state methadone treatment system. However, according to several staff members, during the bidding process for the clinics, he had made certain promises to staff, particularly in terms of the retention of their clinical and financial autonomy; but since the takeover by the corporation, these promises, staff members felt, had not been kept. They believed they had lost much of their autonomy. Despite his experience in working with paraprofessionals and his concern about their position in the system, the corporation's executive director has been described by staff members as aggressive, ambitious, and eager to "make money."

In addition, several staff members felt that the assistant corporation director "checks up" on the clinic's functioning each week. She was at Westend almost weekly but seldom met with the staff other than the clinic director and at times his assistant director. As a result, staff members were either ambivalent or hostile toward the head of the corporation and his assistant director but had no direct means of expressing their negative feelings to them. This is similar to families with a drug abuser as a member which often have problems involving difficulties with expression of anger. Rather than communicating it and receiving a clear response to it, more frequently anger is denied or discounted until finally after much frustration it is expressed explosively and inappropriately.

Generally those in conflict, most often junior staff members and the director but sometimes other staff members and many clients, had an extremely difficult time expressing anger clearly and in "hearing" it when it was communicated to them without its being labeled as inappropriate. Several staff members became overtly angry only when they had been drinking, as many clients become angry only when they are high or withdrawing from heroin.

The problem of expression of anger was also a manifestation of the fear on the part of ex-addict paraprofessionals regarding their job security, which is jeopardized by increased pressures for "professionalization" through academic and professional qualifications in drug abuse.

The clinic director never verbalized opinions about either the corporation's executive director or his assistant but was uncomfortable when anyone on the staff tried to bypass him and communicate directly with the corporation's executive director without his knowledge. Consequently, Westend functioned so that the executive director of the corporation, authoritarian and distant with little communication with the paraprofessionals, was very similar to the peripheral parent in his relationship to the director and the staff of the clinic. Allied against him, in a very "intrusive" relationship with his staff, was the director, who attempted to know about everything taking place at the clinic and be involved in every treatment decision no matter how trivial.

The clinic director's "open door," which he believed represented open communication at the clinic, could perhaps be seen as a metaphor for intrusiveness with his infantilized staff. He constrained his staff members and often discouraged and ridiculed their attempts at therapeutic interaction with clients because of their lack of training, despite the training they had been given as part of the state drug program.

The treatment ideology at Westend Clinic explained most clearly by its director, but at one time or another by almost all the staff, maintained the lack of formal therapy or direct intervention to alter clients' behavior and active overt discouragement of those staff members who attempted it. The therapeutic goal of "getting addicts off the street" required only providing methadone and the ability of staff members to "relate" to clients. This is at least partially a function of the whole state methadone system composed of facilities with dissonant goals and treatment ideology, of which Westend was one.

The System in Context

Because of the recurring patterns of interaction previously described, the addict continues to perceive all the social systems of which he is a part as lacking constraints, while others in these contexts perceive the addict himself as lacking constraints. This becomes extremely difficult to change because, as Bateson suggests, owing to limits on the amount of information any system can store and use, an "economics of flexibility" (Bateson, 1972) requires that an adaptive system internalize as basic premises, out of awareness, the more abstract contingencies in its context and act automatically as if these contingencies were "true" and by this increase their probability of being true. This is as accurate for the state methadone treatment system described in this chapter as it is for any other system. Its basic premises create and maintain social systems that are analogous to the families of clients and to the individual methadone clinic just described. In fact, the maintenance of individuals who are addicted, whether to heroin or methadone, is necessary for the maintenance of those social systems whose function it is to "treat" them, such as the state methadone system. The dissonances in ideology, status of paraprofessionals, and beliefs about addiction create more and more inclusive analogues to the addict's family, intrusive, pseudocon- straining and covertly conflictual, maintained by the flow of clients and paraprofessionals among clinics and the dissonances among and between them for whom "treatment" is ideological, the structure of which main- tains the problem.

As stated earlier, many of the paraprofessional clinics define treat- ment most basically as "getting the addict off the street." In contrast, many of the clinics with a professional director and staff make a more intense effort to push their clients toward abstinence and often have other constraints, such as mandatory group attendance and prompt payment of bills with actual consequences for failure.[15] The paraprofes- sionals believe that reliance on rules (such as those used in a behavior modification schema) rather than on a personal relationship between counselor and client is not "humanistic." Often those clients who are unwilling or unable to conform to the constraints of some of the professional clinics are terminated from them. Both staff and clients at paraprofessional clinics provide myths of how professional clinics have randomly terminated clients for small infractions. The paraprofessionals see such termination as "cold," as of course do the clients; and a great effort is made to get these clients on programs, whatever their status as

15. In actual functioning many clinics that are largely professionally staffed are no more constraining than those staffed with paraprofessionals; they merely select clients who are more compliant.

clients at their previous clinics. As a result, staff and clients at primarily paraprofessional clinics can be described as creating a covert alliance against the more constraining clinics staffed by professionals who "do not understand addicts" because they have not had actual drug experiences or are "just in it for the money." The professional clinics, analogues at a more inclusive level to the peripheral, excluded parent in the addict's family, view this as a lack of expertise, low standards, or "maintenance, not treatment."

The dissonance in ideology is exacerbated and a more inclusive analogue to the client's family is created and maintained between clinics with varying constraints by the changing status of clients. It is exploited by the client at this level also in his attempt, generally successful, at characterizing his social context as lacking constraints. The client acts out his own lack of constraints to validate the expectations of those in his context whose intrusiveness and pseudoconstraints further validate the lack of contraints for him.

The "symptom" for the entire methadone system is the low rate of abstinence of the clients who create the system as they "flow" through it. In the facilities observed, clients transferred from clinic to clinic because they had continuously broken clinic rules or had conflictual relationships with certain staff members, generally concerning the enforcement of these rules. Clients maintain the social system both by the messages they transmit about other clinics and the message that they themselves *are*, defined as "unsuitable" as clients at other clinics. Each client transferred from one clinic to another implicitly creates a perverse triangle by building a relationship with the facility to which he transfers against the clinic from which he has been transferred because he has not been a "good" client. In this process the professional clinics terminate or transfer to paraprofessional clinics their "worst" clients, those who are least willing to be constrained, particularly to stop using illegal narcotics. In the paraprofessional clinics, clients will not be discouraged from remaining on methadone and at times will be actively discouraged from attempts to become abstinent. This validates for the paraprofessionals the necessity of taking care of these clients and the futility of trying to change their lifestyle. For the professionals this reinforces their view that paraprofessionals provide poor treatment.

The more motivated clients often seek out a more constraining professional clinic where they will be encouraged to become abstinent and give evidence of increased improvement, at least by taking the responsibility of paying for their methadone.

The flow of paraprofessionals functions in a fashion similar to that of the clients. Many of those at primarily paraprofessional clinics who are highly motivated express their frustration at the lack of therapeutic interaction with clients where, as stated earlier, it is sometimes actively discouraged. If they are able to transfer, they go to clinics emphasizing more of an abstinence than a maintenance orientation, which demand more constraints and emphasize therapeutic interaction with clients by staff members. At the same time, at these clinics certain counselors have difficulty setting any limits on clients and transfer to "maintenance" clinics where they do not have to frustrate clients, only to maintain a relationship. Both of these groups communicate their negative perspectives of their former clinics and validate the ideology of the ones to which they transfer.

Consequently, many of the drug abusers that Westend attempted to "get off the street" came to Westend because they were terminated from other clinics as a result of conflict with staff members or their refusal to conform to clinic rules. The professionally staffed clinics created the context to which this paraprofessionally staffed clinic's "getting addicts off the street" was the therapeutic response.

Those clients who could not or would not function in professional programs were perceived as victims of the professional clinics' rigid, cold ideology. This perception in turn validated the professional clinics' view of paraprofessional clinics as "giving away methadone to supplement junkies' habits." Almost every client at Westend who had been a client at another clinic had negative comments about that clinic that explained the client's transfer to Westend in such a way that the clinic was at fault and the client an innocent victim "rescued" by the more humane attitude of Westend. Consequently, Westend's functioning was in one sense a response to the functioning of the professional or more constraining clinics in the state drug treatment system, and by this it legitimated the lack of any direct intervention with clients. The type of interaction in which clients often are transferred between clinics amplifies the conflict and mutual denigration between the professional and paraprofessional clinics.

The flow of clients and staff validates for both professionals and paraprofessionals their own beliefs about treatment and about the inappropriateness of the others' approach and lack of knowledge about addiction.

The paradoxical messages that signal "addiction," purposeful behavior defined as out of control, that create social systems composed of methadone clinics and families of addicts trying to "help" or "treat" them, and the clients themselves, are maintained by myths about addiction. These all function as self-regulators because the locus of the problem is transferred from the system into the client. The myth that addiction is a disease inside the addict transforms the paradoxical injunction "Be out of control" that those in his context transmit to the addict, and its paradoxical (but adaptive) response, those behaviors indicative of addiction, his being "purposefully out of control," into an aspect of his nature. The transformation of the problem into the addict is maintained by "treatment" that can be understood as ritual (which in fact was the term several counselors at different clinics used to describe it). By the performance of treatment rituals, the implicit structure of the social system is acted out, the relationships that compose it are re-created, and the dissonances in the system are maintained within tolerable limits. This happens in "staffings" where decisions regarding clients are discussed and the relationships among staff members and clients are acted out. Treatment decisions are contingent on the staff members' relative power, conflict, and relationship to the client rather than on purely therapeutic considerations.

If a client seeks a certain staff member for support or is involved with one whom he can "constrain" in some fashion as described earlier, particularly by manipulating the conflict with another staff member, he can very frequently create perverse triangles so that this staff is allied with him against other staff members. At the same time, this type of functioning inevitably increases conflict, which when it reaches a certain level of intensity, often seems to require someone defined as dysfunctional, either paraprofessional or client, to maintain homeostasis. The dissonance is transformed into conflict "about" the performance of one of the less powerful members of the system, while the structure remains unchanged. Frequently the result is the sudden detoxification or transfer of a client for what seems to be an insignificant reason or alternatively the sudden termination of a staff member or his reinvolvement with drugs after a long period of abstinence.

Consequently, the "treatment" actually creates and re-creates contexts in which the addict, by exploiting certain dissonances, validates his basic premises about himself and his social context as lacking constraints. In addition, the clinics provide few supports or rewards for abstinence; there is no follow-up and abstinent clients quickly disappear, and reappear only when they are readdicted and wish to become clients at the clinic again.[16]

Summary and Implications for the Future

Little attention has been given in the literature on the treatment of psychiatric and social problems to the impact of macrosystems created by the relationships among those providing treatment for the client. (For exceptions see Kaplan, Ryan, Nathan, & Bairos, 1957; Kaplan,

16. Clients who are on methadone are terminated if they miss 14 consecutive days. Abstinent clients must come to the clinic once a month or they are terminated as clients. Neither service nor counseling is provided for abstinent clients.

1952; Roberts, 1979; Polak, 1972.) As discussed in this chapter, there is evidence that in the case of methadone treatment, those providing treatment create and maintain contexts structurally similar to contexts assumed to be pathogenic for the client at the level of the family. There are unresolved dissonances at various levels in the treatment system that function to create more and more inclusive contexts characterized by covert coalitions of the client with some of the treatment personnel against someone else in the treatment system. Thus, as in the addict's family of origin, perverse triangles (Haley, 1967) are formed that are found to be pathogenic in most social systems.

As Shands (1967) states, the functioning of any system can be understood as the transformation of novelty (information) into expectations, or "habits of thought" (Bateson, 1972), that are at a level too abstract to be contradicted by direct experience, so that they are self-validating and provide the focal point by which the system orients itself and "makes sense" of its social context. At the same time, Bateson suggests, "To act or be one end of a pattern of interaction is to propose the other end" (1972, p. 275), so that systems frame the contingencies to which they expect to respond. In the addict's family of origin, a pervasive communication is "Be out of control," and an appropriate response to this paradoxical demand to be spontaneously out of control is a purposeful quest for drugs, defined as a "craving." At the same time, the behavior indicative of his addiction creates a "frame" for a class of responses that are attempts to get him to stop using drugs. These attempts are frequently unsuccessful and validate the expectation that he is "out of control." In addition, a pattern of interaction results in which attempts are made to constrain the addict, which fail if he is persistent, reinforcing those in the system's beliefs in his "craving" (including his own) and in turn increasing attempts to constrain him, which most often fail.

This is a pattern of interaction similar to that of the methadone clinics previously described where very frequently dissonances in the ability of staff members to set limits on the client are transformed into covert coalitions between the client's counselor and another staff member. This pattern often results in their undercutting one another's constraints, so that the client never is actually constrained. The structure of the family, then, is created at this level.

In addition, at a more inclusive level, the clinics themselves vary in their structure and ideology, and the constraints of the more rigid clinics and permissiveness of some of the others result in another analogue to the described type of functioning. At each level of the system under observation, unresolved concealed conflict between two parents, staff members, or clinics generally results in the addict's covertly allying himself with one individual or group against another. The result is that the addict is infrequently constrained because no effective limits are set on him, and he remains irresponsible and is defined as out of control because of his psychopathology and addiction. At all levels the structure is maintained by unquestioned beliefs about the nature of addiction and its treatment, which despite obvious and persistent failure, remain unexamined, so that the continuation of the client's addiction can be seen as functioning to maintain the system unchanged. The final result is that heroin addiction is defined as an untreatable chronic disease.

It seems obvious that the functioning and structure of the present macrosystem of methadone treatment programs reinforce the basic premises that cause the problems. It seems just as obvious that the solution will be found in the operation of the whole system. The system must be based on a uniform set of goals, and conflicts at any level in the system must be made overt and resolved so that the possibility of covert coalitions involving the client may be eliminated.

The failure to conceptualize the entire macrosystem has maintained the perspective that the problem is in the client rather than the social context of which he is a part. The dissonances in interpersonal relationships and the covert coalitions must be eliminated so that the addict can separate and be responsible for his own behavior and function autonomously rather than being rewarded for inappropriate behavior.

The system that allows the flow of clients from clinic to clinic reinforces the problem. The clinics have varying requirements, so that any demand for change in terms of personnel responsibility can be evaded by transfer of the client to another clinic. This validates both for those providing treatment and for the client the supposition that the problem is a chronic one, inside the client, so that treatment failures maintain the label "untreatable"; so each failure is blamed on the client rather than the treatment.

The constraints placed on clients as consequences when they do not follow rules must be uniform to prevent re-creation of the pseudoconstraints that characterize their families of origin.

Implications for the Future

Problems in this state's drug treatment program, as made manifest by the numerous clients involved in the system for years without evidence of successful treatment, prompted formation of a study committee composed of state drug experts to suggest changes in the system.

Having served on this committee, the first author of this chapter describes a systematic perspective adopted for conceptualizing changes in the structure in the system. From this perspective, new ideas emerged for resolving the dissonances that reinforced the addiction and inappropriate behavior of the clients.

As stated throughout this chapter, deviant behavior of clients, along with the dissonances in the system, is maintained by the definition of "addict" held by the clients. A pattern is developed in which clients experience themselves and are defined by those who treat them as lacking control, creating and maintaining contexts without constraint. It is the clients' worldview and socially reinforced character that the restructuring of the state treatment system is to resolve.

Addiction clients, like many other individuals characterized by severe symptoms, often fail to make culturally appropriate changes as their lives progress. Their failures are legitimated by their symptomatic or deviant behavior. Consequently, a newly constructed macrosystem must be able to deal with clients having severe symptoms along with a history of failure to make appropriate life cycle transitions, who act out.

The deviant behavior of these clients is coupled with skills in covertly manipulating differences—within the system—between individuals or groups more powerful than they, exploiting these differences so that they themselves are rarely frustrated, constrained, or responsible. They fail to alter the behavior their treatment endeavors to change.

Because patterns of deviant behavior and manipulation should not be perpetuated, treatment personnel must intervene by consistently imposing penalties and setting limits on inappropriate behavior including continued drug use. At the same time, the system must be structured so that it does not lose clients who test the constraints and find them real.

Primary restructuring in this state's macrosystem consists of establishing clear expectations of clients and clear consequences for continued deviant behavior. The proposed changes are an attempt to force the typical substance abuser to alter his worldview, his behavior, and the social system he creates, all of which have given him reinforcement.

One of the first steps in this restructuring is the classification of clients according to their current drug involvement. Treatment is tailored to this classification. Help offered ranges from primary and secondary prevention for young polydrug abusers in early stages of drug use to rehabilitative procedures for those who have experienced serious, long-term drug involvement. A number of types of intervention are employed for those who have been addicted to opiates for some time, who are often also involved with the legal system.

The "outpatient drug-free intensive model" provides maximum contact with staff. Clients may select this option if they are transferred from another program in which they have been successful. They must agree to accept the responsibility of making progress as a condition of staying in treatment. Clients are given as much vocational counseling as they wish along with frequent group, family, and individual therapy planned in cooperation with their counselors. This is an extensive outpatient modality that allows a maximum treatment of 3 years for each client.

Clients and staff are expected to establish measurable objectives for client progress. The treatment setting is required to provide the necessary services through its own staff and by referral, if necessary, so that these objectives can be met. Clear evidence of progress is required from the client. If the objectives are not met, the client is transferred to a residential setting or another outpatient program such as an "ambulatory detoxification modality." This modality maintains a 60-day program offering no services other than dispensing of methadone. Because there are no take-home provisions, clients must come to the clinic each day for methadone. Frequent random urinalysis is used for testing. In this modality clients are allowed only three admissions in 2 years, with a 90-day wait to reenter the program after having left it or having been dropped. Clients entering this treatment from another outpatient or residential care program are discharged after a single violation, either arrest or a positive toxicology screen for illicit drug use. Self-selecting clients are discharged after two such violations. Discharge results in a 7-day detoxification. Clients who have failed to make progress in other programs enter this modality and are therefore provided with fewer services because of their misbehavior. Those clients who apply for readmission into this modality must not only wait 90 days but must also return to the same clinic, at least for referral.

Another group of clients are stable, employed, or legitimately occupied and seem to need no clinical support other than long-term low doses of methadone. They may have this low dose treatment as long as they remain stable, free from arrest, and free from use of drugs as shown by urinalysis. They have the option of transferring to a more intensive kind of treatment if changes in their lives require more intensive services (e.g., death in family, loss of job).

As described here, the attempted restructuring of the state drug macrosystem is simple. The major intervention is the attempt to establish clear penalties for continued inappropriate behavior. Clients' impulsiveness is not reinforced. Clients continuing to behave inappropriately will be dropped and must wait 90 days before they can be readmitted to treatment. Readmission must then be to the clinic they have left. This eliminates the possibility of manipulating the clinics against one another to avoid client constraints.

Former ambiguous rules, then, and inconsistent enforcement are replaced with clear consequences for misbehavior. At the same time, no negative constraints are imposed for clients making progress in treatment. These clients may transfer freely from one clinic to another or to another type of treatment without being limited in the number of changes they make.

Thus, clients are not penalized while making progress and are not limited in their use of treatment resources as long as treatment is in keeping with mutually agreeable treatment plans. This is in contrast with the too-rigid homeostasis of many of the clients' family systems, which have been demonstrated to be ineffective and must be counteracted by the clinical treatment.

REFERENCES

Bateson, G. *Steps to an ecology of mind.* New York: Ballantine Books, 1972.

Bateson, G. Foreword. In C. Sluzki & D. Ransom (Eds.), *Double-bind: The foundation of the communication approach to the family.* New York: Grune & Stratton, 1976.

Bateson, G., Jackson, D. D., Haley, J., & Weakland, J. H. Toward a theory of schizophrenia. *Behavioral Science*, 1956, *1*(4), 251–264.

Bloch, D. Unpublished mimeograph, 1964.

Bokos, P. Education and training for drug abuse paraprofessional staff. In E. Senay & V. Shorty (Eds.), *Developments in the field of drug abuse.* Cambridge, Mass.: Schenkman, 1975.

Bourne, P. G., Hunt, L. G., & Vogt, T. *A study of heroin use in the state of Wyoming.* Washington, D.C.: Foundation for International Resources, 1975.

Chappel, J. N., Charnett, C. V., & Norris, T. L. Paraprofessional and professional teamwork in the treatment of drug dependence. In E. Senay & V. Shorty (Eds.), *Developments in the field of drug abuse.* Cambridge, Mass.: Schenkman, 1975.

Dole, V. P., & Nyswander, M. Heroin addiction: A metabolic disease. *Archives of Internal Medicine*, 1967, *120*, 19–24.

Freudenberger, H. J. *The staff burn-out syndrome.* Washington, D.C.: Drug Abuse Council, 1975.

Ganger, R., & Shugart, G. Complementary pathology in families of male heroin addicts. *Social Casework*, 1969, *49*(6), 356–362.

Glasscote, R., Sussex, J., Jaffe, J., Ball, J., & Brill, L. *The treatment of drug abuse.* Washington, D.C.: American Psychiatric Association, 1972.

Goldstein, A. Heroin addiction and the role of methadone in its treatment. *Archives of General Psychiatry*, 1972, *26*, 291–297.

Haley, J. *Strategies of psychotherapy.* New York: Grune & Stratton, 1963.

Haley, J. Toward a theory of pathological systems. In G. H. Zuk & I. Boszormenyi-Nagy (Eds.), *Family therapy and disturbed families.* Palo Alto: Science & Behavior Books, 1967.

Haley, J. *Changing families.* New York: Grune & Stratton, 1971.

Haley, J. *Uncommon therapy: The psychiatric techniques of Milton H. Erickson.* New York: Norton, 1973.

Harbin, H. T. Families and hospitals: Collusion or cooperation? *American Journal of Psychiatry*, 1978, *135*(12), 1496–1499.

Hunt, L. G., & Chambers, C. D. *The heroin epidemics: A study of heroin use in the United States, 1965–1975.* New York: Spectrum, 1976.

Jackson, D. The question of family homeostasis. *Psychiatric Quarterly Supplement*, 1957, *31*(1), 79–90.

Jaffe, J. H. Drug addiction and drug abuse. In L. S. Goodman & A. Gilman (Eds.), *The pharmacological basis of therapeutics.* New York: Macmillan, 1970.

Kaplan, M. Problems between a referring source and a child guidance clinic. *Quarterly Journal of Child Behavior*, 1952, *4*, 80–96.

Kaplan, M., Ryan, J. F., Nathan, E., & Bairos, M. The control of acting-out in the psychotherapy of delinquents. *American Journal of Psychiatry*, 1957, *113*, 1108–1114.

Kuhn, T. *Structure of scientific revolution*. Chicago: University of Chicago Press, 1960.

Maruyama, M. The second cybernetics: Deviation-amplifying mutual causal processes. *American Scientist*, 1963, *51*, 164–179.

Mello, N. K. A semantic aspect of alcoholism. In H. D. Cappel & A. E. LaBlau (Eds.), *Biological and behavioral approaches to drug dependence*. Toronto: Alcoholism and Drug Addiction Research Foundation, 1975.

Minuchin, S. The paraprofessional and the use of confrontation in the mental health field. *American Journal of Orthopsychiatry*, 1969, *39*, 722–729.

Polak, P. Techniques of social systems intervention. In J. Masserman (Ed.), *Current psychiatric therapies*, (Vol. 12). New York: Grune & Stratton, 1972.

Preble, E., & Casey, J. Taking care of business: The heroin user's life in the streets. *International Journal of the Addictions*, 1969, *4*, 1–24.

Ramer, B. S. Methadone maintenance for narcotic addiction. *Journal of Psychedelic Drugs*, 1971, *4*(2), 162–164.

Rhodes, C., White, C., & Kohler, M. F. The role of the so-called paraprofessional in the six years of IDAP. In E. Senay & V. Shorty (Eds.), *Developments in the field of drug abuse*. Cambridge, Mass.: Schenkman, 1975.

Roberts, W. Family or agency network: Where to intervene. *Journal of Family Therapy*, 1979, *1*, 203–209.

Rosenberg, C. M. Young drug addicts: Background and personality. *Journal of Nervous and Mental Disease*, 1969, *48*(1), 65–73.

Rosenberg, C. M. The young addict and his family. *British Journal of Psychiatry*, 1971, *118*, 469–470.

Schwartzman, J. The addict, abstinence and the family. *American Journal of Psychiatry*, 1975, *132*(2), 154–157.

Schwartzman, J. Systemic aspects of methadone maintenance. *British Journal of Medical Psychology*, 1977, *50*, 181–186.

Schwartzman, J., & Bokos, P. Methadone maintenance: The addict's family recreated. *International Journal of Family Therapy*, 1979 (winter), 338–355.

Schwartzman, J., Bokos, P. J., & Lipscomb, S. Westend, a methadone clinic: Structural aspects of addiction. *International Journal of the Addictions*, 1982, *17*(2), 271–281.

Shands, H. Novelty as object. *Archives of General Psychiatry*, 1967, *17*, 1–4.

Sluzki, C., & Veron, E. The double-bind as a universal pathogenic situation. *Family Process*, 1971, *10*(4), 397–410.

Stanton, M. D., Todd, T. C., Heard, D. B., & Kirschner, S. Heroin addiction as a family phenomenon: A new conceptual model. *American Journal of Drug and Alcohol Abuse*, 1978, *5*(2), 125–150.

Vaillant, G. E. Sociopathy as a human process. *Archives of General Psychiatry*, 1975, *32*, 178–183.

Watzlawick, P., Beavin, J. H., & Jackson, D. *Pragmatics of human communication*. New York: Norton, 1967.

Weakland, J. H., & Jackson, D. D. Patient and therapist observations on the circumstances of a schizophrenic episode. *Archives of Neurology and Psychiatry*, 1958, *79*, 554–574.

Wikler, A. Interaction of physical dependence and classical and operant conditioning in the genesis of relapse. *Research in Nervous and Mental Disease*, 1968, *46*, 280–287.

Wikler, A. Dynamics of drug dependence. *Archives of General Psychiatry*, 1972, *28*, 611–616.

Wilden, A. Structuralism as epistemology of closed systems. In I. Rossi (Ed.), *The unconscious in culture*. New York: Dutton, 1974.

Family and culture

iii

9

Values and family therapy

HOWARD F. STEIN
University of Oklahoma Health Sciences Center

> *Wohltun, wo man kann—Freiheit über alles lieben—*
> *Wahrheit nie, auch sogar am Throne nicht, verleugnen!*
> —Johann Christoph Friedrich von Schiller[1]

Introduction

One of the most abiding issues haunting any form of therapy—family therapy included—is that of knowing what contexts are significant toward explaining and treating those problems our patients and families present to us. "Boundary problems"—what to include, what to exclude, where to "draw the line"—are universal. Our conceptual and group (e.g., professional) boundaries, however, are, more often than not, monuments to our defenses against knowing rather than the frontier of the knowable. In American society we have arrived at a not exactly amicable division of labor among clinicians who identify and isolate problems in the psyche, in the brain, in organ systems, in the family, in religion, in society, and so on. As a result it is difficult to link artificially bounded realms—this especially because conceptual frameworks and therapeutic techniques tend to be used as ideologies and rituals respectively.

In this chapter I argue that values play a profound role in all healing relationships—family therapy included. In excluding the subject of values from clinical assessment and treatment plans, we exclude valuable data about the family, about ourselves who treat or supervise treatment, about others (in yet other contexts) who influence the family members, and about our assumptions on the value of therapy—family therapy and otherwise. One's very identification of who and what should be treated, selection of admissible clinical data, choice of therapeutic modality, and expectation of outcome are themselves based upon value-laden assumptions. Values not only propel the behavior of identified patient and family, they likewise direct the action of the family therapist. Moreover, family therapy itself as a social movement (Stein,

1. Do good, wherever you can—above all love freedom—/Never deny the truth, not even upon the throne!

201

1983) must be understood to consist of a loosely overarching value system, which in turn links founders and followers of various family therapy schools (e.g., family systems, structuralist, psychoanalytic, para-doxicalist, behaviorist). Each therapist, in turn, brings his or her own hierarchy of values that influences therapeutic means and ends.

The clinical issue is not *whether* values affect the entire treatment process, but *how* they do so, and *how* we can put into use knowledge of that process. It has been repeatedly argued that persistence in treatment, compliance with clinician's treatment plan, improvement, satisfaction, and so forth, have more to do with the patient's (or family's) perception of effectiveness (i.e., that one's expectations of therapy are being fulfilled) and with the quality of the healer–client relationship than intrinsically with the healer's theoretical model or specific skills (Ford, 1978; Kleinman, 1980; Phares, 1979; Strupp & Bergin, 1969). Yet clinicians highly value those theories, authorities, and techniques that they use to organize their inner and interpersonal world and to minimize their own anxieties. As a result, while patients and families may well ascribe the favorable or unfavorable outcome of treatment to the personality of the clinician(s), to their relationship with the clinician, or to the degree of congruence between the clinician's beliefs and theirs, the clinician may attribute success to his or her paradigm or armory of "tricks," and explain clinical failure by blaming the patient (or the patient's family, social class, or culture). The values of family, therapist, and of family therapy itself play a vital role in that "clinical assessment" that takes place *reciprocally* between clinician and family.

Often during the initial "intake" visit, families present us with such aspirations as change, closeness, responsibility, togetherness, freedom, growth (their meanings for these conceptions may be different from the therapist's). In doing so they are conveying values about themselves and others and at least in part about the compliance that they expect from us. For the family in treatment, such variables as the age, sex, ethnicity, physiognomy ("race"), gestural style, and verbal style (authoritarian, compassionate, dramatic) of the therapist are not mere facts but are instead positively or negatively *valued* facts that may unconsciously influence the course of therapy (Abel & Metraux, 1974). The therapist also perceives and interacts with his or her families through these same value-filters (Devereux, 1967). This, of course, is the essence of patient transference and clinician countertransference, which can facilitate, impede, retard, accelerate, terminate, or lead to acting out in therapy. In sum, there is nothing in therapy that is not value-charged.

In this chapter I first discuss the dynamics of human values. Then I consider the process by which family contexts (and values in them) proliferate into society. Finally I suggest a possible relationship between values and strategy in family therapy. Examples from some of my ethnographic and clinical work are used to illustrate theoretical issues.

To identify the place of values in family therapy, we must identify what values *are*, which turns out to be inseparable from identifying what they are *for* in human affairs. Values link seemingly distinct realms (unconscious, family, institution, culture). But how do they do so? Where, in fact, can values be said to be located? If they are personal, familial, and cultural, how does this come about? If we agree that we must consider the macrocontext in conceptualizing and treating family problems, just *where* is this macrocontext located? It is too facile to reply "Out there" (society) as contrasted with "In here" (family), for that seemingly external context is actively created, invested in, maintained, and subtly if not dramatically revised by its participants. We must carefully explore the subtle but systemic relationship between inside and outside.

By considering the part people play in one another's fantasies and thus in social roles (Bion, 1959, p. 134; Stein, 1981), I conclude that the relationship between inside and outside, governed as it is by projection and introjection, differs markedly from our commonsensical—which is to say culturally consensual—view. Although the family is indeed a homeostatically regulated system, it is not a closed one. All the homeostats are not contained within the family. I shall argue that family-derived experiences influence symbols, relationships, and behaviors in institutional settings far removed from one's family of origin. Indeed, the very fantasy of culture as a distinct thing in itself upon which one is dependent and which gives one his or her very identity, recapitulates an idealized mother–infant symbiosis (Stein, 1979d, 1980a, 1980b). In this chapter I offer a psychoanalytic systems theory as a means of interpreting how values link person, family, institution, and society— and as a guide to therapeutic strategy that utilizes values as instruments of change.

The basis for this chapter consists of ethnographic and clinical work in which I have been involved as a medical–psychoanalytic anthropologist. Since the late 1960s I have conducted intensive and intermittent ethnographic fieldwork among Slovak- and Ruthene-American families in the Steel Valley region of western Pennsylvania. While initially interested in traditional ethnicity and American culture, I began to note how family dynamics came to be played out in the imagery of the "new ethnicity" (Stein, 1979d); in popular culture, for example, the generational conflict in the household of "Archie Bunker" (Stein, 1974); and even in the political polarization of American society that culminated in Watergate (Stein, 1973–1974, 1977c). At first a cultural determinist, I soon discovered—because my informants taught me—that culture does not so much explain anything (although it is universally invoked as a form of resistance) as it requires explanation.

What began for me as "pure" ethnographic research among Slavic-American families has evolved into "applied" ethnographic research

among families in the clinical population seen where I have been employed. I would emphasize that in both, my gravitation to a family
framework was less by training or conscious intention, and more by the
ethnographic "discovery" and constant confirmation of the explanatory
power of family process. I study families to learn what problems need to
be solved—and how to solve them. Research is part of therapy.

Work at Meharry Medical College, 1972–1978, with patients, families, medical students, and resident physicians in psychiatry and family
medicine and subsequently at the University of Oklahoma, 1978 through
the present, with patients, families, medical and physician's associate
students, and resident family physicians convinced me that to understand what culture is, one must look closely at how people use, create,
revise, invest in, and repudiate it. Currently I am working with midwestern rural families whose lives are built around wheat farming,
cattle, and oilfield work (Stein, 1982b). Frequent consultation with and
supervision of resident physicians in patient encounters, family sessions, and home visits gave me the opportunity to observe that pathology
was not confined within the boundaries of family systems, but was re-
capitulated and sustained in relationships outside the family—including
the health care system. I am now persuaded that social transference
based largely on a family model keeps society going, so to speak.

My function is therapeutic, both by my own intention and by
others' expectations. I have learned quickly from working with physicians and students in health care professions that countertransference
is perhaps the principal problem in clinician–patient–family communication (Devereux, 1967; Stein, 1982g), one not readily solved by supplying
a different viewpoint, the "correct" answer, or a new strategy. Many of
the communication problems health professionals have with patients,
families, and colleagues reside in their *resistance* to knowledge, to learning
a differing technique, to understanding their own "irrational" feelings
toward patient or family. Were I to circumvent the countertransference
issues, I would essentially be "teaching" my medical colleagues (and
myself) how to split, project, and repress. That is to say, I would be
instructing them to omit or exclude potentially valuable clinical data *in
order to* feel momentarily less anxious. To help them face the uncomfortable truths revealed about themselves in the countertransference, I
first—and continuously—had to learn to face them in myself. Education, I have become convinced, is either therapeutic or pathological
communication (Stein, 1977b, 1979b, 1979c, 1982e).

Others' expectations have likewise influenced my decision to acknowledge that I function as a therapist (which implies clinical intervention), not exclusively as a teacher (which implies a didactic approach,
safely removed from the practical world of blood, gore, pain, and responsibility). On the one hand, to be identified as a therapist, even

informally, is to acknowledge that what one does is expected to have direct consequences, to count, not simply to be an interesting but irrelevant diversion. I have found that in working with family physicians, my "behavioral sciences" or "ethnographic" orientation, broadly conceived, is taken seriously only as I immerse myself in their intensely practical, time-consuming, "hands-on" world. The more clinically salient I become, the more I am identified as a clinician—a role I not only accept but feel honored to be offered.

Moreover, over the years I have found myself becoming somewhat of an "alternate health care resource" to medical and physician's assistant students, graduate students, resident physicians in psychiatry and family medicine, senior physician colleagues, administrators, and families who "insist" that I see them in the capacity of therapist or counselor (many of these people having been actively involved in formal therapies of various kinds). They come referred by professionals or self-referred. I was once embarrassed by this turn of events. Rather than protest that I am ill prepared for this role, I now use it as yet another instrument of education—theirs and mine. I have taken their perception that I am trustworthy and competent and used it to help them become better clinical ethnographers of their lives, families, and—which is why I am employed by them in the first place—patients and patients' families. I have chosen to assume, instead of decline, the therapeutic role imputed to me and use it to help those who have assigned it to become themselves better therapists and to relinquish their need for me. Several of the case vignettes in this chapter derive from this informal role.

The Dynamics of Human Values

The period of the 1950s through the early 1960s witnessed the appearance in American social science of a series of influential papers and books on value orientations by sociologist Florence Kluckhohn (1950, 1953, 1958), anthropologist Clyde Kluckhohn (1951a, 1951b), and psychiatrist John Spiegel (Spiegel & Kluckhohn, 1954). *Variations in Value Orientations*, by Florence Kluckhohn and Fred Strodtbeck (1961), explored the relationships between values, family, and society. In his book *Transactions*, John Spiegel (1971) added the crucial dimension of the relation between intrapsychic defense, value orientation, family, and culture, attempting by it a synthesis of role theory, values, and motivation. Spiegel writes that

> every society faces issues of choice between alternative modes of action arising as possible responses to concrete situations. Generalized solutions to the common human problems posed by these concrete situations are variously elaborated, but the variations in solutions are neither infinite nor

random. They consist, rather, of a limited range of possible choices, and, if one looks at the range of solutions developed in cultures throughout the world, there is consistency and similarity with regard to these products of inquiry from culture to culture. What is varied is the pattern of evaluation which rates one solution as preferable to another. This is one of the specifications—perhaps the principal one—of the word "value": the ranking of an ordered set of choices from most to least preferable. (1971, p. 53)

Later, he defines three tasks which values perform:

[Values] have an evaluative component—that is, they serve as principles for making preferred selections between alternative courses of action; an existential component, which means that the value orientations help to define the nature of reality for those who hold the given values; and finally, they have an affective component, which means that people not only prefer and believe in their own values, but are also ready to bleed and die for them. For this reason, values, once formed, can be changed only with the greatest difficulty. (1971, p. 190)

F. Kluckhohn (1953) posited four overarching problem areas of human life (relationships between people, the relationship between man and nature, man's relationship to time, man's relationship to activity), each containing three distinct value orientations which are in turn hierarchically ranked. The "Relational" value orientation consists of individualism, collaterality, and lineality. In relationships governed by individualism, the family or group prizes the distinctiveness of each person; in decision making each person voices his or her opinion, and the group decides by majority vote. Collateral relationships place the family or group above the individual; indeed, the individual may be said not to exist. Decision making is by consensus so that a sense of harmonious oneness will prevail. Lineal relationships are ruled vertically, in a system of authoritarianism and loyalty, nurturance and dependency, dominance and submission. Stability is preserved as each individual maintains his or her sense of place.

The "Man–Nature" value orientation proposes that man can relate to nature in three distinct ways: mastery over nature, subjugation to nature, and harmony with nature. Man can likewise orient himself to "Time" by preferring the future, the past, or the present. Finally man can prefer three different orientations to "Activity": doing (which emphasizes success, achievement, mastery, improvement), being (which emphasizes spontaneity, the expression of feeling, impulsiveness), and being-in-becoming (which focuses upon personal development, integration, individuation).

Now, dominant values live in uneasy truce with those that are subordinate. That is, they are not only cognitively rank ordered; they are also in conflict with one another in unconscious structure, family relations, and cultural roles. As De Vos (1975) points out, cognitive dissonance is secondary to "affective dissonance." The dominant value orientation is but a conscious representation that in family structures takes the form of what Ferreira (1963) called a "family myth"—a group's internal "party line" by which it distorts and falsifies reality to itself. The family or group proclaims: "This is what we stand for"—and strives to legislate belief into reality.

In the mainstream culture of the United States since the earliest settlement of the colonies, Americans have tended to place individualism in the first-order position, collaterality in the second-order position, and lineality in the third-order position (Spiegel, 1971, p. 353). Yet, Americans, in their preoccupation with combatting tyranny and vigilantly defending freedom, are insecure in their freedom. Seeking freedom *from* oppression, they are unsure of what they seek *freedom for*. Freedom of opportunity, as a cherished value that first declares all men equal and then gives each the opportunity to find success, has on its darker side the psychopathic quality of freedom of opportunism and likewise the unscrupulously lineal quality of a freedom to make others subordinate to one's own success. Enthusiastic boasting masks melancholic brooding over one's fate.

A brief cross-national comparison of the different connotations that the word "freedom" can have is fruitful. Cantril (1960) points out that whereas to Americans freedom means exemption from necessity, to Great Russians freedom implies a recognition of necessity (I would go further than Cantril, and suggest that to Russians freedom contains a heavy submission to necessity, making a mysticism of Fate). Only superficially—that is, from the point of view of dominant values—are Americans and Russians opposites. Americans are fascinated by that dark, repudiated part of themselves, historically represented by the yoke of oppression symbolized by the British and later authoritarian states. Russians are likewise captivated by what appears to be American license (indeed, the U.S. Constitution was the model for the ill-fated Decembrist revolution in 1825).

Spiegel notes the "incompatibility between our [American] democratic ideals and our authoritarian practices" (1971, p. 347).

> Freedom from something—from the conqueror, from the sense of inferiority, from want, from lawlessness—becomes the slogan to rationalize the seizing of power for the purpose of subjugating someone else. Identification with the oppressor perpetuates the authoritarianism of the fighter for freedom. The Lineal principle, the unconscious endorsement of authoritarianism, persist behind the mask of Individualism. (1971, p. 353)

Spiegel then goes on to contrast the "operative" pattern of relational preferences (individual, lineal, collateral) with the "ideal" ranking pat-

tern (individual, collateral, lineal). The inconsistency (reflecting ambivalence) between ideal and operative makes for conflict at the family and
societal (and, I would suggest, international) levels.

But the matter does not end here. One must consider as well the
family and cultural value orientations of those who emigrated to the
United States and their descendants in relation to the American culture
value configuration in which they invested and which in large measure
they reinvented anew. Where, one must ask, are "American" values
located? What is the psychogeography of the American Dream (Stein &
Hill, 1977a)? From a decade of ethnographic and, more recently, clinical
research among "white ethnic" families of central, east, and south
European origin, I would conclude that their traditional familial–cultural
hierarchy of value orientations is precisely that which the founders and
succeeding generations of Americans sought to reject. Feudal peasant
values placed the family group, the village, and traditional authority of
elders and priests far above the inconsequential self. Feudal peasant
time was dominated by the vagaries of the present and loyalty to the
past; the future was more feared and bowed to than eagerly anticipated.
One sought mystically to live peacefully with Mother Nature and
tragically to accept her cruel and capricious yoke; the very thought of
mastery or domination was dismissed as sheer hubris. Little thought
was given to the development and enhancement of the self; life consisted of unabating toil with moments of religious and drunken release.
Certainly while "doing" occupied first or second rank, it did not connote
mastery; instead, within a universe of closed possibilities, relationships,
and cyclic time, one's physical toil only affirmed the supremacy of
Nature, the feudal lord, and God.

Yet, at the same time, this only *apparently* changeless system har-
bored the seeds of that elusive American Dream that would throw the
venerable worldview to the winds. Immigrants imported their forbidden dreams and ambitions to America as well as discovered them
there. On the one hand, the traditional value hierarchy contained the
seed of the radical value inversions that underlay American culture. On
the other hand, the conflict—internally, between family members, and
in American society itself—between traditional loyalties, new opportunities, and repressed impulses also made for the very pathology we
now see commonly in family therapy.

Values and value orientations are thus far more subtle and dynamic
matters than one might at first consider them to be. Humans—not just
social scientists and family clinicians—tend to reify values into invariant
"they" as a defense against ambivalence, as a hedge against mortality
and fallibility. One speaks of "serving" values, as though they had a life
apart from oneself. For instance, those who demand a papal infallibility
or the inerrancy of some revered master (one among the many founders

of schools of family therapy?) display only their frightened doubt and insecurity in a sought-after obeisance to One Who Knows. By magically hypostatizing values into an impersonal, Platonistic "it," one displaces (and misplaces) the locus of values and responsibility for them from self to environment, tradition, family, culture, or whatever. Only as a result of misplaced concreteness, which is to say externalization, can one act in accordance with values that are not self.

Lamentably, the pioneering work of the Kluckhohns and Spiegel on value orientations—not unlike the fate of Sigmund Freud's stages of psychosexual development, Erik Erikson's eight stages of psychosocial maturation, or Abraham Maslow's hierarchy of needs—has tended to be reified, hypostatized, and mechanically used as though one were completing a scorecard of human behavior. As suggested above, "doing" means something very different to a peasant fatalist than it does to a boundlessly optimistic capitalist. What we sorely need in family ethnography, assessment, and treatment is less an uncritical application of Kluckhohn's categories than our own self-critical abstraction of contending value orientations *from* family behavior that we observe (from "body language" of spatial interaction to fantasies and dreams). I have found the old distinction between an *active* and *passive* orientation to problem solving to be invaluable, for it helps me to understand how families and family members experience problems (e.g., independence–dependency, initiative–helplessness). The alloplastic–autoplastic distinction enables one to assess the extent to which manipulation of the environment or manipulation of the self, respectively, are valued solutions to problems. Such distinctions as act-upon/acted-upon and initiator-of-action/recipient-of-another's-action are useful in determining a family's and family member's valued locus of control (Schwartzman, 1982).

Just as values can be classified by their *content*, they can also be categorized by the *context* to which they refer. For present purposes a few distinctions are essential. One can speak of explicit in contrast to implicit values (C. Kluckhohn, 1951a), which corresponds to the distinction between manifest and latent values. These pairs, in turn, may or may not correspond to the distinction between values held consciously and those held unconsciously. From the viewpoint of the observer, one must distinguish between stated values and those values that the observer infers from statements, affect, and behavior. This latter derives from Richards's (1956, pp. 118–119) distinction between expressed and deduced purposes. Moreover, one must distinguish between operant values and espoused values (i.e., those values that in fact underlie behavior vs. those values that a person says that he or she is guided by). Furthermore, some values are held idiosyncratically, some are shared only within the family system, and still others extend beyond the family to society. Finally, some values are uniformly adhered to and are thus (or appear to be) context-free, whereas others come into play only in certain contexts or situations. For the clinical ethnographer as for the family therapist, these distinctions are far from academic. It is important to know what frame of reference to assign the asseveration by a father in his first family therapy session, "In our family, the children always come first." Is it a family fiction that flies in the face of observed fact? It is a value rigidly adhered to irrespective of situation? It is an ideal which he "somehow" always manages to subvert? and so on?

Conscious preference is not all there is to our rank ordering of value hierarchies. Instead, a strong case could be made for the hypothesis that staunchly held dominant values are implemented as defenses against (i.e., rationalized reaction formations) subordinate values. Thus, dominant and subordinate values are far more intimately linked than as mere alternatives to one another: They symbolize the patterned defenses *together with* those fantasies, anxieties, wishes, and conflicts they defend against.

Let me illustrate this point with an example from my research among Slavic-Americans (encompassing Slovaks, Ruthenians, Poles, etc.). Early in my work with Slavic-American families, I was struck by the generosity with which guests and family members alike were treated. Abundant food and drink were not only proffered but lavished. Frequently invited into the home for dinner, I was urged helpings of "seconds" and "thirds" far beyond either my satiation or protests. My jovial hosts almost invariably turned sad or sullen, solemnly worrying lest I be hungry, or issuing a stern warning, disqualified with a smile, that "If you leave here hungry, it's your own fault." It was as though I were an extension of their need to feed, a container of their need to be generous. To say "No" was to violate their boundary of them-in-me. I felt it to be a struggle for the control of my body; likewise have a number of insightful informants.

The virtues of generosity are proclaimed as well as acted upon. The good Slav is the generous Slav, one who is altruistic to a fault. To admire something is to be virtually assured of being given it—or a reasonable facsimile—promptly (to ward off the evil eye, even when it is no longer consciously believed in). The ability to give is the measure of one's self-worth, and not that of the proverbially bountiful "mother" alone. Indeed, the entire family contends with one another to outgive, which becomes endless.

Yet the value of generosity does not stand alone. One bestows as a way of receiving: bestowing in order to receive, yet denying that one expects or wishes for anything other than the recipient's welfare. The recipient is placed in a position of guilt-induced reciprocity: One can never give enough in return to erase or balance the debt. One becomes "eternally indebted," as many Slavic informants referred to it with resignation—as they offered me a meal with a twinkle! Beneath the appearance of freely bestowed love lies the frightened quest for a total control that forever binds the recipient to gratitude. One thus can only receive—and merit receiving—by giving. The fact that generosity is bestowed *in exchange* for control is not, and *must not be*, acknowledged to oneself or used to confront another. The message "This is freely given" is disqualified by "This must exact the price of your very self-hood"— which message you must not recognize. "You need me" is a transformation of "I need you." "You need what I have to offer" originally means "I need you in order to give to you."

In a sense, the oral satiation is poisoned with the aggression of the giver; moreover, one must only see the pure motives and disavow noticing any hostility. One south Slavic-American woman in her late 30s stated: "One must not unmask generosity for control, because once one perceives the pattern, the controlled person can break out simply by refusing the generosity. Christmas dinner is a compulsory gift (compulsory to receive [I would add, equally compulsory to bestow]; Stein, 1981). The dominant value "generosity" is utterly dependent upon the *devalued* wish to receive; likewise the second-rank value of control is disavowed, although it is the price of accepting the gift in the first place.

"Generosity" is a reaction formation to "receiving"; inasmuch as the individual (unconsciously) seeks to avoid being at the mercy of anyone, he or she wishes to be a giver in good standing (i.e., on the top side of a complementary relationship, always struggling from under the bottom side). Likewise, although control is the goal, generosity is proclaimed to be the only goal. Among Slavic-Americans to unmask generosity for control is less liberation than liberated rage against and overwhelming guilt toward the giver. The therapist working with Slavic families must recognize the value of generosity to be a compromise formation and homeostat whose defensive and interpersonal function is to perpetuate the family—and ethnic—symbiosis.

Thus understood, "generosity" is a condensation both of the wish to receive and the defense against that wish implemented in the process of binding by giving. I would also add that symptom formation proper occurs only when the balance within this normative sham is upset; for example, when one comes to realize that the food is poisoned by affect, that either self or other is hostile rather than benevolent, or when one considers an alternative to the cycle of reciprocity. Another way of putting it is that what we would identify as bona fide symptom formation consists of *new* symptoms that depart from those normative familial-cultural patterns, which are symptoms that have stabilized over long periods. It is the observer's diagnostic punctuation, not the family's behavior, which distinguishes between the former as "pathology" and the latter as "culture."

It behooves us not to take manifest values—what people say they live by, their public "party lines"—at face value but to allow for, if not expect, the possibility that the explicit is systematically related to the implicit. Thus the classical Greeks' "golden mean" must be understood *in conjunction with* their irrationality and violence; "the ostentatiously Apollonian facade of Pueblo culture . . . screens a witches' cauldron of meanness, envy, hate, and fear" (Devereux, 1980, p. 308); the grandiosity and competitiveness of Kwakiutl chiefs and of the potlatch cannot be understood apart from day-to-day cooperativeness; "the strongly male-valor-oriented culture of the Plains Indians contains unusually elaborate devices for the repression (negative implementation) of cowardice" (Devereux 1967, p. 210); the Jewish devotion "to life" can only be understood in relation to Jews' preoccupation with death (Stein, 1977a, 1978a); the Slovak (and generically Slavic) emphasis on generosity is inextricably tied to the unspoken, because unconscious, need for control, security, and dependency (Stein, 1976, 1978b); the Russian peasant's piety and submissiveness are reaction formations against orgiastic violence (proverbial in warfare, bouts of vodka); and so forth. Devereux has brilliantly summarized these relationships in what might be called formulas or principles:

> *Minimization of non-X is a culture trait as important as the maximization of trait X.* (1967, p. 210)

> *The elaborateness of a given trait is not a measure of its cultural nuclearity*, since its complexity may be due to attempts to use it as a counterpoise for a culturally maximized "nuclear trait." The elaborateness of such a counter-trait is simply a good measure of the *total* socio-cultural mass of *both* conjugate traits, taken together. (1967, p. 211)

> The mandatory hypercathecting of one attitude is itself a byproduct of the attempt to deny one's ambivalence about it. (1967, p. 212)

> Each culture contains also the negation of its manifest pattern and nuclear values, through a tacit affirmation of contrary latent patterns and marginal values. *The complete real pattern of a culture is a product of a functional interplay between officially affirmed and officially negated patterns* possessing mass. (1967, p. 212)

In dealing with American culture and with those "ethnic" American families in which American and traditional ethnic values conflict, it is essential that we not overplay the ideological dimension of American values to the neglect of more deeply seated values against which the official ideology is used to defend self and family alike. The core constellation of American values including self-reliance or inner-directedness,

autonomy, independence, mobility, privacy, individuality, and future orientation are systematically linked respectively with other-directedness,
hierarchical authority, dependency, fixity, community, consensus or
conformity, and past orientation. Americans pride themselves on their
freedom but are fascinated with foreign tyranny and the pomp of
British royalty. American parades, football homecoming games, beauty
contests—all have their kings or queens.

Official core American values represent attempts to distance oneself from the more underlying and enduring values—historically because
psychohistorically prior. Mobility can be seen as flight from dependency,
being tied down to place or relationship. Self-reliance can be seen as a
vehicle for pulling oneself away from domination by hierarchical authority. One flees into the future in order to escape from the past. A
profound melancholy underlies cheerful optimism. Americans believe
that they can master anything, yet dread being mastered by anyone or
anything ("Better dead than Red"), which is why one must remain
vigilantly "on guard for freedom" by keeping one's powder dry. A
frightening (because persecutory) symbiosis lurks beneath one's proud
independence and achievements. This holds not only for "old Americans"
(i.e., Yankees) or long-acculturated ethnics but persistently and anew
for each new wave of immigrants or internal immigrants (e.g., blacks,
Hispanics) eager to trade old lives for new.

Moreover, the language of American culture can be confused with
the language of metacultural developmental psychology. For instance,
"individualism" is often wrongly assumed to mean *individuation*, whereas
the former is a panicky riddance from relationship and the latter is the
growing awareness of personal distinctiveness. Likewise, "mobility"
refers to the wish-become-need to keep on the move, to avoid settling
down too permanently, whereas "motility" denotes the capacity of the
growing baby to feel and explore its environment with (optimally) a
minimum of anxiety and a maximum of autonomy.

One familiar defensive gambit that troubled ethnic families play
(and which credulous therapists play into) is to characterize the interior
of their families as blissfully untroubled were it not for the evil external
American culture that is eroding traditional roles, values, beliefs, loyalties, and the like. This defense of externalization is used by individual
and poorly differentiated group alike to preserve the illusion, conviction, and feeling of internal harmony: "*We* have no problems" or "We
had no problems until *you* [American culture, education, therapy] tried
to change us," are common rationalizations. Conflicts over separation,
Oedipal resolution, generational conflict, and so on, are ejected from the
family, which can thereby feel disinculpated from participating in its
own problems. I have found this to be the case with problem families
some of whose members have contributed to and embraced the identity

and ideology of the "new ethnicity," which dichotomizes between traditional ethnic values and family life as "all good" and American values
and nuclear family as "all bad" (Stein, 1975, 1979d, 1980b; Stein & Hill,
1973, 1977a, 1977b). What appear on the surface as conflicts *between*
American and traditonal ethnic values are in fact conflicts *within* the
ethnic and American value systems alike.

In the social sciences, discussion of values as moving forces in
human life has tended to concentrate on the cognitive or ideational
dimension of values. The emotional or affective side of values tends to
be viewed as primarily an effect. However, this view of the relationship
between the cognitive and affective side of values has it precisely
backwards. It is affect that is primary. Spiegel refers to "the way
cultural values are built into the personality as a mechanism for the
control of anxiety" (1971, p. 316). Caudill writes, "Values, as more
representative of cognitive orientations to life, can be linked to the
preferred patterns of impulse gratification and restraint which are more
representative of emotional orientations to life" (1962, p. 201). Sander
also argues that value orientations are heir to primitive splitting.

> The world and self in the infant's blurry eyes are either good *or* bad and
> thus hopefully within the sphere of the infant's omnipotent control. . . .
> This "splitting" tendency of seeing human nature as good or evil, the
> environment as beneficent or menacing, of man as master of, the slave of,
> or in harmony with nature, are matters of "basic value orientations."
> F. Kluckhohn (1953) first systematically studied how all cultures express
> and reflect such generalized views, giving its members a sense of their
> relationship to the world. (1979, p. 123)

I should hasten to emphasize that although values can be understood to be built upon splitting derivatives of the mother–infant dyad,
the father–mother dyad (the nuclear family) and various extensions of
the family are contexts which frame the former dyad. What appears
from the point of view of the mother–child dyad as *causation* can be seen
from the point of view of the family as *punctuation*. Moreover, the
proverbial "fit" between values of one generation and another must be
imperfect as is parental love imperfect to meet voracious infant need.
Or again, parental ambivalence toward their own values makes for the
values of their children hardly conflict-free. Further, the failure at exact
replication of values—or stated differently, the constant creation of
values—stems from the fact that values are learned, invested in, acted
upon, elaborated, and are only then in the life cycle offered to one's
children: How one transmits them is never precisely how one acquired
them. One sees a rather continuous *oscillation* between projection and
introjection not only in the individual but also between generations.

The complex process of formation, cathexis (investment in), internalization, and externalization of values cannot be reduced to the simple-minded culturalist notions of one-way internalization of cultural morality or of unmediated internalization of parental superego into a child who is but the passive recipient of values (see Hartmann, 1960). Spiro (1967) argues that the credibility of particular beliefs rests upon a prior motivation to believe. In similar fashion one includes ideas, values, and concepts into one's "libidinal field" (Weisman, 1958). The cognitive component of values builds upon the prior affective component, which the former comes to represent or symbolize, and is experienced as an independent entity outside the self to which one gives one's allegiance.

Properly speaking, values and similar cognitive organizational schemata (beliefs, expectations, attitudes, etc.) should not be seen themselves as motivation for action but as motive derivatives, the secondary elaboration of defenses. For instance, De Vos writes, "Individuals 'freeze up' when asked to learn something that might threaten an incompetence that is a protective part of one's identity, be it sexually or socially defined. For example, many boys and men 'cannot cook.' Just as many women and scholars 'cannot learn' to fix a leaky faucet" (1980b, p. 114). Here, the "value" placed on cooking is contaminated, so to speak, by its association not only with female role but with female identity: Males protect themselves from fantasied emasculation by disassociating themselves from what they experience to be an intrinsic part of femininity. The converse is true for women and scholars with respect to the underlying *meaning* of being capable of repairing a dripping faucet or changing an automobile tire. One devalues what he or she cannot or dare not have, at the same time admiring, even envying, those who do possess it. Male birth envy and female penis envy are but two obvious examples.

Cultural examples abound. East Central European Slavic peasants, themselves valuing patience, obedience to authority, and thrift—which in turn are based on dependent, symbiotic family relations and repression of sexuality—viciously detested the Gypsies (*Czigany*). To the Slavs, Gypsies embodied the uninhibited Freudian id and the compromising superego: lazy, perverse, dishonest, lascivious, irreverent, untrustworthy. Everything the Slavic peasants could not and should not want to be, the Gypsies—in Slavic eyes—seemed to indulge. To American whites, especially in the South, blacks were devalued as embodying rampant id. In an Oedipal vein, Jews characteristically place supreme value on submission to the Law (sacred or secular) of the Father God, while projecting all Oedipal hostility and rebellion upon "alien" Gentiles. Christian Gentiles, in turn, identify with the obedient, sacrificial Christ the Son, and project all counter-Oedipal hostility and castration fears upon the Jews (Stein, 1977a). Moreover, Jews of Russia, Poland, and the Ukraine placed highest value upon the devout, intellectual, pious, scholarly, sedentary life, while distantly admiring yet detesting the Ukrainian Cossacks with their fierce aggression, manliness, and mobility. In Erikson's (1968) framework, the "positive identity," which includes that which is positively valued and associated with the conscious self, is inextricably bound up with the "negative identity," which includes that which is negatively valued and dissociated from the conscious self. It is simply insufficient to ask what values behavior implements without simultaneously asking what unconscious defenses these values implement.

Spiegel (1971) offers a particularly poignant illustration of the relationship between the subjugation-to-nature value orientation and identification among Irish-Americans:

> While it is perfectly true that one aspect of the Irish-American patient's resistance is associated with the Subjugation-to-nature value position, this is by no means the whole story. The value orientation accounts for the patient's resignation, his inability to conceive of the possibility of change, in the cognitive area. A real change within the personality has not been in his experience, and he just doesn't see that it is possible. However, there is an emotional as well as a cognitive side to this kind of resistance. On the emotional side it is associated with the identification with the angry, critical parents. The attachment to the internalized parental images is intensely ambivalent and masochistically satisfying. The treasuring of the sense of sin is, from one point of view, a conscious derivative of the highly libidinal, unconscious cathexis of the internalized, scolding parents. In addition, the scolding parent within becomes a tender forgiving parent whenever a confession takes place. The alternation between sinning and confessing is necessary to the maintenance of the internal, libidinal dynamics. Furthermore, sinning or the alerting of the sense of sin in the external object is the primary way of getting the object's attention.
>
> These considerations are directly pertinent to the transference problem in the management of such a patient. It is not only that the patient remains cognitively unaware of the possibility of change. In addition he has no wish to change in the direction which the therapist expects him to. Giving up the crushing sense of sin means, essentially, renouncing the relation with the internalized parents. (p. 333)

To relinquish or change one's values symbolically enacts a separation from, loss of, or murder of the parents or other significant love-objects. In therapy as in "culture change," the perceived threat to one's values is experienced as a threat to one's internal representations and to one's present and past object-ties.

No discussion of the direction and goals of family therapy is complete that does not consider the issue of the "self" as a value in therapy.

One must be careful to distinguish between the self as a *cultural* value in the West (e.g., as reflected in egoism) and as a *biological* direction in development (e.g., individuation) which parent–child relations can foster or undermine (see Kohut, 1971, 1977; Mahler & Furer, 1968; Mahler, Pine, & Bergman, 1975). When working with the family anywhere, it is essential to learn how individual members experience themselves, others, and the family group.

It is edifying to compare the Western value system with that of Japan. In Japan the family is experienced as identical and coextensive with the self. In Confucianism, whose "moral principles . . . supported the legitimacy of [the Japanese] family and state" (De Vos, 1980a, p. 121), there is

> no place for individualistic concepts of the person. There are no individuals as such—only family members whose roles change through the life cycle. At no time is the person regarded as separate from his family and social roles, and maturation is a deepening of understanding of one's place in a system, that is, part of a yet larger social unit. One's ultimate duty, as one's ultimate psychological security, is to be found in family or group continuity, not in the continuity of the self. (De Vos, 1980a, p. 121)

> The Japanese continue to reject psychoanalytic theories not because they are about an irrational unconscious per se, but because delving into this unconscious threatens family cohesion. Tensions experienced through a conflict of occupational expectations or family role versus disruptive private feelings are most frequently resolved in Japan by directing the individual back toward the family. The goals of attempts to alleviate psychiatric problems are therefore defined in terms of family or occupational integration. (p. 122)

From within the Buddhist ideal of detachment,

> drives are examined not to control them but to obliterate them, to make them inconsequential. To release oneself is not to continue to participate in the world but to withdraw from it and, indeed, to withdraw from any sense of self. (p. 123)

The equation of self with role or function, indeed the submergence of self within role, is certainly not limited to the Japanese (see Stein, 1981). The Japanese are here cited only as an illustration of the symbiotic psychic organization of human groups throughout human history until very recently.

The very *idea* of a distinct, differentiated, autonomous self has only come about in recent centuries owing to advanced child-rearing methods that fostered the individuation and less conflict-ridden separation of child from parent and family (see deMause, 1982) and can be said to represent a potential and an ideal rather than an accomplished fact. The Freudian *and* family therapy revolutions are themselves historic phenomena that attest to our conflictual awakening from age-old group symbioses and enmeshments. Most cultures could abide unflinchingly by the motto of the SS: My honor is my loyalty. Likewise, much of cultural behavior can be characterized as group-psychic organization based upon projections outward *from* family *to* society (Friedman, 1980) —calling to mind Bowen's (1978) concept of "undifferentiated family ego mass" writ large. Poor self–other differentiation is the rule, not the exception, in social life, as people use one another projectively (La Barre 1969, 1972).

Here, once again, we can ill afford to take American official values at face value. Autonomy based upon individualism is a lifelong counter-dependent obsession. Self-reliant "disengagement" is not the opposite of symbiotic "enmeshment" in one's family; it is a counterphobic reaction to it. For many throughout American history, the preeminent value of freedom denoted an unstable quality of flight from the very dependency it presupposes. The American fear of symbiosis (reaction formation to the wish) tends to determine not only the form of many of our social problems but our purported solutions to them as well— "therapy" being one. Schulz recently writes:

> In recent years an emphasis has been placed on the avoidance of de-pendency process by keeping the [psychiatric] patient functional in the community. This approach, first learned on a large scale in the Korean War, was later transplanted to the community psychiatry movement and has revolutionized treatment compared to what was available 30 years ago. Secondly, when hospitalization does become necessary the choice is usually a short-term treatment unit. In short-term treatment, separation reaction is avoided by means of discharge planning commencing on the day of admission. Finally, and not least significant, is the increasing reluctance of third-party payors to reimburse for long-term care. All of these factors contribute to shortened lengths of stay with the expectation of maximum functional adaptation. But, are we thereby eliminating potential benefits from the working through of dependency conflicts? Does the apparent bypass of separation issues deny our patients an important contribution of longer-term treatment? (1981, p. 133)

I do not in any way deny that keeping people functional, or re-habilitating them to socially acceptable roles, works. I do wish to em-phasize that *functionality is itself a paramount value, not a context-free given.* As culture hero Archie Bunker begrudgingly declares, "Them that works eats." I suggest that functionality is our positively valued symptom, and any hint of dependency is our negatively valued symptom. Likewise, "working through" does not denote only a therapeutic process but an orientation to problem solving that is itself valued or devalued. Clearly the preeminent value placed upon "keeping the patient functioning" could *only* be implemented as long as the staff or therapists work out *their own* fear of dependency through the patients whom they serve by restoring them to "maximum functional adaptation." Countertransference toward the patients preserves the staff's own "maximum functional adaptation," as staff and patients collude on avoiding or minimizing separation anxiety. So long as Americans can keep "doing" (e.g., the emphasis placed upon occupational and recreational therapy in psychiatric hospitals), they can forestall, if not entirely circumvent, the emotional issue of powerful ties to others. Inadvertently mental health workers help to perpetuate the cultural problem in the very act of performing the cultural therapy—which they perform for reasons of their own defense as well as for the good of patient or family.

Values, Society, and the Proliferation of Family Contexts

It seems to me that we cannot—even if we try—stray from human biology, because human relationships, language, symbolism, and culture "itself" (i.e., ourselves as we reify aspects of ourselves outside) are all expressions of that species-specific biology and efforts to cope with that biological inheritance. The experience of childhood and of being a familial animal constitute much of the substance from which culture is built (La Barre, 1951, 1968, 1972). Through culture we tend to respond to, if not continuously recreate, society and nature as though they were our bodies, our early mother–infant symbioses, our families, and the contents of our primitive psyches.[2]

The family is not the agent of the internalization of (impersonal, external) culture, as we have thought for nearly a century; instead, culture is a result of the externalization and re-creation of family. Culture is created and sustained by the proliferation outward of family contexts. As Hall (1977) has written, people experience and respond to others, society, and the environment as though these were unconsciously "extensions" of oneself. This, of course, is at the heart of transference–countertransference phenomena: the splitting off or dissociation of parts of oneself and safely locating them projectively outside oneself in another person or object. One thereby preserves while

2. Although in this chapter I shall be designating society to be that web of relationships that are heir to *family* relationships, symbolized and ritualized in cultural form, I wish to acknowledge (but cannot pursue) the point advanced by the psychoanalytic "school" of British object-relations, particularly W. R. Bion, and pursued by small-group theorists and psychohistorians, that the more disturbed the group (e.g., the macrosociety), the less it is governed by an externalization and reenactment of family dynamics and roles and the more it is governed by what Volkan (1976) refers to as "primitive internalized object relations," dominated by a splitting of affects and of self- and other-representations (cf. Bion, 1959, pp. 127–174).

eliminates that part of oneself (and of the early relationship with which that part is tied). In society, one can indefinitely expand the original context as one proceeds from the family outward with social transference willingly abetted by others who include one in their own family.

Externalization can likewise account for the fact that every society has its officially diagnosed "identified patients" or "symptomatic members" who bear or contain valued and devalued qualities of and for the others in the system (from the adored "Lamb of God" who self-sacrificially takes away the sins of the world, to the overdosed addict who magically removes the evil from his family; see Stanton, 1977). The symptom bearer—whether hero, villain, or fool—is the "not me" made flesh. I think of a 4-year-old Slovak-American girl whom the parents both branded and proudly displayed as "little miss destructiveness." Struggling to keep their home and lives in order, they watched with glee and helplessly as their daughter toppled toys throughout the house and got into everything—only to erupt with wrath when she had gone too far. They first enticed her to act out their rebellion, only to punish her for doing precisely what they wanted.

Although the *content* of cultural fictions varies enormously, the *process* or *context* that requires and sustains these fictions is universal: Through our shared fiction or "group fantasy" (deMause, 1982), we consensually negate reality and agree that our highest ideal or our fatal flaw is not located in ourselves but within the loyal deviant. From this group diagnosis, pronounced by its official diagnosticians, we conclude that we must treat the affliction encapsulated within the "identified patient."

Ruth Benedict wrote, "Every culture besides its abnormals of conflict has presumably its abnormals of extreme fulfillment of the cultural type" (1934a, p. 64). Indeed, "Any society, according to its major preoccupations, may increase and intensify even hysterical, epileptic, or paranoid symptoms, at the same time relying socially in a greater and greater degree upon the very individuals who display them" (1934b, p. 275). "Society . . . supports them in their furthest aberrations" (1934b, p. 275), just as it supports those whom it officially condemns. Moreover, "Tradition is as neurotic as any patient; its overgrown fear of deviation from its fortuitous standards conforms to all the usual definitions of the psychopathic" (1934b, p. 273). Mead distinguishes "between normative behavior which is also modal behavior and modal behavior which is felt to violate the ethical norms of a society" (1962, p. 125).

Type A behavior, for instance, is among our primary symptoms of choice—an exaggeration, if not a caricature, of the value of hard work. If Type A behavior manifests itself in those "abnormals of extreme fulfillment of the cultural type," then surely those who exhibit "neurotic fatigue" (Devereux, 1980, pp. 237–243) in their reaction formation against aggressiveness would dynamically be the opposite side of the coin, namely, the "abnormals of conflict." One could likewise juxtapose anorexia nervosa and obesity as dynamically based value opposites. The anorectic is a "good kid," perfectly compliant to the nth degree. The obese person, by contrast, is out of control, "gone to pot" in negativistic reaction formation to any self-limiting. The point to be emphasized is that while in our shared cultural language these are designated as "diseases," they in fact are *metaphors of linked and contesting values*.

Anyone familiar with the now prodigious literature on family process that attests to the systemic relation between family "deviants," "standard bearers," and normals will recognize from Benedict's account the isomorphism beyond the analogy between family dynamics and sociodynamics. But even this misses the more profound point: The form of the structure is the same because the process or dynamic is identical. In society we re-enact and re-create family symbols, values, conflicts, and relationships through externalization. In society we delegate to others and accept projective delegation from others (Stierlin, 1976) in the same way and for the same reasons that we do so in family life. Society is a macrocosm of the family (not conversely). This situation in turn stabilizes the family dynamics that constitutes its source; in similar fashion, intergroup or international relations (from diplomacy to war) build from a family model that in turn stabilizes intrasocietal and intra-familial relationships (Stein, 1982a).

La Barre argues that "we must consider more deeply the problem of the *dynamics* of the 'abnormal' milieu, in which the abnormal individual is at home" (1956, p. 545). Moreover,

> It is true that group fantasy confines and delimits our private psychoses, but if the culture of the group comes to resemble a psychosis itself, by a kind of *folie à deux* to the nth degree, then the group is worse off than when it started. In this unconscious and unwitting way, all social groups are in the long run either therapeutic, that is, adaptive to a real world, or anti-adaptive. Man is like an existentialist spider who spreads a moral net of symbolism over the void out of his own substance—and then walks upon it. But the final safety of the net depends always upon the integrity and the soundness of the postulated points of support with reference to a real physical world. (La Barre, 1962, p. 67)

Every society has precisely the kinds of deviation it needs and creates; likewise, deviancy is a form of social negativism that requires what (and whom) it often violently opposes.

Prizing conformity, consensus, and law and order, Americans are held spellbound by those who violate the sacred. These latter are the tricksters whom we seduce to seduce us. The untamed wilderness of the western frontier and of the moral frontiers of society continues to captivate Americans. It is a mainstay of popular culture. Old "cultural crimes" are in fact timeless: from Billy the Kid and the notorious James Gang, to the sordid activities of the "underworld," to immigrant Italian anarchists Nicola Sacco and Bartolomeo Vanzetti, executed in 1927 for allegedly murdering two guards during a Massachusetts payroll robbery (yet about whom books continue to be written; see Jackson, 1981).

Consider, for instance, delinquency, criminality, or madness as disapproved of and tabooed but strongly held *values*, not merely feared conditions, despised behaviors, or seemingly refractory "social problems." Pioneering in work on unconscious family dynamics, Johnson and Szurek (1952) argued that superego lacunae in the parents made for delinquent behavior in the offspring. And Devereux (1956), anticipating a central tenet of family therapy, argued in an essay titled "The Wrong Patient" that "quite often the child expresses the illness of its symptom-free milieu" (1978, p. 371; see also his essay on "Female Juvenile Sex Delinquency in a Puritanical Society," in Devereux, 1980). Children live out the forbidden impulses of their parents. Offspring unconsciously obey their parents when they disobey them. In their impulsivity, they act out in behalf of parents who unconvincingly inhibit themselves. Prohibition masks the command for exhibition.

These same persons who are a family's loyal deviants (Stierlin, 1974) subsequently make themselves available as the "deputy lunatics" (Devereux, 1956) for those *societal* normals who—like the delinquent's family—are able to sustain their own incomplete repression through the vicarious acting out of their hated tricksters. This is, incidentally, likewise true for beloved societal extremists who embody group ideals and repressions (our macho John Waynes who act out *for* us; Kwakiutl chiefs who potlatch *for* empathizing tribesmen): It is the affective division of labor that determines which pathology will be punctuated as positively valued and which as negatively valued. In mainstream American culture, for instance, both the crime-catching sleuth and the criminal are admired, the former openly and the latter secretly. What is more, in the social as in the family system, police, criminal, and permission-giving audience presuppose one another. Each role, in a sinister way, completes the other. The disobedient rebel is in fact quite compliant in his only apparently solo negativism (Stierlin, 1974).

In society as in the family, the normals "condemn with admiration" (Devereux, 1937) those who violate what normals dare not. Society's normals are deviants in disguise (Edgerton, 1978). In their extremism deviants are loyal. Normals both condemn what they covet and covet what they must condemn. In society as in the family, exemplar and violator are parts of a system; each presupposes the other and requires the other for stability. In social roles, whether familial or societal (or intersocietal), every member not only plays a part in the etiology and sustenance of the pathology contained in the identified member; each member also contains that pathology. Likewise, the abnormals require the normals against which to define themselves and against which they maintain themselves by opposition. They help to perpetuate the very system they so hate.

Deviant behavior everywhere holds unremitting fascination among society's and family's normals. Witness, for instance in American society, the sustained popularity of cowboy or Western genre television shows and movies; also those which feature "action" stories of police, criminals, and detectives. By prosecuting the guilty, normals protest their innocence and shore up their commitment to law and order—all the while taking a moral holiday as the derelict first does his mischief. If indeed normals need their criminals to do their "dirty work," it is little wonder that penal reform in the criminal justice system is so slow, that the prison system ambivalently punishes as it half-heartedly rehabilitates. Likewise, the ever-insolvable family intrigues, conflicts, affairs, illegitimate births, separations, abandonments, and varieties of madness that are the sustenance of American radio and television soap opera serials, mirror publicly in popular culture the identical *irresolutions* that plague private family life (see Stein, 1974). Television, cinema, and art provide us with our tribal folklore, legend, and myths that represent to us our espoused and unconscious values.

Although at the level of theory, it is perhaps unparsimonious to multiply contexts if a simpler explanation is to be found, at the level of human behavior one is struck by the regularity with which people multiply early object-relation and familial contexts in subsequent relationships all their lives—in marriages, child rearing, occupation, religion, political allegiances, *ad nauseam*. Yet it is that "simpler explanation" that families loathe to accept. People seek new relationships that replicate formative ones. Indeed, "society" is heir to that indefinitely expanded multiplication of the family context. This fact compels us to ask anew: What is society for? The old shibboleths about adaptation through pooled experience are partially true but incomplete. Through social relationships, symbolized in the cultural ethos, we pool our adaptive failures. Just as in our religions we anthropomorphize the environment (La Barre, 1972), in our more mundane institutions (from economy to polity) we familomorphize society. Externalizing family pains and failures, we re-create new "families"—and failures. One might define society as that network of relationships whose purpose (whatever other purposes it might be said to have) is the reenactment and mastery of failures in one's family of origin.

In this context, I am persuaded that a principal goal of family therapy—only rarely articulated—ought to be a diminution of externalizing onto the various "public" stages of the macrocontext (including the family of procreation). The direction of therapeutic change would consist of a painful return of conflicts, wishes, fantasies, and anxieties *from* their symbolization and expression in multiplied contexts *to* the original private familial (and thence childhood) context from which origins family members have sought to divert their attention. One could say that the direction of therapeutic change is from externalization to greater internalization and finally to (internal representational) differentiation, separation, and resolution. The reason that this direction is so prohibitively difficult to attain is that people adhere to their contexts in order that they retain their symptoms.

Obviously, even in those varieties of family therapy in which the therapist assembles as many members of the family "cast" as possible (e.g., Carl Whitaker's requirement that three generations be present— which is itself a value), it would be impossible to gather all those (deceased as well as living!) who constitute the family's macrocontext. It is important, nevertheless, to determine which persons are *not* present in the treatment room in terms of their meaning to the family, especially the persistence of the family homeostasis and the official pathology of the labeled member. These, for instance, can provide valuable clues as to why family therapy is *not* progressing (see Schwartzman, 1979, for a discussion of the recreation of the drug addict's family). I make this point not to "reinvent the wheel," so to speak, in family therapy, but to illustrate an inexorable *clinical* conclusion derived ethnographically. In working closely with families, I have learned of the powerful influence of family "ghosts" even when demonology is no longer believed in.

For example, a young diabetic man in his early 20s, married and with an infant, repeatedly made the rounds, so to speak, in all the community hospitals, regularly coming into emergency rooms in ketoacidosis, demanding and receiving hospitalization (to which he felt entitled and which the ER staff could not refuse). He also frequented "his" family physician (one of many) for control of his frequently out-of-control condition. His wife would often smuggle into the hospital such forbidden foods as soft drinks, hamburgers, french fries, and so forth; on his birthday she even brought him a cake. The hospital staff had become so angry toward him that they "looked the other way" when his wife violated the treatment plan and hospital rules. Both he and his wife were repeatedly "instructed" in diet, lifestyle, and insulin injection, yet although they comprehended intellectually the physician's instructions, they never quite complied. After one of his hospitalizations, his wife promised the physician she would come to his office to pick up a manual of instruction on managing her husband's diabetes but never did show up. The booklet sat there for months. The physician, I might add, was an empathic fellow, far from calloused. Yet he, like other health care personnel in the area, also spoke with admiration about his patient's daredevil, seemingly carefree lifestyle, saying once that were he the patient, with perhaps only a few years left, he might also live it up, do what he pleased, and take chances with himself.

The diabetic patient came from a home in which his mother was rather indulgent and seductive, although rejecting toward him. He extrapolated his self-destructive acting out at home to all later relationships, which, like that with his mother and other family members, profited vicariously from his only apparent impulsiveness. The world is structured as he first experienced it. One can find analogues of his family drama throughout his later life. "He acted out responses to the deutero-learned behaviors in his family of origin, in other contexts, and by this created contexts with similar structure and basic premises" (Schwartzman, 1982)—which process offers us insight into how "culture" is created and perpetuated.

On each successive "stage" (private physician, hospital system, criminal justice system) he was tempted by others (for their own needs) to act out. Subsequently they helped and punished him when he made close calls with death. He and they dared each other; his death wish corresponded to their sacrifice. Not only the "identified patient" but the family and macrosystem (which ostensibly valued health care) were out of control. They could not adequately care for him (i.e., help him to control himself) because they needed him to be out of control for them. They consciously devalued him as an "abuser of the health care system"; they unconsciously valued him as a trickster—who would eventually catch up with himself and die (for them: just reward). It was well nigh impossible to limit the patient's dangerous gambling if an endless succession of care givers were, so to speak, giving him an endless supply of chips at the gambling table. In the macrocontext, he sought out relationships that would place him in a dependent, receptive position *and*, in never living up to his voracious needs, leave him frustrated—further justifying his (projective) perception that *the world* is no damn good. Should he eventually destroy himself, he will also have died for us. He lives in a social system whose rules and values he violates and *in behalf of* which he violates them. (I discuss this case at length in Stein, 1982c.)

This example illustrates what I believe to be a general principle of therapeutic success or failure: To the extent that the system which participates in the symptom and symptomatic member(s) can be contained, family therapy is more likely to be successful; conversely, to the extent that the system which participates in the symptom and symptom bearer(s) cannot be contained, family therapy is more likely to fail. The latter, unfortunately, is true because although "the family" may well be in treatment together, members of this same family have re-created numerous successor families in which the old "traded dissociations" (Wynne, 1965) flourish. Thus, what is most necessary for therapy to take place—second-order change, that is, some means of challenging basic premises and altering a self-maintaining system—is what all participants (including the therapists) flee from. *It is difficult to contain "the family" in family therapy* if the participants in family therapy have extended the boundaries of the family to be coextensive with society itself. Like the psychotic's ego boundaries which expand to become coextensive with the universe, the metasystem of family therapy continues to expand indefinitely as some members do not appear for therapy, as family members triangulate a host of outside lay "helpers" or seek treatment elsewhere, and as the therapist enlists the aid of consultation or other experts to whom the family is referred.

Consider the following two clinical examples:

One resident physician in her mid 30s with whom I had worked a year placed supreme value upon "unbroken unity" in relationships. Whether in intimate relationships with men, in occupational groups of peers, or in religious community, she sought the "feeling of family" that she never had in her family of origin. She conducted an anguished search for idealized relationships in which she could merge and through which she could acquire a self. By-passed in a recent promotion, she felt jolted from her security and unity, "discounted" (a word she frequently used to describe how she felt treated in relation to others who were given preferential treatment despite *her* hard work, superiority, and merit). Only after months of resistance (in the analytic sense) had she come to recognize and acknowledge the anger behind the hurt and the family origins of her futile quest long displaced from her family of origin. She had long insisted on the screen memory that her parents "had done the best they could; they just didn't know better" to avoid looking at the early family origins of her intense separation anxiety, her dread of rejection, her fear of being overlooked, and her vacillation between clinging to relationships at any cost and renouncing everything for professionalism. Slowly, in discovering her rage, she discovered her self, that is, her personal distinctiveness. She voiced anger and terror over her father's "emotional abandonment" of her and her mother's "consuming" of her. Gradually she began to need less and to look less for "perfect" relationships in which she would find "unity." She needed less to *value* the security of finding "unity" in society once having discovered why she was seeking it, that is, its roots (which she had all along been avoiding) in her family and childhood.

Some years ago, while conducting an ethnographic study of an inpatient psychiatric hospital ward, I met a Jewish man, perhaps in his mid-30s, who had been diagnosed as paranoid schizophrenic. He would often walk with a stereotypic shuffle or stomp his feet. He spoke with few people and seemed angry with most. One day he took me into his confidence and told me that the head nurse was "cane" (kāyn). I had no

VALUES AND FAMILY THERAPY

idea what *cane* connoted. I was reluctant to dismiss it as some incomprehensible privatism or monosyllabic schizophrenic word salad—after all, he knew what it meant; it was I who could not understand him. But I had no frame of reference to fit it in. The head nurse had told me that for some time he had been calling her *cane*, but dismissed it as the inconsequential workings of a crazy mind.

Now, I knew that nurse and patient disliked one another and avoided contact. Although the patient was paranoid, he was not equally distrustful and suspicious of all staff and patients. I wondered why this particular nurse should be selected to be whatever it was that *cane* meant. She seemed a rather aloof, sometimes rejecting woman, concerned for order and control. But from my perception of her behavior, I failed to understand what it was about her that made her *cane*. What is more, the staff talked often about him, especially *his* bizarreness and belligerence which *their* withdrawal and avoidance heightened. Much of the unresolved conflict *among the staff* was targeted onto him. A symptomatic individual means that something is unresolved: in this case, within him, between his parents, and among the ward staff.

One day I confessed to him that I never was able to figure out what *cane* was. He was silent, then barely whispered: "You're Jewish aren't you?" "Yes," I replied. He continued: "You see, she's Cain, and I'm Abel. You remember from the Bible? She's German, you know. I think she's after me, you know, the way Germans killed Jews." I asked him whether he had told his secret to anyone else, especially his psychiatrist. "No, I can't. He wouldn't understand. I think he's Cain too—Italian. Weren't the Italians allies of the Germans in World War II?"

Now, to my eyes, although the head nurse was not especially kindly toward this patient, whatever she was doing did *not* include persecuting him. In his own family, he was the target of much persecution, which he dare not acknowledge. He projected his feelings of persecution, rage, and guilt within his family onto the ward personnel, using imagery of the Holocaust. He had borrowed, or rather coopted, a Biblical symbol of fratricide, used it as a personal myth to symbolize persecutory fantasies and relationships in his family of origin, and externalized it onto the staff of the psychiatric ward. Here the drama was played out anew. Staff members, for reasons of their own, played into the fantasy by further avoiding and isolating him. To avoid rejection from him (even "normals" seek affirmation from those they spurn as "crazies"), they rejected him, "confirming" in their behavior his myth of himself and his relation to the world.

Moreover, his cultural borrowing of Jewish symbolism to represent his personal conflict was not altogether privatistic. In Jewish lore Jews often represent themselves with reference to the Biblical allegory: the Jews as the innocent, dutiful, proto-monotheistic, carnivorous, victim

Abel and the non-Jewish world as the envious, barbaric, pagan, herbivo-
rous, murderous Cain. Abel was God's favorite; the impulsive Cain
became God's outcast. For this patient, the Cain–Abel story was a
Biblical lesson about relationships in the real world. The symbol was
experienced as though it were a palpable reality, the cultural "belief"
now a "delusion" (Devereux, 1980). He *was* Abel; the nurse *was* Cain. By
resorting to his *ethnic* fantasy, the patient could project and displace the
site of the anxiety *from* his own psyche and family *onto* the outside world
and find in its behavior "proof" of the ethnic myth. His unconscious
role-choice allowed him to depersonalize the entire matter. The patient
assumed an ethnic role in an interethnic drama. He delusionally expanded "family" until it became coextensive with "world." Personal
history was symbolically fused with ethnohistory, vividly "confirmed"
by it.

Values and Therapeutic Strategy

For healers, primitive or modern, therapy often seems less an opportunity to help than tantamount to a compulsion to change. It is as though
they must prove to themselves through their patients that they are able
to heal. In this way the patients become an extension of the healers'
fantasied omnipotence. Thus, the value of healing or change can itself
interfere with therapy! The "need to heal" or "need to change" amounts
to a countertransference distortion to be analyzed—not indulged (Stein,
1982g).

   Governed by an implicit activity bias, health and mental health
practitioners in American society feel not only that they are skilled at
their healer role, but that they should be able to effect a cure. With man
seen in terms of the machine and computer metaphors (Stein, 1982f;
Stein & Kayzakian-Rowe, 1978), practitioners apply their practical,
empirically based, know-how to the "repair" or "reprogramming" of
faulty families, organ systems, and minds. One veteran physician's
assistant, fresh from replumbing his own home, remarked wistfully, "I
wish I could fix people the way I fix pipes. Isolate the problem, take out
what's defective, put in what works, and you're through." The combined
doing–mastery–future–individualistic dominant value orientation com-
mits those in the healing professions to frequently unrealistic reliance
upon one-way technique apart from the therapeutic relationship in
which the technique is used. It likewise leads clinicians to a feeling of
having to "do something" (e.g., alleviate the pain, remove the anxiety,
change the family structure) in order to feel that they are acting
competently.

It has been my experience from over 10 years' work supervising family physician and psychiatry residents in behavioral science that the greatest and most recurrent source of dread is that of loss of control, of helplessness—of failing to be able to "do something" that works and reverses pathology of every kind. (I might add that frequently this urgent need to repair others, to make them well and happy, is an attempt by clinicians to master old childhood losses and guilts; to overcome the depression from the past in the present and future; to "restore" the complete, idealized mother mirrored in the recovery of one's patients.)

In the late 1970s, I had been supervising a family physician over a several-month period with a young couple whose stormy, brief marriage had been characterized by a fear of intimacy, extramarital affairs and provocations to engage in them on the part of both members, mutual recrimination, and so forth. Following one particularly difficult session, the physician and I left the consultation glum and—as is my practice—discussed various aspects of the session. He said, dejectedly, "Something's wrong today. Before today we've always ended on an upbeat note. It's as though today we weren't able to do anything for them." I commented, "I'm feeling it's as though today they weren't able to do anything for us—that's my problem." He exclaimed, "That's it!" with a recognition of our unconscious investment in the direction and outcome of the marriage therapy. We then devoted the remainder of the "debriefing" to a discussion of our countertransference reaction to the couple, the implicit values of marriage and of counseling which we were inadvertently imposing upon the couple, and so forth. We spoke of the Hollywood and Walt Disney sentimentality on the movie screen and on television that "confirms" our childhood wishes and expectations for couples somehow to "live happily ever after." We discovered the extent to which—even momentarily—we were dependent upon the couple's ability to resolve their profound problems, that is, the extent to which we had projected our needs onto them and into the therapy in which we had to "do something" to rescue them. Therapeutic intervention had become projective intrusion, and ever so briefly, we became part of their problem, implemented by our value orientation.

In working ethnographically or clinically with families, I find it imperative initially to "join the defense," so to speak, and accept their "actuality" (Erikson, 1968) as their motivated distortion of whatever "reality" might hold for them. The therapist(s) must have their acceptance, trust, and respect before he or she will be allowed to intervene—even as their very presence in the treatment room is a conscious request to do something. The therapist must "communicate" in the language of the client and family, accept their "definition of the situation," including their rigidly held values, as true and necessary for them in order to be subsequently allowed to influence them to change. Spiegel sensibly writes:

> A pattern of values which is rank-ordered along . . . defensive lines will, quite obviously, be difficult to modify; in addition, a precipitous alteration will run risks of severe personality disruption. It must be handled with care. Therapeutic interventions must be carried out within its structure rather than in opposition to it. (1971, p. 253)

With respect to the goal or direction of treatment, family therapy ought to be indifferent or neutral toward familial–cultural values: They are neither intrinsically good nor bad, they simply are (see McGoldrick, Pearce, & Giordano, 1982). It is the therapist's obligation to learn their function in the group-psychic economy of the family; that is, values are a part of the diagnostic process. With respect to therapeutic technique, tactics, or strategy, values acquire an additional importance, not as ends in themselves, but as instruments the therapist can use toward change, as paradoxical means toward ends. I realize that it is almost heretical to say this today, as many therapists and anthropologists alike have become celebrants and advocates of ethnic sectarianism (Stein, 1975, 1977b, 1979d, 1980b; Stein & Hill, 1973, 1977a, 1977b), having set up cultures and values as objects of aesthetic veneration while resisting insight into just what ethnicity is used *for*.

The structure I would have for those who contend that values are to be "respected" as entities or ends in themselves applies to those who fecklessly argue that all so-called healing or curing techniques are equally valid, therapeutic, even interchangeably effective (e.g., Torrey, 1972; see review by La Barre, 1974). With our ideologies of pluralism, relativism, and "salvage anthropology" (sophisticated rescue fantasies), we blind ourselves clinically to essential distinctions. All techniques of change are not necessarily therapeutic—this despite the infinite elasticity of the word (see Devereux, 1980; De Vos, 1978; La Barre, 1962, 1975, 1978). Genuine therapy must rigorously be distinguished from ritualistic acting out that often goes by the name of therapy (whether by patient, family, or therapist). Possession is not cured by exorcism; the problem of forbidden hostility is not resolved by vodun (*voodoo*). Symbolic–ritual solutions perpetuate and further camouflage the problem they purport to solve. Only that which leads to conflict resolution, to a change in premises, does not result in "more of the same" behavior or a mere change from symptoms disturbing to others to symptoms shared by all (see Slipp, 1981).

I would point out that this credulous acceptance of indulgence of symptom exchange as bona fide therapy is not limited to our view of healing practices among so-called primitives. In contemporary American life, we unquestioningly tend to consider our clinical work done and the patient recovered when the confirmed alcoholic has foresworn his or her vice and has become addicted to his or her Alcoholics Anonymous group, to compulsive productivity at work, or to obsessively devoted family life. Here, recovery is falsely equated to conformism with the symptoms we approve of and share (Kellermann, 1981; Stein, 1982d).

Therapy, *of whatever kind*, I take to be intrinsically that process by which individual patient, family, or group develop the capacity (which we commonly define as strength) to face and accept, however painfully, the truth about oneself, one's relations to others, and one's relation to the world. All else is either preparatory or acting out. Therapy is always experienced, at least in part, as a threatening intrusion, even when it provides relief from the oppressive burden of maintaining perennial defensiveness. For to relinquish these burdens is to relinquish those relationships they symbolize and perpetuate. There can be no therapeutic "gain" without there being a concomitant "loss," including a feared loss of one's cherished values.

In a different context, anthropologist Nancy Scheper-Hughes writes of her return visit in 1980 to the community of "Ballybran" in County Kerry, Ireland, which she had written about in her celebrated book, *Saints, Scholars, and Schizophrenics: Mental Illness in Rural Ireland.* Many of those whose lives she had studied read her account of themselves in her book, published in 1979. Their sense of loss that accompanied a new and disconcerting vision of themselves parallels poignantly the feared loss of values in therapy (even as people enter into therapy for change of some kind):

> They have lost a hitherto unchallenged native interpretation of the meaning of their lives as ones based on the implicitly cherished values of familistic loyalty, obedience, and sacrifice. *Illustration:* I was told that one young village lass has not been the same since identifying herself in the pages of the book. Until that time she herself (and the parish at large) viewed her decision to give up a disapproved "love match" in order to stay home and care for her widowed father and three unmarried brothers as the good, moral "Christian" thing to do. As was said: "her father and brothers 'had right' to claim her." But now there is an alternative view, and a hint of pity has been introduced: "Oh, what a shame, the poor creature." Worse a suggestion of something tainted: "Could she be overly attached to them?" (Scheper-Hughes, 1981, p. 371)

Therapy likewise offers "an alternative view," one gradually recognized to be the reality beneath the personal defense and family camouflage. Therapy is subversive as it is liberating, for in it we come to question what we hold most dear; in lifting our blindness we also curse our sight.

Elsewhere I have written:

> Far from ritualization being selected-for as an adaptive response toward the attainment of "practical outcomes," it is in fact dangerously maladaptive: the reality to which we are adapting, under the influence of ritual, is a timeless dream-world made in the image of our anxieties, conflicts and wishes. The very ritual process which we use to defend us against the Unknown (our-selves and reality) makes us even more vulnerable and helpless. And this, for the simple reason that we use symbolism to *misdefine the problem*, and ritual to *solve the wrong problem*. It is no wonder that the ritual process among groups is identical to the vicious cycle of psychopathology among lone neurotics or psychotics: every new, erroneous solution becomes a new problem for which yet another ritual must be devised, further removing the participant from the source of the need for the ritual in the first place. The "context" upon which ritual is ultimately "dependent" is the unconscious. (Stein, 1979a, pp. 516–517)

This perspective in turn helps us to answer such questions as: What ought to be the goals of family therapy? And whose goals? The family's? The identified patient's? The therapist's? "Society's"? Does therapy consist—as some aver—of conformity to some cultural standard? If so, then to which? And by what rationale? Ought we to impose our (cultural, professional) values on our patients—ever so gently, perhaps? Or ought the family to set the standards for treatment? What (and who) is our authority? Culture does not exist apart from what its members— those who feel and identify themselves as the same as or one with the group, itself also a psychic representation—use, create, reinvent, and revise it for. Far from imposing values, bona fide therapy helps patient and family not to need those self-defeating defenses that have given their lives the quality of drivenness, necessity, rigidity, and changelessness; that have profoundly distorted perceptions of the self, other, and environment; and that have been devoted to a vigilant denial of the separateness of self and other (Beavers, 1976; La Barre, 1972; Speer, 1970).

From this the relationship between therapy and culture becomes clear: The only legitimate use values (and other cultural trappings) have is that of "cultural levers" (Devereux, 1969, pp. xxvi–xxxiv), not things in themselves to be respected. Devereux writes, "Every properly executed psychotherapy—and psychoanalysis more than any other form of psychotherapy—ultimately abolishes, and is intended to abolish, the levers used in the therapy, simply because every genuinely psychotherapeutic device is, in the last resort, self-abolishing" (1969, p. xxvii). He then offers two illustrations.

> My systematic exploitation, *for therapeutic ends*, of the cultural—and therefore largely supernaturalistic—meaning of dreams and of dreaming in Wolf culture promoted and accelerated the obtaining of insight. The insights so

> obtained *first* to an objective and non-supernaturalistic attitude toward
> dreams and dreaming and *then* to the complete disappearance of that
> (magically tinged) reliance on dreams which had made possible their initial
> utilization as cultural levers for therapeutic ends. Similarly, the device of
> providing ego support to the patient by permitting and even encouraging
> him to identify his therapist with the Wolf guardian spirit *first* enabled the
> patient to tolerate new and painful insights which, *in turn*, sufficiently
> strengthened his ego to make possible a complete "demythologization" of
> the guardian spirit—and therefore also of the therapist. This then permitted
> the patient to emancipate himself both from the guardian spirit image and
> from the therapist, and to cease to be dependent on either. (1969, p. xxvii)

Finally:

> Any use of cultural levers—and especially of irrational and/or ideological
> levers—which is self-reinforcing, in that it impedes the gaining of *culturally
> neutral* insights capable of abolishing these levers, constitutes a misuse of
> culture and is not genuine therapy. (1969, p. xxxiii)

For a number of years before I had learned Devereux's valuable
concept of *cultural levers*, I was implicitly using it in supervising resident
physicians in psychiatry and family medicine; and I find it a valuable
resource in family therapy. I have emphasized that the "home visit" not
only provides a wealth of diagnostic data *in vivo* but has strategic value
as well. For families have genuinely expressed gratitude for my interest
in their world and not merely their "sickness." In a sense, from an
ethnographic point of view I reinvented a wheel which I only subsequently
discovered to have been independently and previously invented in family
therapy circles. Ethnographically, my rationale in prescribing home
visits was that while the clinic afforded a look at only a single "character," the home facilitated the careful observation of not only the
wider "drama" but the "performance" on its natural "stage." I have
necessarily had to work through terrifying fantasies of being over-
whelmingly outnumbered, annihilated, swallowed up, and the rest.
Having (relatively) weathered those anxieties, I find that by my taking
their milieu (which is to say, cultural world) seriously—indeed, my
willingness to enter into its intimacies and frights—families are somewhat disarmed and thus more willing to peer beneath their resistances
embodied in and "staged" in that very milieu.

While teaching in Nashville, Tennessee, I coordinated a weekly
seminar on psychosocial aspects of religion with Reverend Julius Thomas.
Students at the American Baptist Theological Seminary, many of them
already pastors of churches, participated. One of the principal methods
we used to bring religion home, so to speak, in these groups was to
utilize cultural levers fully. Recognizing the high *value* that these semi-
narians placed upon Biblical exegesis as a form of uncovering ultimate
truth and upon sermons as a vehicle for communication with their

congregation about the meaning of life and the right way to live, we asked our students to choose what for them were the most important or illuminating passages in the Bible and what for them were some of their own most important sermons and to discuss them in class.

What began as "cultural" guides to the nature of life gradually were secularly revealed to be inadvertent guides to the royal road to the unconscious. Discussions that began ostensibly to outline the nature of deity, sin, and salvation, came to reveal the nature of self. We came to recognize as manifestations of human biology the subject matter of theology. In ways exciting and perplexing, we discovered (or continuously rediscovered) religious symbolism as vehicles for the self, which once externalized, became detached and thereby acquired "a life of their own." The group came to understand religious beliefs and commitments to be something of a group-created, administered, and interpreted Rorschach card—a tool that they could not only use better to understand their own personal motivation, but which they could then use as a form of "transitional phenomena" to better understand and minister to their congregation.

As a final example, consider the value of the "cowboy ethos" held by many midwestern United States families whose lives are built around grain farming, livestock, and oil drilling. Among males this ethos consists of a constellation of themes that include physical labor as a means of expressing and proving one's manliness (not simply earning a living), emotional detachment and fierce self-reliance (while one is devoted to his family as its titular head and supporter), a matter-of-factness and dogged practicality (with little room for airy speculation or sentimentality in the presence of others), a preference for ample "breathing space" for solitude if not isolation (a "don't-fence-me-in" attitude whose obverse side is nostalgia such as reflected in country-and-western songs and ballads). Having worked closely with midwestern rural families in family medicine settings (Oklahoma), I would assert as a general principle that fathers and husbands tend to want to have nothing whatsoever to do with family therapy. It is both an affront to their principles and a threat to their fragile autonomy. Often whole nuclear families scheduled to assemble for family therapy appear without father—who usually will have plausible excuses (relayed by his wife) related to work.

Initially I accepted as valid the explanation that the father/husband had to cancel because of the long, unpredictable hours on the oil rig or the seasonal requirements of wheat farming, and so forth. What I failed to realize was that the exclusively economic argument was often a family- and culturally sanctioned rationalization for the fear of becoming involved in therapy. Wives would frequently make excuses for their absent husbands, while in the next breath complaining painfully that they feel that their husbands virtually desert them to lose themselves in work. It became clear to me that in many cases the economic argument was in fact a cultural argument, that for males, ostensibly instrumental behavior was profoundly expressive. Work—especially rugged work with all-male teams—was a way of constantly reaffirming a man's independence, of maintaining his distance from the very women and children whom he loved, but who he also feared would shackle him. At work, a man could be a man; at home, he was never certain. Given the compensatory, masculine protest-quality of the work ethic, how could one begin to do a "systems" family therapy?

I have found two strategies that have been productive. One, in which the husband/father consistently refuses to enter therapy or comes only reluctantly and intermittently, consists of exploring with the wife/mother and children the "family myth" (Ferreira, 1963) that any possibility of change not only requires the presence of the husband/father, but revolves around him (privately, he will persuasively argue precisely the opposite!). To "buy into" the family system of "traded dissociation" (Wynne, 1965) ensures that no change will occur: One simply—and complicitously—listens empathically to the wife/mother's plaintive cry and accepts her helplessness as her "cross" to bear. By focusing upon her options (and that of the children as well), and by patiently helping her to understand her quietly fierce resistance to the *exercise* of alternatives to her present course, she comes to induce change by acting directly herself instead of waiting for him to change himself. It frequently turns out that directness is a recourse she fears most in relation to him, for her security has lain in her indirectness, if not deviousness, in choreographing her own life and home life to appear as though it were built around him, while filling some of her own needs. Her separation anxiety, her fear of being bereft and abandoned, has led her to cling and to resent having to cling. Over the course of family therapy in this cultural context, the woman slowly develops sufficient self-confidence to stand up to her husband—and more with him than against him.

A secondary strategy that I have developed is useful when the husband does regularly attend the family sessions but spatially locates himself peripherally, often toward a corner or protectively separated from the unruly brood by a table corner. Commonly the wife is eager to get therapy underway, whereas the husband is fearful for what might happen. As a means of attempting to reduce his anxiety, I initially take an active interest in his work, and inquire (as a male) into his male world, gradually using it as a cultural lever to promote an understanding of what he uses work *for*, while respecting his wish to save face with his family (and himself).

Initially, I accept—rather than attempt to exploit—his uneasiness and sense of vulnerability. For one thing, the intimacy of family problems holds uncertain danger that, through work, he has been trying to avoid; for another, he fears to be implicated in the problem rather than be the steadfast breadwinner; and thirdly, he is embarrassed that what should be an exclusively private matter will now be dealt with publicly. I do not wish to be perceived as an agent of the wife/mother; nor do I wish to worsen his fears of emasculation. By inquiring into his work, especially into his routine and into the value of work for him, I temporarily identify with him, facilitating his identification with therapy. In my experience husbands/fathers quite literally come out of the corners once they feel safe in these corners—safe, that is, in that I shall not try to pry them out of the little turf they have.

These all are rather standard strategies in family therapy. Here I merely draw attention to the use of cultural content or coloration as vehicles for identification and subsequent leverage (e.g., the midwestern "cowboy" ethos, the previously discussed Slavic ethic of generosity, etc).

Finally, I wish to address the issue of "value change" during the course of family therapy. Here my goal is never to prescribe values for the family, but to help them to take leave of dysfunctional ones to which they adhere because "they keep us together." The family to be discussed is a multiproblem family with whom I worked for several months in collaboration with a resident physician in family medicine. Before summarizing the case, I first schematically present three family values that governed dysfunctional family interaction: (1) the most important thing is to keep the family together; (2) the kids come first; (3) avoidance is better than conflict. One can see how *family values can function as the content and rationalization of "family myth"* (Ferreira, 1963).

Case: The Runaway

Jenny Kraft is a 17-year-old who some months earlier developed classic signs and symptoms of anorexia nervosa. She is the eldest female sibling and "standard bearer" in a "reconstituted" family of eight children. Her father is a farmer and cattle rancher who spends every waking hour tending his fields and cattle. Her stepmother is a conscientious woman who cares for home and children, and who feels overwhelmed by domestic responsibility. Husband and wife interact little directly, and mostly over various conflicts with the children. The marital role is not only subordinate to the parental role, it is virtually nonexistent. The eldest daughter's anorexia had temporarily united them in their concern for her welfare. However, it also had absorbed the entire burden of their marital problems, unresolved issues in their families of origin, hints of voyeurism and incest among the other children, and so forth. Both parents are remarried divorcees who are adamant about making *this* marriage work—*for the sake of the children and out of a dread of being alone.*

Her parents first "dispatched" her, into individual therapy with their family physician and consultant. Only gradually did they agree to become involved. Individual and family therapy revealed that Jenny had begun to use self-starvation as a desperate attempt to establish distinct personal boundaries, especially from her stepmother, a woman in her 40s to whom she felt very close but whom she was never able to please. She calls her stepmother "Mom" affectionately and regards her as her mother. (Her biological mother had abandoned the family when Jenny was 8.)

She was also using her symptoms to stave off sexual development, for to become a woman was to be trapped. Her stepmother enlists her to be a junior mother, so to speak, consuming all of Jenny's time and energy outside school. Her father expects her to bring home perfect grades, and both parents closely supervise such high school activities as gymnastics and cheerleading. Her stepmother follows every move she makes, checks up on her, demands constant reports from her. Her parents' approval is very important to her. She tries hard to live up to their exacting expectations.

The age of 17 is significant for Jenny's stepmother, for it was at that age that she left her parental home, married, began bearing children, and shouldered enormous responsibilities in a small northwest Oklahoma farm community. Jenny, who has been flirting on and off with marriage during this year, feels almost compelled to get married this year, and is likewise repelled by the idea. She vacillates between wanting to be a dutiful daughter and wanting to make a complete break with her family—the prospect of marriage being one vehicle for the latter (as it was for her stepmother). She also alternates between clinging and fleeing.

Some months into therapy, Jenny ran away from home with her (then current) boyfriend, sending her parents into a desperate state-wide search for her. She returned of her own choice within 2 days, having escaped detection, remorseful for having caused her family so much grief. In a subsequent family therapy session, the atmosphere was grave. Father was silent, averting eye contact with his family; stepmother fought tears and anger. The penitential errant daughter first spoke; her father said that he was shocked, felt let down. I turned to the stepmother, who looked at me and immediately away: "Don't ask me to say anything," she struggled to say, in obvious agitation. "I'm having a hard enough time holding myself together." I did not press. Soon, however, out of the ensuing silence the stepmother sobbed, but then spoke through her tears with resolution in her voice, "I wish to God I had the courage to run away."

This was a moment of profound insight on her part, and marked a turning point in the treatment. She made no immediate connection between her own feeling of imprisonment, her paralysis to do anything other than continue to bear the family's burdens in silence, her own inability to run away, and her stepdaughter's acting out of her forbidden wish. The stepmother came to understand that the more she felt confident enough to stand up to her husband with her own principles, needs, expectations, and limits, the less she would feel the panicky need to take flight from an impossible situation—*or* to need to encourage her stepdaughter to do (in her behalf) what she could not herself do.

In the next family session, which her husband did not attend ("because of work"), the stepmother was openly angry about having allowed her fears of being alone, abandoned, helpless, and the like, to dominate her interactions in holding the family together. I was also pleasantly surprised to discover this woman's sheer physical attractiveness. On previous occasions she had let her appearance "go to pot," so to speak. On this day, she had fixed her hair nicely, wore a stunning outfit, and smiled for the first time since I had met her. She realized that others would take responsibilities only if she did not assume them herself. The roof to their home was leaking; she had notified her husband about it and resolved to do nothing further: "I don't *have* to do it all anymore. I've reached my limit. If he doesn't fix the roof that's *his* problem. I'm not afraid of standing up for myself anymore. I made it on my own and could make it again if I had to." She less needed her depression as an escape from an unbearable reality which she had helped to fashion (and as punishment for the wish to escape); and she less needed to bear her current reality masochistically.

Jenny's anorexia nervosa and vacillation between flight and clinging likewise began to resolve. They both could elect to stay only when they could choose to stay rather than feel compelled to stay. Jenny no longer had to become a runaway on behalf of her stepmother; and the stepmother no longer needed to delegate her (now less) forbidden wishes to Jenny. Moreover, the stepmother and Jenny had undergone a major, but subtle, *value change*. The paramount value of "togetherness at any price" gave way to a prizing of personal distinctness and self-respect. The prior skewed parental (exclusive) emphasis upon the children gave way to a valuing of the separateness of the parental dyad and of greater individual autonomy within that dyad. The children were less often out of control (and sexualizing it with one another) when the parents less needed them to be unruly. Finally, the value of conflict avoidance ("peace at any price") gave way to a valuing of greater verbal directness—and thereby of diminished acting out.

I should also add that it was necessary for the therapists to overcome their own tendency to accept cultural values "at face value," that is, as intrinsic forces and as widely shared—therefore not to be examined. Cultural materials do not *affect* people apart from how they are *used* by individuals and families. It would have been easy to dismiss as *un*clinical the cultural (American) values that family togetherness is paramount or that "the kids come first." Likewise, it would have been easy to buy into the midwestern value of conflict avoidance. To do so, however, would have bought into the family prescription, to the effect that "We're fine, it's just that Jenny isn't eating." We approached values clinically; that is, we inquired into their individual and interactional *function*.

   In summary, I have grown increasingly aware of the familial use of cultural paraphernalia (ideas, values, beliefs, loyalties, etc.) as permanently installed "transitional phenomena" (Winnicott, 1953) to be respected, accepted, and carefully investigated (with the family) for their function, not arrogantly manipulated or simply disregarded in favor of my own (or some favorite theorist's) strategy for intervention (see Maduro, 1975). "Wild analysis" in psychoanalysis (Freud, 1957) surely has its parallel in family therapy or any other avowedly therapeutic form. Therapeutic "dive bombing," whether toward deep insight, structural change, paradoxical injunction, or whatever, is acting out rationalized as being in the family's (or patient's) best interest. It conveys disrespect toward the family in treatment and is a tactical error that results in missed opportunities (see Stein, 1982h). Perhaps the preeminent value in family therapy (if not all truly therapeutic forms) is the therapist's unspoken respect for those whom he or she treats—even as they devalue one another.

REFERENCES

Abel, T. M., & Metraux, R. *Culture and psychotherapy*. New Haven, Conn.: College & University Press, 1974.
Beavers, W. R. A theoretical basis for family evaluation. In J. M. Lewis, W. R. Beavers, J. T. Gossett, & V. A. Phillips (Eds.), *No single thread: Psychological health in family systems*. New York: Brunner/Mazel, 1976.
Benedict, R. Anthropology and the abnormal. *Journal of General Psychology*, 1934, *10*, 59–82. (a)
Benedict, R. *Patterns of culture*. Boston: Houghton Mifflin, 1934. (b)
Bion, W. R. *Experiences in groups*. London: Tavistock, 1959.
Bowen, M. *Family therapy in clinical practice*. New York: Jason Aronson, 1978.
Cantril, H. *Soviet leaders and mastery over man*. New Brunswick, N.J.: Rutgers University Press, 1960.
Caudill, W. Anthropology and psychoanalysis: Some theoretical issues. In T. Gladwin & W. C. Sturtevant (Eds.), *Anthropology and human behavior*. Washington, D.C.: The Anthropological Society of Washington, 1962.
deMause, L. *Foundations of psychohistory*. New York: Creative Roots, 1982.
Devereux, G. Institutionalized homosexuality of the Mohave Indians. *Human Biology*, 1937, *9*, 498–527.
Devereux, G. The wrong patient. In *Therapeutic education*. New York: Harper, 1956.

Devereux, G. *From anxiety to method in the behavioral sciences*. The Hague: Mouton, 1967.

Devereux, G. *Reality and dream: Psychotherapy of a Plains Indian*. New York: New York University Press, 1969. (Originally published, 1951.)

Devereux, G. The works of George Devereux. In G. D. Spindler (Ed.), *The making of psychological anthropology*. Los Angeles: University of California Press, 1978.

Devereux, G. *Basic problems of ethno-psychiatry*. Chicago: University of Chicago Press, 1980.

De Vos, G. A. Affective dissonance and primary socialization: Implications for a theory of incest avoidance. *Ethos*, 1975, *3*(2), 165–182.

De Vos, G. A. Comment on Weston La Barre's "Hysteria and psychopathy: Two sides of Freud's coin." *Dialogue*, 1978, *2*(2), 17–19.

De Vos, G. A. Afterword. In D. K. Reynolds, *The quiet therapies: Japanese pathways to personal growth*. Honolulu: University Press of Hawaii, 1980. (a)

De Vos, G. A. Ethnic adaptation and minority status. *Journal of Cross-Cultural Psychology*, 1980, *11*(1), 101–124. (b)

Edgerton, R. B. The study of deviance: Marginal man or everyman? In G. D. Spindler (Ed.), *The making of psychological anthropology*. Los Angeles: University of California Press, 1978.

Erikson, E. H. *Identity, youth and crisis*. New York: Norton, 1968.

Ferreira, A. J. Family myth and homeostasis. *Archives of General Psychiatry*, 1963, *9*, 457–463.

Ford, J. D Therapeutic relationship in behavior therapy: An empirical analysis. *Journal of Consulting and Clinical Psychology*, 1978, *46*(6), 1302–1314.

Freud, S. "Wild" psycho-analysis. In *Standard edition of the complete psychological works of Sigmund Freud* (Vol. 2). London: Hogarth Press, 1957. (Originally published 1910.)

Friedman, E. H. Systems and ceremonies: A family view of rites of passage. In E. Carter & M. McGoldrick (Eds.), *The family life cycle: A framework for family therapy*. New York: Gardner Press, 1980.

Hall, E. *Beyond culture*. Garden City, N.Y.: Doubleday/Anchor, 1977.

Hartmann, H. *Psychoanalysis and moral values*. New York: International Universities Press, 1960.

Jackson, B. *The black flag: A look back at the strange case of Nicola Sacco and Bartolomeo Vanzetti*. Boston: Routledge & Kegan Paul, 1981.

Johnson, A., & Szurek, S. A. The genesis of antisocial acting out in children and adults. *Psychoanalytic Quarterly*, 1952, *21*, 323–343.

Kellermann, G. *Sobriety: Effective distancing or recovery?* Paper presented at symposium on alcoholism, Georgetown University, April 1981.

Kleinman, A. *Patients and healers in the context of culture*. Los Angeles: University of California Press, 1980.

Kluckhohn, C. The study of culture. In D. Lerner & H. D. Lasswell (Eds.), *The policy sciences*. Stanford, Calif.: Stanford University Press, 1951. (a)

Kluckhohn, C. Values and value orientations. In T. Parsons, & E. Shils (Eds.), *Toward a general theory of action*. Cambridge, Mass.: Harvard University Press, 1951. (b)

Kluckhohn, F. Dominant and substitute profiles of cultural orientations: Their significance for the analysis of social stratification. *Social Forces*, 1950, *28*, 376–393.

Kluckhohn, F. Dominant and variant value orientations. In C. Kluckhohn & H. A. Murray (Eds.), *Personality in nature, society, and culture*. New York: Knopf, 1953.

Kluckhohn, F. Variations in the basic values of family systems. *Social Casework*, 1958, *39*, 63–72.

Kluckhohn, F. R., & Strodtbeck, F. L. *Variations in value orientations*. Evanston, Ill.: Row Peterson, 1961.

Kohut, H. *The analysis of the self*. New York: International Universities Press, 1971.

Kohut, H. *The restoration of the self*. New York: International Universities Press, 1977.

La Barre, W. Family and symbol. In G. Wilbur & W. Muensterberger (Eds.), *Psychoanalysis and culture*. New York: International Universities Press, 1951.

La Barre, W. Social cynosure and social structure. In D. G. Haring (Ed.), *Personal character and cultural milieu.* Syracuse: Syracuse University Press, 1956.

La Barre, W. Transference cures in religious cults and social groups. *Journal of Psychoanalysis in Groups,* 1962, *1*(1), 66–75.

La Barre, W. *The human animal.* Chicago: University of Chicago Press, 1968.

La Barre, W. *They shall take up serpents.* New York: Schocken, 1969.

La Barre, W. *The ghost dance: The origins of religion.* New York: Dell, 1972.

La Barre, W. Review of *The mind game: Witchdoctors and psychiatrists* by E. Fuller Torrey. *Social Casework,* 1974, *55*(1), 57.

LaBarre, W. Anthropological perspectives on hallucination and hallucinogens. In R. K. Siegel & L. J. West (Eds.), *Hallucinations: Behavior, experience and theory.* New York: John Wiley, 1975.

La Barre, W. Hysteria and psychopathy: Two sides of Freud's coin. *Dialogue,* 1978, *2*(2), 2–19.

Maduro, R. J. Hoodoo possession in San Francisco, *Ethos,* 1975, *3*(3), 425–447.

Mahler, M., & Furer, M. *On human symbiosis and the vicissitudes of individuation.* New York: International Universities Press, 1968.

Mahler, M., Pine, F., & Bergman, A. *The psychological birth of the human infant.* New York: Basic Books, 1975.

McGoldrick, M., Pearce, J., & Giordano, J. (Eds.). *Ethnicity and family therapy.* New York: Guilford Press, 1982.

Mead, M. Retrospects and prospects. In *Anthropology and human behavior.* Washington, D.C.: The Anthropological Society of Washington, 1962.

Phares, E. J. *Clinical psychology.* Homewood, Ill.: Dorsey Press, 1979.

Richards, A. *Chisungu.* London: Faber & Faber, 1956.

Sander, F. *Individual and family therapy.* New York: Jason Aronson, 1979.

Scheper-Hughes, N. *Saints, scholars, and schizophrenics: Mental illness in rural Ireland.* Los Angeles: University of California Press, 1979.

Scheper-Hughes, N. Cui bonum—For whose good?: A dialogue with Sir Raymond Firth. *Human Organization,* 1981, *40*(4), 371–372.

Schulz, C. G. The value of working through: An introduction to the subject of separation. *National Association of Private Psychiatric Hospitals Journal* (special issue devoted to separation), 1981, *12*(4), 133.

Schwartzman, J. Methadone maintenance: The addict's family recreated. *International Journal of Family Therapy,* 1979, *1*(4), 338–355.

Schwartzman, J. Personal communication, 1982.

Slipp, S. (Ed.). *Curative factors in dynamic psychotherapy.* New York: McGraw-Hill, 1981.

Speer, D. C. Family systems: Morphostasis and morphogenesis, or is homeostasis enough? *Family Process,* 1970, *9*, 259–278.

Spiegel, J. *Transactions: The interplay between individual, family, and society.* New York: Science House, 1971.

Spiegel, J., & Kluckhohn, F. *Integration and conflict in family behavior* (Report No. 27). Topeka: Group for the Advancement of Psychiatry, 1954.

Spiro, M. *Burmese supernaturalism.* Englewood Cliffs, N.J.: Prentice-Hall, 1967.

Stanton, M. D. The addict as savior: Heroin, death, and the family. *Family Process,* 1977, *16*(2), 191–197.

Stein, H. F. The silent complicity at Watergate. *American Scholar,* 1973–1974, *43*(1), 21–37.

Stein, H. F. *All in the Family* as a mirror of contemporary American culture. *Family Process,* 1974, *13*(3), 179–215.

Stein, H. F. Ethnicity, identity, and ideology. *School Review,* 1975, *83*, 273–300.

Stein, H. F. A dialectical model of health and illness attitudes and behavior among Slovak-Americans. *International Journal of Mental Health,* 1976, *5*(2), 117–137.

Stein, H. F. The binding of the son: Psychoanalytic reflections on the symbiosis of anti-semitism and anti-gentilism. *Psychoanalytic Quarterly,* 1977, *46*, 650–683. (a)

Stein, H. F. Identity and transcendence. *School Review*, 1977, *85*, 349–375. (b)

Stein, H. F. The triumph of the son, the vengeance of the father: A contemporary American cultural drama. *Psychoanalytic Review*, 1977, *64*(4), 559–584. (c)

Stein, H. F. Judaism and the group-fantasy of martyrdom: The psychodynamic paradox of survival through persecution. *Journal of Psychohistory*, 1978, *6*(2), 151–210. (a)

Stein, H. F. The Slovak-American "swaddling ethos": Homeostat for family dynamics and cultural continuity. *Family Process*, 1978, *17*, 31–45. (b)

Stein, H. F. Commentary on C. W. Kiefer & J. Cowan, "State/context dependence and theories or ritual" (*Journal of Psychological Anthropology*, 1979, *2*(1), 53–83). *Journal of Psychological Anthropology*, 1979, *2*(4), 515–517. (a)

Stein, H. F. The new pluralism, education, and the problem of human values. *Journal of General Education*, 1979, *31*(1), 1–11. (b)

Stein, H. F. The salience of ethno-psychology for medical education and practice. *Social Science and Medicine*, 1979, *13B*, 199–210. (c)

Stein, H. F. The white ethnic movement, pan-ism, and the restoration of early symbiosis: The psychohistory of a group-fantasy. *Journal of Psychohistory*, 1979, *6*(3), 319–359. (d)

Stein, H. F. Bowen "family systems theory": The problem of cultural persistence, and the differentiation of self in one's culture. *The Family*, 1980, *8*(1), 3–12. (a)

Stein, H. F. Culture and ethnicity as group-fantasies: A psychohistoric paradigm of group identity. *Journal of Psychohistory*, 1980, *8*(1), 21–51. (b)

Stein, H. F. *Social role and unconscious complementarity.* Paper presented by G. De Vos at the Annual Meetings of the American Anthropological Association, Los Angeles, California, December 3, 1981.

Stein, H. F. Adversary symbiosis and complementary group dissociation: An analysis of the U.S./U.S.S.R. conflict. *International Journal of Intercultural Relations*, 1982, *6*, 55–83. (a)

Stein, H. F. The annual cycle and the cultural nexus of health care behavior among Oklahoma wheat farming families. *Culture, Medicine and Psychiatry*, 1982, *6*(1), 81–99. (b)

Stein, H. F. The contest for control: A case of diabetes mellitus in psychosomatic, familial, health care, and cultural contexts. *Journal of Psychoanalytic Anthropology*, 1982, *5*(2), 173–196. (c)

Stein, H. F. Ethanol and its discontents: Paradoxes of inebriation and sobriety in American culture. *Journal of Psychoanalytic Anthropology*, 1982, *5*(4), 355–377. (d)

Stein, H. F. The ethnographic mode of teaching clinical behavioral science. In N. Chrisman & T. Maretzki (Eds.), *Clinically applied anthropology: Anthropologists in health science settings.* Boston: D. Reidel, 1982. (e)

Stein, H. F. Man the computer. *Continuing Education for the Family Physician*, 1982, *16*(3), 19. (f)

Stein, H. F. Physician–patient transaction through the analysis of countertransference: A study in role relationship and unconscious meaning. *Medical Anthropology*, 1982, *6*(3), 165–182. (g)

Stein, H. F. Toward a life of dialogue: Therapeutic communication and the meaning of medicine. *Continuing Education for the Family Physician*, 1982, *16*(4), 29–45. (h)

Stein, H. F. An anthropological view of family therapy. In D. Bagarozzi, A. P. Jurich, & R. W. Jackson (Eds.), *New perspectives in marriage and family therapy: Issues in theory, research and practice.* New York: Human Sciences Press, 1983.

Stein, H. F., & Hill, R. F. The new ethnicity and the white ethnic in the United States: An exploration in the psycho-cultural genesis of ethnic irredentism. *Canadian Review of Studies in Nationalism*, 1973, *1*(1), 81–105.

Stein, H. F., & Hill, R. F. *The ethnic imperative: Examining the new white ethnic movement.* University Park: Pennsylvania State University Press, 1977. (a)

Stein, H. F., & Hill, R. F. The limits of ethnicity. *American Scholar*, 1977, *46*(2), 181–189. (b)

Stein, H. F., & Kayzakian-Rowe, S. Hypertension, biofeedback, and the myth of the machine: A psychoanalytic–cultural study. *Psychoanalysis and Contemporary Thought*, 1978, *1*(1), 119–156.

Stierlin, H. *Separating parents and adolescents: A perspective on running away, schizophrenia, and way-wardness*. New York: Times Books, 1974.

Stierlin, H. *Adolf Hitler: A family perspective*. New York: Psychohistory Press, 1976.

Strupp, H. H., & Bergin, A. E. Some empirical and conceptual bases for coordinated research in psychotherapy: A critical review of issues, trends and evidence. *International Journal of Psychiatry*, 1969, 7, 18–90.

Torrey, E. F. *The mind game: Witchdoctors and psychiatrists*. New York: Emerson Hall, 1972.

Volkan, V. *Primitive internalized object relations*. New York: International Universities Press, 1976.

Weisman, A. D. Reality sense and reality testing. *Behavioral Science*, 1958, 3, 228–261.

Winnicott, D. W. Transitional objects and transitional phenomena: A study of the first not-me possession. *International Journal of Psycho-Analysis*, 1953, 34, 89–97.

Wynne, L. C. Some indications and contraindications for exploratory family therapy. In I. Boszormenyi-Nagy & J. Framo (Eds.), *Intensive family therapy: Theoretical and practical aspects*. New York: Harper & Row, 1965.

10

Social change, disequilibrium, and adaptation in developing countries: A Moroccan example

FROMA WALSH
University of Chicago and
Center for Family Studies/The Family Institute of Chicago,
Northwestern University Medical School

While development efforts in Third World countries have concentrated on socioeconomic and technological advancements, insufficient attention has been directed to the systemic impact of rapid social change. This chapter addresses the disruptive transitional processes and adaptational challenges that confront individuals and their family and social systems in societies undergoing rapid development. Viewed as a period of profound disequilibrium, the transition holds potential for disorder as well as for creative new solutions. Social planning and intervention efforts must be attuned to the process of change in human systems in order to facilitate successful adaptation.

Tasks of Developing Nations

Whereas certain development priorities are specific to the sociocultural, economic, and political context of each Third World nation, a number of critical social concerns are shared throughout most of Africa, Asia, and Latin America. Ways must be found to ameliorate widespread poverty, overpopulation, unemployment, illiteracy, malnutrition, and disease.

The situation confronting planners and service providers in Morocco —a North African, Islamic society of Arab and Berber descent—is a case in point. The government of Morocco has launched an ambitious social action program to modernize the country and to improve the standard of living of its people. Most Moroccans live in impoverished conditions, with the annual per capita income under $500 and inflation rising dramatically (Moroccan Ministry of Planning, 1978). The population

244

growth rate is over 3%, with nearly half the population under the age of 15. Urban population is expected to double in just 13 years owing to migrants from rural areas in search of income. Unemployment estimates range as high as half the work force, with illiterate and unskilled youth and women most affected. Despite a government commitment to universal education over the past two decades, 76% of the population is illiterate and fewer than half of school age children attend school. In rural areas where most Moroccans live, jobs are scarce, the illiteracy rate is over 90%, and school enrollment is under 15%. Women and girls, mostly secluded in homes or working in fields, are least educated with 86% illiterate (98% in rural areas) and only 15% attending school (only 5% rurally). Harsh and unsanitary living conditions, malnutrition, disease, and lack of basic health care and information contribute to a high infant mortality rate (130 per 1000 live births) and a life expectancy of just 53 years. Half of all village children die before the age of 5. A severe shortage of medical facilities and trained health personnel exists, with just one hospital for every 234,000 Moroccans and only one physician for every 14,000 persons.

Clearly, in Morocco as throughout the Third World, the tasks of socioeconomic development present a formidable challenge for social intervention. To develop human resources and income-generating capacities, programs in basic education and literacy are required as well as training geared to new demands in expanding industrial, technological, managerial, and professional fields. To improve the standard of living, education and services promoting health, child care, and family planning are necessary. Unfortunately, social intervention efforts, although well intended, have too often been directed in a fragmented, piecemeal fashion to specific targeted problems and particular segments of the population without attention to the linkages between the pieces and the systemic ramifications of change efforts. Perhaps most essential to the success of development efforts is an understanding of the process of change in human systems and the transitional turmoil that accompanies rapid social change.

Human Systems and Social Change

All human systems are governed by basic regulatory processes to insure their survival and vitality, although the particular norms and mechanisms may vary in different cultures (Walsh, 1982). Of special relevance to social change are the universal systems properties of ecological fit, circular influence, and the counterbalancing processes for stability and change.

Ecological Fit

Human systems are so organized that individuals, families, communities, and societies form nested layers of increasing inclusion and complexity (Bronfenbrenner, 1979; Schwartzman, 1982). Each system level operates in constant interchange with the others, in a reciprocal interlocking of interactional patterns. In stable societies, as in traditional cultures, there is an ecological fit among the levels, with each level complementing or reinforcing the others, each a functional part of a larger systemic pattern (Bateson, 1979).

The family occupies a central mediating position in this hierarchy, functioning as the primary link between the individual and the broader society. In all cultures historically, the family has served a major socializing function, transmitting societal values and norms to its members and, through acculturation processes, preparing offspring to function in the social world (Lidz, 1963).

Morocco is typical of Third World countries in the importance that the family holds in the society and for Moroccans as individuals. The family is regarded as the foundation of Moroccan life (Geertz, 1979). In the Moroccan conception of the nature of society and humankind, every person is seen as an active agent attempting to create a meaningful life within an arbitrary world. Family relationships provide the essential core of meaning to life in this worldview. The family is defined broadly for Moroccans; it is a tangled web of valued and trusted relationships including extended kin, friendship, and patronage ties (Geertz, 1979). These relationship networks are based on reciprocity, loyalty, and obligation, and function as the essential link for individuals to their broader social context. Through its relationship rules, sanctions, and taboos, the family upholds the values and practices of a traditional Islamic culture. Particular esteem is accorded to women as preservers of home and family in carrying out their functions as wives and mothers. Nomadic Berber tribes, in fact, speak metaphorically of women's importance as the tent pole: the center pole holding up the tent.

Circular Influence

In a system, individual members or component parts are related in a mutually causal network. Change in any member or part affects all others and the group as a whole, whose reactions in turn affect all in a circular chain of influence (Buckley, 1968). This principle applies as well to relationships among systems levels. In a cycle of action and reaction, change at one level affects all other levels, which in turn affect the first change in a circular feedback loop. Change at the societal level will have the greatest impact on all other system levels because it is most in-clusive. Therefore, when a society is undergoing the massive changes involved in rapid development, the impact will be felt throughout the social system, at community, family, and individual levels of functioning (Halleck, 1976: Landau, 1981; Schulman, 1979). The importance of ecological fit and circular influence should be taken into account as should the reactions at each level that will influence the process of social change.

Social action programs launched in developing nations to benefit disadvantaged segments of the population have generally been directed to classes of individuals, such as skills training of youths. When intervention is at the lowest systems level, the individual, without giving sufficient attention to the family, there are two important ramifications. First, in not including intervention at the family systems level, the potential power of the family as a mediating influence is not used to advantage for change efforts. Second, change at the individual level will indirectly have consequences for the family, because it changes the individual's relationship to his or her social context.

When the ecological fit and the circularity of influence between individual, family, and community are not taken into account, the result of change efforts can be potentially destructive at each level. A common experience in development projects in countries such as Morocco has been the provision of advanced formal education and nonformal technical skills training for youths without sufficient attention to systemic ramifications of such training. Too often there is a failure to assess and provide job opportunities to meet the new demands, resulting in a situation where youths with increased abilities and rising aspirations remain, nevertheless, unemployed. It is a case where an attempt to solve one problem creates another frustration. Moreover, the consequences for family and community bonds are too frequently disintegrative as youths leave home to seek employment elsewhere. Losing the important supportive network of family, neighbors, and patronage leaves the individual lonely, vulnerable, and at a considerable social and political disadvantage (Geertz, 1979). In Morocco,

> such separation and personal powerlessness are all the more difficult to bear because they are interpreted by everyone in terms of a cultural counterimage of the *normal* family situation—an image that is both valued and a part of most people's early experience—of intricate and manifold ties and frequent interaction. (Geertz, 1979, p. 338)

With the training and migration of youths, families can no longer expect sons to remain near home to assist them or to carry on small family businesses, crafts, or plots of land. Young wives and children are abandoned with increasing frequency, contributing to a rising divorce rate, currently estimated between 40 to 60% of all marriages in Morocco.

A vicious cycle of migration and dislocation typically ensues. Rural youths flocking to the cities find a scarcity of jobs fitting their skills and lack a social orientation or support network to adjust to modern urban life. When unable to send money home to their families, contact is frequently cut off in shame. New families, which cannot be supported, may be started in the urban slums. Further migration is then fantasized as the only route out of poverty and disgrace, to the developed nations of Europe and North America mythologized as lands of wealth, promising jobs, and a better life.[1] Unfortunately, most who manage to migrate abroad repeat the vicious cycle, earning marginal wages, living in ghettos, isolated by language and culture from the society surrounding them, and further dislocated from their families and communities. A further consequence of the cutoff is the likelihood that the extended family will become unable or unwilling to support wives and children left behind. Abandoned wives lose their social status and lacking basic income-generating skills, too often must resort to begging or prostitution (Davis, 1978), even introducing young daughters and sons into prostitution as a desperate means of survival.

Thus, social intervention, albeit for the economic betterment of a needy segment of the population, generates a chain reaction of influences disrupting the established social order. If not taken into account, this process may be to the detriment of the individuals being helped as well as their families and communities. In the case above, training individual youths altered their relationships to their families and communities without addressing those by-products. Individual change must be simultaneously accompanied by assessment and intervention at family and community levels. At the family level, the importance of kinship bonds, both economic and emotional, must be recognized so that reciprocal ties of support and obligation can be sustained or renegotiated. Moreover, local job demands and potentials should be assessed so that training fits local job opportunities or new jobs are developed to fit acquired skills.

Stability and Change

The maintenance and growth of all human systems are regulated by counterbalancing processes of morphostasis and morphogenesis (Maruyama, 1968; Speer, 1970). A stable structure, or pattern, is essential to the integration and continuity of a system. "Morphostasis"

---

1. A 1981 Peace Corps volunteer survey found that almost none of the Moroccan rural youths receiving technical skills training (e.g., mechanics) expected to work in their local area after training. Most fantasized going to Casablanca, France, or the United States, with one hopeful youth imagining he would go to the hometown of the volunteer!

(homeostasis) is the process of maintaining consistency and stability through self-correcting action that minimizes deviation to within pro-scribed limits from systems rules or norms. At the same time, systems require mechanisms for flexibility or adaptive variability when confronted with new demands (Buckley, 1968). Morphogenesis is the deviation-amplifying process that facilitates change and accommodation to new demands. Such pressures for change, when great enough, require systems to undergo "second-order change," which is not simply an increase in permissible deviations from the established norm but rather a reorganization of the systems with new rules to fit new requisites. The impetus for structure-changing processes can come from internal pressures within the family, as in the transition to a new developmental stage over the course of the life cycle (Hoffman, 1981). The impetus for change may instead come from environmental forces. The transition from a traditional to a modern society in countries undergoing rapid development necessitates such second order changes for individuals and their families. Beyond the acquisition of new competencies, be it the learning of technical job skills, basic education, or health care information, individuals and their families undergo fundamental changes in the nature of their relationships as well as assumptions and rules for guiding their behavior and making sense of their lives.

In traditional societies, there is generally a congruence of normative values and practices among the culture, the family, and the individual. As in all ongoing relationship systems, these norms evolve over time. In traditional societies they have been maintained over centuries. These norms, or rules, both explicit and implicit, organize social interaction and function to maintain stability and continuity. They provide expectations about roles, actions, and consequences that guide behavior and family life. Values originating in extrafamilial influences, especially culture and religion, exert leverage on family relationships, affirming and enforcing family norms (Jackson, 1965; Spiegel, 1971). Thus, morphostatic processes maintain stability and continuity by reinforcing tradition and counteracting change. This tendency to preserve sameness, or the status quo, is in conflict with the morphogenetic forces activated by profound societal change. When these pressures for change are too sudden or too powerful, fundamental values and assumptions are challenged and the continuity of the system is threatened.

It is important to be aware of these counterbalancing tendencies for stability and change to understand why many apparently beneficial development efforts are met with apparent resistance. The failure of social change efforts to achieve their goals is often explained away as due to the ignorance, inertia, or "primitive" superstitions of beneficiaries of the new services. Even the term *underdeveloped countries* carries the negative connotations of backwardness and deficiency; *old* ways are

250 FAMILY AND CULTURE

viewed simply as obstacles to progress. Social planners and change agents must also appreciate the positive aspects of traditional cultures, the rich heritage and cherished values and beliefs that have long provided a shared sense of identity, meaning, and purpose and which are embodied in rituals and practices of daily living. What is viewed as resistance to change, thus, involves an effort to preserve those established patterns that have functioned so essentially for so long. Development implies a depreciation of such values just as change threatens their loss. Thus, social change interventions are likely to be countered by a conservative tendency in attempts to maintain cohesion and continuity in goals and relationships (Marris, 1974).

A case in point regards the role of women in development in Moslem societies such as Morocco. Despite longstanding government commitment to the advancement of women and to universal formal education, the vast majority of women remain uneducated and illiterate and the gap between the level of school enrollment for boys and girls has persisted (Jones, 1980). Nonformal educational programs for girls and women, in government sponsored centers throughout Morocco, remain focused in practice almost exclusively on traditional domestic skills, such as cooking and sewing. Attempts to implement training in income-generating skills have, with rare exception, made few gains (Maher, 1978).

To understand how it happens that there is so little progress in women's education and job training it is useful to consider the blockages to change related to cultural and family values, beliefs, and rules of conduct. In Moroccan society where the family is the foundation of social life, family stability and family honor are considered of paramount importance. They are viewed as contingent on the maintenance of chastity of the female family members (virginity of unmarried daughters and fidelity of wives and mothers). The ideal woman is submissive to her husband and a virtuous wife and mother who remains at home and out of the public eye. To insure chastity the worlds of men and women are kept relatively separate. Two customs serve this function: seclusion of women in the home and their concealment from the eyes of men in public by means of the veil and cloak-like jellaba. Although these practices seem extreme to the Westerner, they are regarded as necessary given the Moroccan conception of sexuality, based on a belief in the highly sensual and passionate nature of human beings. Sexuality is regarded as a natural, God-given drive, and a matter not for internal control but for external regulation, mainly on the part of the social community, backed by the sanction of the judgment of Allah (Mernissi, 1976). In the traditional Moroccan view,

> women are seen as possessing extremely intense sexual desires which, untempered by an equally well-developed reasoning ability, are capable of wreaking havoc on the established social order. Men, in turn, are ex-

tremely vulnerable to this feminine sexual onslaught, simply because the best among them still possess passions of their own. To place a man and woman together in any situation in which this quintessential force would have the opportunity to take its "natural course" is considered both socially foolish and morally suspect. (Rosen, 1978, p. 158)

From this perspective, education is viewed, at best, as irrelevant to the domestic role ideal for women. More dangerously, in taking young women out of seclusion and preparing them for jobs in the public sphere in contact with men, it threatens their reputation and thereby threatens family honor and stability. Furthermore, it destabilizes the marital balance based on husband's/father's dominance and on gender role complementarity. When women's advancement and training for economic self-sufficiency is perceived as in drastic conflict with core family values and beliefs, it becomes more understandable that families fail to send their daughters to be educated or withdraw them by the time of puberty. Ways must be found to overcome this conflict if women are to benefit from development.

Transitional Stress and Disequilibrium

Profound societal change generates enormous stress on individuals and their families during the transition process from traditional to modern ways of life. Multiple, concurrent changes are mutually interactive and the stresses accompanying them are likely to be cumulative in their impact. The pace of social change is a critical factor in stress impact. Rapid change is far more disruptive of the social order than slow, gradual change.

The transition from a feudal agrarian society to a modern industrial urban society, which took place over the course of many centuries in Europe and North America, has occurred over a single generation, and only in recent decades, in most Third World countries. For the oil-rich nations of the Middle East, change has come most suddenly and dramatically. Those nations formerly under colonial rule long witnessed many of the material benefits of the modern world, but were for the most part denied access to them and generally lacked educational and employment opportunities to prepare them for self-determination and survival in the modern world. In Morocco during the French protectorate period (1912–1956), two separate worlds simultaneously coexisted, one for French settlers and the other for native Moroccans, with a rigid boundary between the two. Adjacent to the old Moroccan city (the medina), the French constructed a new city (the *ville nouvelle*), with villas, schools, shops, cafes, and cinemas largely restricted to Westerners. Ironically, the gates of the walled medina, constructed in the Middle

Ages as a fortress to protect inhabitants from outside marauders, were, under French rule, locked after dark for the protection of the foreigners outside the walls.

As Third World nations now attempt to bring the benefits to the modern world to their people, the rapid pace of changes being introduced poses a paradoxical situation fraught with transitional dilemmas. The paradoxical nature of the rapid transition from traditional to modern society is evidenced in numerous incongruities, conflicts, and disparities in everyday life. Changes are taking place so rapidly that the old comingles with the new in a rather incongruous juxtaposition of traditional and modern images. It is common in Moroccan city streets to see a woman cloaked from head to foot in the traditional jellaba, her face veiled, riding a motorbike to an office job, where she removes jellaba and veil to reveal the latest Paris fashion. Returning home to her parents or husband, she is expected to remain cloistered with other women of the household.

Such incongruous images reflect deeper conflicts of traditional versus modern values, roles, and rules of conduct. For individuals struggling with the clash between old and new, an internal conflict, or ambivalence, is common. Within families the clash occurs most often in intergenerational conflict, as youths who are more likely exposed to modern influences confront the established values and practices of their parents. The family, attempting to uphold traditional norms and to maintain its stability is likely to oppose societal changes that threaten it. As we have seen, the persistent gap in school enrollment between boys and girls in Morocco, particularly in rural areas, despite the government thrust for universal education, may be better understood by taking into account the conflicting value orientations of traditional families and the modern world represented by—and influenced through—education.

The disparity between the haves and the have-nots generates other severe pressures. The increasing gap between rich and poor nations and the unequal distribution of wealth and advantage within a society create inevitable tensions. For those lacking access to perceived benefits of the modern world, there is a gross disparity between the possibility and the probability of attainment.

This dilemma is compounded by the technological advances in mass communication and transportation that now connect remote parts of the world through satellite television and jet transit. Although such contact can contribute to a mutually enriching interchange of information and a necessary economic interdependency, the dominance of Western values, lifestyle models, and consumer goods threatens the integrity and continuity of diverse cultural patterns by imposing the desirability of foreign norms. New demands and rising aspirations are catalyzed that may be contextually inappropriate, and this attainment may be unrealistic. Television, in particular, brings rather startling images of the modern world into homes and local cafes around the world. Families in Marrakesh, many living in impoverished conditions without running water, now disrupt their traditional evening meal to gather around their television sets in fascination to watch "Dallas." It is difficult to imagine how they reconcile such images of wealth, power, and glamorous (albeit corrupt) lifestyles with the realities of their daily lives.

The period of transition from traditional to modern is also characterized by disorientation and unclarity. Basic premises about reality that have functioned for centuries are shattered by unfamiliar situations and unpredicted consequences. Although the presence of new technology may be quickly accepted, its operation and implications are not as readily comprehended. A peasant crossing a highway on a donkey may not be surprised to see a Mercedes approaching but may not realize that a speeding car cannot stop suddenly to avoid hitting him. The result is a tragically high rate of traffic accidents in rural areas.

An unclarity, or confusion, regarding rules of conduct, roles, and expectations complicates social interaction. Traditional norms may be discarded as irrelevant without a clear conception, or paradigm, to serve as a guide in new situations. Western models, which, it should be underscored, are often culturally inappropriate to other societies, are themselves too often perceived only in superficial, stereotyped, or distorted media images. Contextually relevant models tend to be lacking in a period of rapid social change. Thus, a young Muslim woman attempting to have "modern relationships" with young men may find that lacking models and experience to negotiate new relationship rules, her reputation is likely to be compromised.

Dysfunction and Adaptation

The transitional upheaval, or disequilibrium, generated by rapid social change can lead to dysfunction or can result in successful adaptation. From a systemic perspective, one of two dysfunctional consequences may occur if the strain is too great between morphogenetic forces for change and morphostatic pressures to remain the same. An escalating spiral of changes may produce a runaway effect, so that the conflicts and confusions inherent in the transition process result in chaos. At the other extreme, the threat to the systemic equilibrium may lead to a homeostatic rigidity, characterized by a rejection of change and a retreat from reality demands for accommodation. Disorder experienced at individual, family, or broader community and societal levels may be symptomatic of these seemingly unresolvable tensions.

For individuals caught in the turmoil of transition, there is likely to be a loss of meaning and self-esteem accompanying the inability to make sense of their experience and to resolve the binds. Radical change in the context of meaning, as well as a feared loss of attachment to family and community and of continuity with the past through tradition, can contribute to intense emotional upset, grief, identity diffusion, and even psychological disintegration (Marris, 1974). It is well established that change events are associated with a range of mental and physical disorders (Rahe, 1979). Increased substance abuse, crime, and delinquency have become major social problems in societies undergoing rapid development, particularly in urban areas receiving the largest influx of rural youth.

Disorder at the family level can be seen in two increasingly common dysfunctional patterns. First is the rise in marital and intergenerational conflict when forces for change and for tradition become polarized within the family. Second is the dissolution of family units through divorce, abandonment, and severing of ties within extended-family networks. A major contributant to family breakdown is the cutoff accompanying migration. The most severe dislocations may be experienced months and even years later (Sluzki, 1979).

The breakdown of communities and of entire societies may occur when tensions escalate beyond the power of governments either to resolve problems or to meet rising expectations that they, themselves, have contributed to through development efforts (Zonis, 1984). The political consequences may be anarchic runaway in revolution or retreat from change in repressive and reactionary policies. The recent rise in religious fundamentalism in many Islamic societies reflects such a repudiation of modern Western ways and a reassertion of traditional values and codes of conduct. The abandonment of Western dress and return to the chador by many Iranian women cannot be explained simply as compliance to more authoritarian family and government stances. In fact, the view has been expressed by Iranian women that in returning to traditional dress and conduct, they hoped to regain a position of respect that they felt they had lost by adopting Western ways.

Disorder, thus, can arise at each system level out of the psychosocial disruption inherent in the transitional process of social change. Although disequilibrium may be inevitable during such periods, its outcome is not necessarily pathological nor regressive. The paradoxical dilemmas inherent in the transition from traditional to modern life can also be a stimulus for creative, adaptive solutions to the complex tasks of development. Successful adaptation requires second order changes, involving conceptual and structural reorganization of the nature of experiences and relationships. Resolution, or rebalancing of systemic forces for change and stability, will not occur simply through acceptance or rejection of models transferred from other cultures. Nor will it be achieved by either abandonment of tradition or attempted retreat into the past. Rather, successful adaptation involves a transformation, so that individuals, their families, and their communities fit together in a new ecological balance that integrates the traditional and the modern. When ways are found to synthesize the old and the new, continuity between past, present, and future is maintained by them. Significant values and relationships are not simply lost but rather are transformed to be functional in new circumstances.

Through experimentation and innovation, each society must find its own solutions to the tasks of socioeconomic development and to the paradoxical dilemmas posed by rapid social change. In fact, the image of the Moroccan women in Paris fashions concealed by veil and jellaba, which strikes the foreign observer as seemingly incongruous, could also be seen as a transitional attempt to combine the traditional and the modern, preserving the cultural distinction between public and private domains and respecting the taboo against revealing oneself to the eyes of strangers.

Social Policy and Strategies of Intervention

The *process* of rapid social change requires more attention in the planning and implementation of social programs in developing societies. Two critical aspects of this process have been underscored here, each with important implications for social policy and strategies of intervention.

First, efforts toward social and economic development require broad-based intervention programs that address the *connections* between multiple, interrelated priorities and the reciprocal influences of individuals, their families, and their communities. Change efforts directed at any single priority or any particular system level will have reverberating consequences for other aspects of life and other system levels. In this circular chain of action and reaction, efforts for change are likely to be resisted by systemic processes aimed at maintaining stability when the equilibrium of a system is threatened. These systemic properties of circularity, hierarchy, morphogenesis, and morphostasis need to be taken into account in the planning and implementation of any social intervention.

Second, the process of rapid transition from a traditional to a modern society poses numerous paradoxical dilemmas and uncertainties that have a destabilizing effect for individuals, their families, and the broader social system. This disequilibrium, inherent in the period of transition, needs to be anticipated and understood so that social intervention strategies can recognize dysfunction associated with the turmoil and assist in facilitating more adaptive alternatives. By realizing that the transitional upheaval can also be a stimulus for creative growth, social interventions can better help individuals and their families in necessary reorganizations of their experience and their relationships.

Thus, educational programs directed toward children and youths must take into account the contextual ramifications of such change. They need to gain the family's support if they are to succeed, and to intervene in such a way that success does not leave the child and family in opposition or in dissolution. Rather, family values, purposes, and concerns need to be understood and respected and ways found to join with parents in the education of their offspring.

The major task in social intervention is to assist individuals and their families to adapt to a rapidly changing social world. It is important not to erroneously diagnose and treat adaptational problems as individual or family pathology without attending to their social context (Elkaïm, 1981). It can be useful to normalize distress and disorientation as symptomatic of the societal upheaval, and as an expectable, understandable, and temporary disequilibrium accompanying the process of transition from traditional to modern ways. In this way individuals and their families gain awareness of ways in which their problems are shared by others caught up in the same dilemma (Elkaïm, 1981). It may be useful to help them to recognize fears of loss of value and familiar traditions and to grieve losses suffered when traditional patterns are given up (Marris, 1974). It is still more useful to help them recognize that change brings about creative gain as well as loss, especially if it is planned.

Most valuable is to facilitate transformations that integrate valuable elements of tradition with useful aspects of the modern in a new way. This may involve reframing or recasting experience in a different light so that seemingly irreconcilable options can be seen as potentially compatible. It is not necessary to give up tradition altogether to become modern. Rather, the task is to find new ways of expressing and carrying on tradition that are more functional in mastering the challenges of the modern world. What may have functioned successfully in the context of the traditional world may require alteration to fit new demands. Yet, although rules of interaction may need to change, it may not be necessary to give up fundamental values underlying them.

In the Moroccan case, where women's emancipation is viewed as incompatible with traditional values of family stability and honor, several possibilities present themselves for changing the linkage of family honor (the value) as contingent on chastity (criterion of the value) as contingent on seclusion (the means of enforcing the criterion). New means can be found so that chastity can be safeguarded in ways other than seclusion. Another option is to promote other ways besides chastity for preserving family honor and stability. By appreciating and joining with fundamental family values and beliefs, social change efforts will become less threatening and innovative possibilities for adaptation will become more likely.

Modalities of social intervention need to be selected as appropriate to the problem and its context, based on a careful systems assessment. Individual, family, group, and community intervention approaches may be of different utility for various aspects of a problem and may be combined to integrate change efforts at all levels. For example, family-planning efforts, typically carried out through contraception information and services for women, need to be directed to husbands as well, with extended family and community pressures also taken into account. Changing a wife's practices in this vital matter without the approval and collaboration of her husband sets the wife in violation of their relationship rules of husband's dominance and against traditional family and cultural values of procreation. (In fact, in many cultures failures to conceive a male heir is the most common grounds for divorce by the husband, sanctioned by both extended families.) Thus, programs cannot simply educate wives to alter their fertility without addressing the implications of that change for her marriage and family, as well as her community status.

Particular intervention strategies must respect and can effectively utilize the values and preferred modes of social interaction in each society. In Morocco, for example, the social world is divided into two groups: family (kin), who can be trusted, and nonfamily, who cannot. Thus, trust will be an issue when social interventions are attempted by professionals who are not from the extended family network or community. Local change agents will likely be more readily trusted; strangers will need to build trust through their actions. Moreover, the network of family and social relationships is for Moroccans an intricate web of social indebtedness and contracted ties built up through individual efforts. Individuals bargain out the relationships they are going to have with one another. When relationships lead to conflict, they can be canceled or renegotiated in regularized ways. Social intervention can apply such rules of interaction in working with family members, drawing on their sense of mutual obligation, indebtedness, and reciprocity. A bargaining process can be utilized to renegotiate relationship rules, creating new contractual arrangements, employing methods of personal confrontation and exchange of information that are important in Moroccan daily interaction.

Finally, regardless of particular priorities and strategies of intervention, the central importance of the family in traditional societies must be taken into account. Successful adaptation to the challenges of rapid development requires programs that will respect and strengthen the family foundation.

ACKNOWLEDGMENTS

In conceptualizing the issues presented in this chapter, the author drew upon her experiences in Morocco, first (1964–1966) working for the Moroccan Ministry of Youth and Sports as a Peace Corps volunteer and more recently (1981) serving as consultant to the Moroccan Ministry of Social Affairs, the United States Agency for International Development, and Human Resources Management in development of a cosponsored social service training program in Tangier, Morocco.

Appreciation is also due to Celia Falicov, PhD, and Jay Lebow, PhD, for their useful comments on this chapter.

REFERENCES

Bateson, G. *Mind and nature: A necessary unity.* New York: E. P. Dutton, 1979.

Bronfenbrenner, U. *The ecology of human development.* Cambridge, Mass.: Harvard University Press, 1979.

Buckley, W. Society as a complex adaptive system. In W. Buckley (Ed.), *Modern systems research for the behavioral scientist.* Chicago: Aldine, 1968.

Davis, S. Working women in a Moroccan village. In L. Beck & N. Keddie (Eds.), *Women in the Muslim world.* Cambridge, Mass.: Harvard University Press, 1978.

Elkaïm, M. Family system and social system: Some examples of interventions in an impoverished district of Belgium. In M. Andolfi & I. Zwerling (Eds.), *Dimensions of family therapy.* New York: Guilford Press, 1981.

Geertz, H. The meaning of family ties. In C. Geertz, H. Geertz, & L. Rosen (Eds.), *Meaning and order in Moroccan society.* Cambridge: Cambridge University Press, 1979.

Halleck, S. Family therapy and social change. *Social Casework,* 1976, *57,* 483–493.

Hoffman, L. *Foundations of family therapy: A conceptual framework for systems change.* New York: Basic Books, 1981.

Jackson, D. The study of the family. *Family Process,* 1965, *4,* 1–20.

Jones, M. Education of girls in Tunisia: Policy implications of the drive for universal enrollment. *Comparative Education Review,* 1980, *24*(2), 106–123.

Landau, J., & Griffiths, J. The South African family in transition: Training and therapeutic implications. *Journal of Marital and Family Therapy.* 1981, *7,* 339–344.

Lidz, T. *The family and human adaptation.* New York: International Universities Press, 1963.

Maher, V. Women and social change in Morocco. In L. Beck & N. Keddie (Eds.), *Women in the Muslim world.* Cambridge, Mass.: Harvard University Press, 1978.

Marris, P. *Loss and change.* New York: Pantheon Books, 1974.

Maruyama, M. The second cybernetics: Deviation-amplifying mutual causal processes. In W. Buckley (Ed.), *Modern systems research for the behavioral scientist.* Chicago: Aldine, 1968.

McGoldrick, M., & Walsh, F. A systemic view of history and loss. In M. Aronson & L. Wolberg (Eds.), *Group and family therapy: 1983.* New York: Brunner/Mazel, 1983.

Mernissi, F. *Beyond the veil: Male–female dynamics in a modern Muslim society.* New York: 1976.

Minuchin, S. *Families and family therapy.* Cambridge, Mass.: Harvard University Press, 1974.

Moroccan Ministry of Planning. *Annuaire statistique de Maroc*, Rabat, 1978.

Rahe, R. Life change events and mental illness: An overview. *Journal of Human Stress*, 1979, *5*, 2–10.

Reiss, D. *The family's construction of reality*. Cambridge, Mass.: Harvard University Press, 1982.

Rosen, L. The negotiation of reality: Male–female relations in Sefrou, Morocco. In L. Beck & N. Keddie (Eds.), *Women in the Muslim world*. Cambridge, Mass.: Harvard University Press, 1978.

Rosen, L. Social identity and points of attachment: Approaches to social organization. In C. Geertz, H. Geertz, & L. Rosen (Eds.), *Meaning and order in Moroccan society*. Cambridge: Cambridge University Press, 1979.

Schulman, G. The changing American family: For better or for worse. *International Journal of Family Therapy*, 1979, *1*, 9–21.

Schwartzman, J. Normality from a cross-cultural perspective. In F. Walsh (Ed.), *Normal family processes*. New York: Guilford Press, 1982.

Sluzki, C. Migration and family conflict. *Family Process*, 1979, *18*, 379–390.

Speer, A. Family systems: Morphostasis and morphogenesis. *Family Process*, 1970, *9*, 259–278.

Spiegel, J. *Transactions: The interplay between individual, family, and society*. New York: Science House, 1971.

Walsh, F. Conceptualizations of normal family functioning. In F. Walsh (Ed.), *Normal family processes*. New York: Guilford Press, 1982.

Zonis, M. Self-objects, self-representation, and sense-making crises: Political instability in the 1980's. *Political Psychology*, 1984, *5*(2).

11

Culture as intervention

JOHN R. FARELLA
MacNeal Memorial Hospital and
University of Illinois Medical School

> *Once I asked my mother, "What relation is my father to you? What relation do*
> *you call him: I call you my mother, and I call my father my father. What do you*
> *call my father, and what does he call you? How are you related to each other?*
> *When I said this to her she said, "He's my husband." She said it in a loud voice,"*
> *and she scared me with what she said. She said, "A man and woman who are*
> *together like that are husband and wife. The man is husband to the woman, and*
> *the woman is wife to the man. That's why they call each other my husband and*
> *my wife. You'll be that way when you grow up to be a man. You'll have a wife*
> *just like these men now." I said, "I don't want to go near a woman who's not*
> *related to me, because she's not my mother." She said. "You don't know*
> *anything about it yet, because you're small. When you grow up to be a man,*
> *you'll get a woman and when she wants to leave you you'll be hanging on to her,*
> *even though she's not your mother. You'll be hanging on to her . . . just as if*
> *she were your mother. . . ."*
>
> *It's pretty dangerous to have a wife or a husband. . . .*—Dyk (1938,
> pp. 47–48, quoted in Witherspoon, 1975, pp. 27–28)

Introduction

The basic argument in the family system perspective is that what is seen
as dysfunctional or symptomatic in larger or more inclusive context
(say, a society) is adaptive or functional for a smaller or less inclusive unit,
in the case of this literature, the family.

Although this, at least in its explicit form, is a relatively new[1]
argument for the mental health professions, it is a fairly old and well-
accepted theoretical stance in the social sciences (and, of course, the life
sciences). This is true especially with regard to anthropology and
sociology.

---

1. Bateson (1956) and Jackson (1957) are two "family systems" pioneers.

Perhaps because of this "newness," there are certain implications of this theoretical stance that have either been overlooked or only tangentially considered in the family therapy literature. In general, if one accepts the premise that there are entities related in a systems–subsystems fashion, it follows that these are not limited to the systems we refer to as individuals and as families or the subsystems that comprise families.

Specifically, the systems or contexts of which the families are part have either only implicitly been considered or, occasionally, tangentially explicated under the rubrics of ethnicity, networking, milieus, and a variety of other labels. My argument is that other levels, particularly and most importantly more abstract or more inclusive levels, have to, at least implicitly and often overtly, be taken into account.[2] The so-called subsystems of the individual have, by the nature of the model and the context of the mental health professions, been taken into consideration and turned over to the medical professions. But the more inclusive cultural and social systems are usually considered or handled as a series of labels or adjectives that are added on to modify the "basic" family concept. For example, certain ethnic groups are seen as having "matriarchal" families, others are seen as more likely to be enmeshed, and so on. The more abstract context, culture, is added on to the less inclusive context, family, as in "black family" or "Jewish family" or whatever. It is an error in the conceptualisation of level of abstraction.

For therapy to be effective, it must be at the level of *all* involved systems or contexts. Most often this is implicit in the intervention or, more precisely, in the structure of the intervention. Haley (1963) has described a part of this rather nicely in the chapter "The Therapeutic Paradoxes" in *Strategies of Psychotherapy*. He is generally arguing that certain paradoxical situations or injunctions are necessarily a part of any therapeutic relationship. These injunctions are an artifact of what is probably the most basic assumption of Western epistemology—the tenet that entities can be classified into relatively discrete binary (either/or) categories.

The therapist–client relationship is such that the basis for classifying the relationship itself is called into question in a paradoxical way. For example, it is a voluntary relationship within a compulsory framework (e.g., scheduled appointments); it is, on the one hand, assumed that clients can not help behaving as they do, but, on the other hand, that they can change their behavior; it is a framework where one seeks out an expert who takes charge by placing the patient in charge, and so forth.

---

2. Schwartzman and Bokos (1979) make an attempt at this. They describe the drug addict's treatment milieu and, in turn, the more inclusive milieu of treatment for heroin addiction in general.

Although he does not label it as such, Haley is talking about culture. It is the same sort of thing that anthropologists talks about when they describes a Navajo Indian ritual or a Catholic Mass or when Emily Post instructs us on which fork to use first at a formal dinner. It is the sort of thing that people think about and (apparently) make rules about, including, importantly, rules about how to classify relationships, behaviors, and things.

The therapeutic interaction is framed or structured in terms of a rather abstract set of rules, assumptions, or basic premises about how the world, particularly the world of humans, works. By the structure of therapy, that is, by virtue of the structure of the relationship between the therapist and the client, certain of these assumptions are called into question. Thus, a part of the intervention, because of the nature of the relationship between the therapist and client, implicitly and necessarily takes these rather abstract cultural basic premises into account. Therapy, in fact, can be defined in the most general sense as a process of socialization with the goal of undoing, or altering, socialization.

The Western Treatment of Alcohol Abuse

As noted, the questioning of basic assumptions and categories is usually inherent in the therapeutic relationship. In certain cases, however, this implicit structure can be inadequate and even antitherapeutic.

Historically the psychotherapeutic attempt at treating alcoholism provides an example of this. Both the therapist and the patient were operating in terms of the epistemology that was at the base of the problem. Bateson summarized it this way:

> I shall argue that the "sobriety" of the alcoholic is characterized by an unusually disastrous variant of the Cartesian dualism, the division between Mind and Matter, or in this case, betwen conscious will or "self," and the remainder of the personality. (1972, p. 311)

The pre-Alcoholics Anonymous (AA) approach to the treatment of the alcoholic intensified this dualism. It consisted mainly of periods of trying harder and failing; trying even harder, and again failing, and so on. The alcoholic's family, and usually the therapist, were part of this. Encouragement to be strong, to use one's will power, and so on, only exacerbated the problem. In systems terms it was a classic deviation-amplifying system.

Alcoholism treatment was a "trouble case" for psychiatry and for Western medicine in general. At the heart of this was this question of Occidental epistemology. The Cartesian duality is a cornerstone of medicine and at the heart of psychiatry; the concept of "mind" is the whole basis for the psychiatric specialization. But the variant of this epistemology held by the alcoholic was the cornerstone of the disease.

Both psychiatry at this time[3] and the alcoholic accepted the immanence of mind. But whereas this produced benefits for psychiatry, it was a disaster for the alcoholic. Another way of stating this is that the sociocultural premises implicit in the situation and in the resulting communicative acts were antitherapeutic.

In "The Cybernetics of 'Self': A Theory of Alcoholism," Bateson (1972) pointed out that AA was an intervention that attacked, or struck at the heart of, these very general cultural basic premises. Specifically he argued that AA "resolved" this particular Cartesian mind–body problem for the alcoholic. The first two steps of the AA contain what will become the basis for a new epistemology for the alcoholic. These are:

1. We admitted we were powerless over alcohol—that our lives had become unmanageable.
2. Came to believe that a Power greater than ourselves could restore us to sanity.

Bateson summarizes what this means for the alcoholic:

Implicit in the combination of these two steps is an extraordinary—and I believe correct—idea: the experience of defeat not only serves to convince the alcoholic that change is necessary; it is the first step in that change. To be defeated by the bottle and to know it is the first "spiritual experience." The myth of self-power is thereby broken by the demonstration of a greater power.

In sum, I shall argue that the "sobriety" of the alcoholic is characterized by an unusually disastrous variant of the Cartesian dualism, the division between Mind and Matter, or, in this case, between conscious will, or "self," and the remainder of the personality. Bill W's stroke of genius was to break up with the first "step" the structuring of this dualism.

Philosophically viewed, this first step is not a surrender; it is simply a change in epistemology, a change in how to know about the personality-in-the-world. And, notably, the change is from an incorrect to a more correct epistemology. (1972, p. 313)

What occurred then was a change in cultural basic premises or, in Bateson's term, a change in epistemology. With this there were many other changes that, paradoxically, altered the various contexts of which the alcoholic was a part. It was a phenomenon that the society generally associated with mind (the will) that was labeled a disease (which can be

---

3. It could be argued that today psychiatry is arguing for the immanence of the body. The various dopamine hypotheses and the use of lithium carbonate are two examples of this. But the Cartesian epistemology is unchanged. Whether one accepts mind *or* body as immanent, one still accepts the dualism.

defined as being outside of the control of will or as "just happening").
The disease was incurable but treatable, and the primary treatment was
delivered by those who had the disease, not, except in unusual instances,
by physicians. Alanon groups were started for the family members,
where the paradoxical concept of "tough love" was espoused. That is, if
you really loved the alcoholic, you would in the short run do unloving
acts toward the person, so that he or she would change. This was a
"higher and more difficult form of love." And so on.

AA was a program that ultimately treated *all*[4] contexts or systems
to which the alcoholic belonged. It further offered an alternative to a
very abstract basic premise of Occidental culture that was paradoxical
and, in the case of the alcoholic, therapeutic.

Navajo Basic Premises

The Navajo are a group of Native Americans that live in northern
Arizona, southwest Colorado, southern Utah, and northern New Mexico.
Their reservation is about the size of West Virginia, and the 1980
census had their number at about 175,000.

They live in camps made up of several related nuclear families.
People say that traditionally the expectation was toward matrilocal
residence. That is, when a man married, it was considered proper that
he move near his wife's family of origin. In the families I lived with, this,
in fact, was the most common practice. Navajos are also matrilineal.
Descent is through one's mother's side. In contrast, Anglo-Americans
are patrilineal, descent being through our father's side of things.

Navajo social structure has to be the most well-studied in the
world, so I'm not going to go into much of a summary of it here. For
those who are interested, a book by Gary Witherspoon (1975), *Navajo
Kinship and Marriage*, is the best work on the subject.

Bateson provided us with an example of how highly abstract
cultural basic premises affect both symptom maintenance and therapy.
For the Navajo or any other people, it is no different. And the way to
understand the culture is through the study of these premises.

For the Navajo everything (with a single possible exception that
will be discussed below) is divided into male and female. In many ways
this gender division approximates ours; in important respects, however,
it differs. For one thing, it refers less to "objective" things (like genitalia)
than to abstract essences. *Maleness* and *femaleness* would be terms that

4. The relatively recent advent of employee assistance programs should be mentioned in
this regard. Basically, there are potential consequences for alcoholics that do not get into
treatment.

approximate the ideas. But these sound artificial in English. The eastern Yin–Yang distinction is similar but probably more abstract. At any rate, the bik'a–ba'aad[5] distinction is one of gender, although not necessarily one of sexuality. It is very nearly as abstract[6] a distinction as can be made by the Navajo. In addition, it has a very central social and cultural meaning.

To begin with, a person is not simply male *or* female but in all cases, both. Behaviorally and psychologically each of these "parts" or aspects of an individual has important implications.

The male aspect of a being is, most importantly, powerful, Male thought is characterized as being of large scope, of extending over great distances. As part of this, male thought is associated with ceremonial or ritual power. This male symbolism without a doubt derives from the hunting traditions of the people, from their Athapaskan roots. In English, Navajos refer to it as the "game way." And, like the game, there is a risk and uncertainty that is a part of the male strength. If un-restrained, it can go "wild."

The complement, and the restraining aspect of a being, is, of course, the female side of things. This clearly derives from the agricultural traditions of the people. Here we have domesticity, thought that is stable and restrained but not of great scope or magnitude. The two together are obviously complete. They form a whole that is both stable and powerful. When a "person" is "in balance" with regard to these dual elements, there is stability or the appearance of stability.

Let me again state that we are not just talking about men and women; we are talking about aspects and, in some ways, essences. The most complete being is, naturally enough, the hermaphrodite. And for the Navajo, there is a little bit of hermaphrodite[7] in each of us. Further the level of "completeness" varies over a person's life span.

From birth to adolescence, people are viewed as children; that is to say that their status as minors supercedes their gender identity. When adolescence is reached, a boy and girl are treated very differently. At first menses there is a ceremony for a girl. It is called *Kinaalda*,[8] and it marks a rather clear status demarcation. There is nothing similar for boys. The social status of males from puberty until 50 or 60 is very

5. When I use Navajo terms, I leave off the diacritics marking tone and nasalization.

6. These terms can also be used very concretely. The examples that come to mind are vulgar or obscene connotations.

7. The term I translate *hermaphrodite* is *nadlei*. I believe that this refers less to external genitalia than it does to internal balance, but on this point some very knowledgeable younger Navajos disagree with me.

8. In passing it should be noted that *Kinaalda* is a celebration, primarily of the girl/woman's fertility.

vaguely defined. In fact, it is not defined at all except for a set of negative expectations. The most common of these is that the male will "run wild." Another way of stating this is that a woman is seen as having a rather stronger ego boundary than a man. In old age, when one is a grandparent, this changes. A man and a woman are (in terms of social expectations) almost indistinguishable. Their roles don't vary that much. They are both seen as being "in balance" or complete.

This description of individuals is rather artificial, however, as the units that matter to the Navajo are social. Further, the social units, not the individual, are seen as primary, as opposed to how we as Westerners view it, taking ego or a monad as the "basic unit" of society.

In general terms then, Navajos conceive of man and society in terms of relatively weak boundaries around individuals and rather strong boundaries around certain social units. In addition, these social units are the systems that matter, the "building blocks" of society.

The primary unit is mother–child and especially mother–son. This mother–child relationship is viewed in terms of a range of levels of relative concreteness. Conceptualized abstractly, it describes a nurturer–nurturee relationship. Many of these applications seem metaphorical to Westerners. Examples are "my mother, the earth," or "my mother, the sheep," or "the corn." Concretely the term for "mother" can be used the same way as in English (Witherspoon, 1975, pp. 15–23).

In human society a key dilemma is the relative loyalties (Boszormenyi-Nagy, 1973) between one's family of origin and the family that one creates through marriage. There are certain characteristics of the Navajo situation that makes this a practically irresolvable dilemma for the male.

As stated, the mother–child relationship is the crucial social and symbolic (or cultural) unit. An understanding of the relationship is an understanding of all of Navajo society and culture. Witherspoon summarizes its nature:

> A mother is one who gives life through birth to her children, and then sustains the life of her children by giving them both physical and emotional sustenance. The acts of giving birth and sustenance are imbued with meaning from the cultural system, and this meaning can be described as intense, diffuse, and enduring solidarity. (1975, p. 20)

A part of the cultural meaning that Witherspoon refers to is found in the Navajo deities, Earth Woman and Changing Woman. Both are referred to as "our mother." Both are looked upon primarily as sources of strength and security by current Navajos. Note also that these relationships are viewed as "enduring" or "continuing." Another way of stating this is that the mother–child relationship continues at an intense level throughout life.

The husband–wife relationship is at the opposite end of the symbolic continuum. Whereas the mother–child relationship is viewed in terms of relative safety and security, the other is viewed as relatively weak and insecure. Primary complementary themes in Navajo stories or mythology are the safety of the mother–child relationship as portrayed by Changing Woman and Earth Woman on the one hand, and the danger and insecurity of the husband–wife relationship on the other. The latter stories emphasize jealousy, anger, grief, loss, and separation, at the same time emphasizing the necessity for men and women to be together so that "things will continue," that is, so that reproduction will be assured.

A Navajo male fits very uncomfortably into all of this. In the language of family therapy, it seems built in culturally (and today socially) that he is the "peripheral parent." Witherspoon (1975, p. 34) goes so far as to argue that fathers are related to their children through the mother, that is, that the father–child relationship is a second-order relationship mediated by the mother. It would look like this:

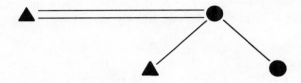

As noted above, a part of this is that Navajos are culturally matrilineal and socially matrilocal. The husband today is often geographically removed from his own family or origin. Additionally, this means a man may be living in a community where he has no close "blood" relations and where the people he lives with (his in-laws) have something of an antagonistic relationship with him.

In summary, men are in something of a chronic anomalous position in Navajo society. They are virtually without status between adolescence and old age. Or to state this more correctly, their position in society is contingent on their relationship to women. They move from an idealized relationship of safety with their mother in their family of origin to a relationship of danger in their marriage. They often live in a community where they have no close relationships and where the people with whom they have the most contact are their in-laws. As with all in-laws, these individuals have a primary loyalty to their daughter/sister. Culturally men are in a structural position relative to their children that is peripheral. This structural distance is often repeated socially. In short, men occupy a position in Navajo Reservation society today that is isolated and anomalous for the greater part of their lives.

Alcohol Abuse on the Navajo Reservation

Alcohol use as a symptom can be viewed as a "solution" to these social dilemmas. A crucial part of this argument is that this "symptom" is an attempt to maintain traditional values and, especially, traditional social relationships.

I emphasize this point because alcohol most commonly is seen as an external (white or Anglo) imposition onto a people (Native American) who can't handle it. I instead argue that it is a relatively new means of solving traditional dilemmas and, further, that the goal that is sought and effected in its use is to remain traditional by maintaining traditional cultural and social relationships.

The cultural basic premise to be maintained, as discussed above, is that a male must maintain a relationship with a stable female symbol.

The most commonly talked about social solution is to pair a young man who is behaving in an out-of-control, irresponsible way (including alcohol usage) with an older woman. This can take a variety of forms. It can have the young man living with an aunt, or a grandmother or an older sister. These are fairly common but temporally limited solutions, for the young man is expected, at a fairly young age, to marry and to leave home.

Fairly often then, and as a solution to immaturity, a relatively younger man marries an older woman. Often the woman has been married before and has children. The stated purpose is control, to have him behave. In fact, this behavioral control theme is quite common in all marriages of partners below the age of 30. Symbolically, such marriages are anomalous in a variety of ways.

First of all, they are attempts to combine the relative safety of the mother–son relationship with the comparative uncertainty and danger of the marriage relationship. As noted above, the one is characterized as being totally positive, the other as very dangerous. The obvious solution is to, in a variety of ways, marry your mother, or more correctly, to transform the relationship of risk, husband–wife, to one that is safe, mother–son.

Alcohol, and the irresponsible behavior associated with it, do this in two ways. It both puts one's wife in the position of mother when one is behaving irresponsibly, and it maintains the son's loyalty to his family of origin. That is, because his marriage never quite works, he still maintains a primary focus on his family of origin.

Socially there are other crucial aspects to this. If the male is in a matrilocal setting, he maintains or at least sporadically has a certain contact or closeness with his in-laws. An essential characteristic of alcohol (for Navajos) is that it puts females on one generation (ascending) and males on another generation (descending). Men drink with their sons, uncles, sons-in-law, whatever. When they are drinking, they are all of one generation; they are peers, that is, they are brothers. So along with "my wife = my mother," we have "my son (or son-in-law) = my brother." Drinking transforms a world where all but blood relatives are excluded to one where all are brothers. It also, of course, is ammunition for the exacerbation of the in-law conflict when one is sober.

At any rate, the use of alcohol on the Navajo Reservation may, in part, be viewed as a means of maintaining certain traditional social and cultural values, goal states, or homeostases. By using a behavior that is defined as foreign or new (the consumption of alcohol) to maintain old or traditional relationships, one adapts to the Navajo context but is, of necessity, a failure in the larger context. Indians who drink do not do well in the Anglo world of which they are a part.

This can also be looked upon in terms of the redundancy of structure in a systems hierarchy—a phenomenon at one level being replicated at all levels. Alcohol functions, first, to maintain one's loyalty to one's family of origin. The symptom functions to continually replicate that context. It does this, in part, by regulating intimacy in the symptomatic individual's marriage. As stated, alcohol abusers do poorly as husbands or, more generally, as peers to their wives. The other part of this is that it symbolically restructures the marriage into a new family of origin. Generally speaking then, alcohol represents the repetitive (or chronic) choice of a less inclusive context, as represented by maintaining one's place in one's family of origin, over the more inclusive context, as represented by marrying out. That is, marrying out can be viewed as the choice of being a part of the society at large rather than staying home.

On the larger scale, the structural choice represented by the symptom is repeated. Alcohol abuse is an adaptation to the relatively restricted sociocultural context, the Navajo Reservation, that fails in the more inclusive context, the western United States. Again, the symptom always represents the same choice—the less inclusive over the more inclusive context.

The Native American Church

Alcohol use, then, may be seen as an adaptation to a sociocultural dilemma as well as a problem in its own right. Focusing momentarily on the problem aspect, there are several common attempts at solution. We have already mentioned one of these, the pairing of a relatively younger male with a relatively older woman. A second type of solution is identical symbolically. That is traditional ritual. Without going into detail, the emphasis is on stabilizing the "out of control" male element with a stable (symbolic) female element. With this attempt at symbolic homeo-stasis, there is also a corresponding social emphasis on the female side of things. Generally, the patient's relationship to his matrilineal kin is emphasized in the ritual and in the preparation for it.

If, however, we see alcohol, the symptom, functioning as an attempt in part to maintain or re-create a mother–son relationship, returning to one's family of origin in a society that has a matrilineal descent system is obviously an intervention that is destined to fail. That is, it is a part of, and a perpetuation of, the symptomatic behavior.

At this point it is necessary to summarize the essential points of the discussion thus far. First, the "goal" of the syndrome associated with alcohol abuse on the reservation is the maintenance of a "one down" or descending generation relationship with a stable female symbol. Second, the attempts we have described that overtly are aimed at altering this symptom are structurally and symbolically identical to and a part of the symptom itself. That is, they assure that change will not occur or that things will stay the same. In contrast, the Native American Church with peyote as a sacrament resolves these dilemmas in a multileveled and paradoxical manner. It is structured so that what Watzlawick, Weakland, and Fisch (1974, p. 77) call second-order change will occur.

At the physiological level, Native American Church members define peyote and alcohol as mutually exclusive. Le Barre (1969) has pointed out that the substances are not "truly antagonistic;" but, of course, what matters in this case is the view of the believers, not that of the experts. Thus, we have as a symptom—physiological helplessness over a substance (alcohol)—and we have an intervention that in essence states, "By ingesting this substance (peyote), you will be helpless *not* to be helpless over the other substance (alcohol)."

This is rather clever. It is a solution that depends on a logical hierarchy, and it is paradoxical. The solution first of all accepts the basic premise of drinking as a symptom,[9] that is, the belief that "I can't control it" (the use of a substance). It then provides another substance that is highly controlled through ritual and that has the characteristic that it also makes one helpless over alcohol but in an opposite direction. That is, you can't drink.

Culturally, the situation is very similar. The Native American Church can be defined as both Christian and traditional. The Christian element is differentially emphasized depending on the particular "church." But the potential is always there. The traditional part can be seen in a variety of ways. Basically the idea is that peyote is represented in

9. Any symptom can, of course, be defined as being out of the individual's control.

the Navajo origin stories, that it was lost to the people and then returned by way of Plains Indians.

The way this is handled in these stories is quite interesting. The words used in the narratives are terms that have referents on several levels of abstraction.[10] The reference to peyote can be seen as a specific interpretation placed on an abstract usage. In a sense, it is much like a pun.[11]

So this is a relabel at a cultural level. We have something that is "new" (or a change), the Native American Church, described as "old," conservative or "traditional," by its being a part of the creation story. In fact, it goes beyond this. Adherents to the Native American Church will state that it is the only true "traditional" religion in existence today and that the "other" Navajo religion is no longer what it should be.

The "new" part of the Native American Church includes, and this is crucial, regular weekend meetings. This is very different than the rather sporadic seasonally limited, problem orientated meetings of the other traditional religion.[12]

But the most interesting part of all of this is at the level of symbol system. Peyote (the plant) and the medicine (*azee'*) is symbolically female. In fact, it can be referred to simply as *azee' ba'aad* (*female medicine*). This is novel in the Navajo universe in that it apparently violates the rule that "all things can be divided into male and female." What this has meant traditionally is that all things can be divided into a male and a female on the same level.

10. *Man* is an example in English. Taxonomically it would be represented thus:

11. The word used in Navajo is *azee'*. This is usally translated as *medicine*, but it can have a more abstract connotation than what we usually associate with the term. It can, however, also be used very specifically in a particular context. Thus, if a person is in the context of a ceremony, they will refer to, say, the herbs as *azeè*. If it was not in that context, a more specific term would have to be used. It would be similar to the way we use the term *sacrament* in English. The term has a variety of uses, and in the context of, say, this paper some explanation would be required if I used the term in a particular way. But, if I were at Mass in a Catholic Church and used "the sacrament," it could have only one meaning. *Azee'*, the abstract usage in the origin story, is interpreted by Native American Church members as a specific reference to peyote.

12. A ceremony is called, at least overtly, to treat a specific problem in a particular patient. In addition, the rite, Blessingway, is utilized at significant life events of a family and individual (e.g., birth, marriage, first menses). Thus there are no guaranteed regular meetings.

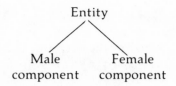

What peyote does is set up a higher level or a metalevel. That is, the highest and most powerful level is solely female. Implicitly it also alters the basic rule that each level in the hierarchy has the male and female in balance. Thus, instead of the male and female being equal but different, we have them now arranged hierarchically with the female being the most powerful. It is also fairly obvious that this symbolically re-creates the basic Navajo social relationship, mother–son. In fact, peyote is referred to in ritual as "My Mother Peyote."

This symbolic structure exactly replicates the essential structural feature of out-of-control alcohol use—the centrality of the mother–son relationship. Or stated more generally, alcohol produces the situation in which the female is of the ascending, and the male of the descending, generation. The symbolic structure of the Native American Church is identical to the structure of the symptom.

In addition, this hierarchical male–female relationship is permanent but periodically reinforced and reiterated through the ritual and, as a part of this, through the ingestion of the female medicine, peyote. Following the all-night ceremony, some of the participant's wives serve them "traditional" prewhite food.

Symbolically then we have the traditional requirement of a relationship between a stable female element and a strong but relatively unstable masculine element. The relationship is contingent on a metalevel and is therefore more constant than those relationships limited solely to the world of humans.[13]

Thus, peyote is defined as an attempt to return to, re-create, or reinforce an old or traditional life pattern that results in, or is, an adaptation to a more inclusive (in this case white American) context. The more the goal of remaining or returning to a traditional state is focused on, the more there is acculturation or change.

The emphasis in this paper has been on a particular aspect of this. Alcohol (associated with other behavior) is viewed as adaptive in a restricted (Navajo Reservation) context. Specifically, it functions to transform a relationship that is egalitarian and dangerous (marriage) into one that is, momentarily, hierarchical and safe (mother–son). As a part of this, it also functions to maintain loyalty to the male's family of

---

13. In some sense this is similar to the AA members' relationship to "God" or a higher power, as, for example, in the second step.

origin, which is another reinforcement of the mother–son relationship. And as a part of placing male drinkers on the descending generation (sons), it provides peer contact in an otherwise often hostile environment. Men who are drinking are all brothers, and their wives are all mothers.

Peyote creates a metalevel, a metamother or female symbol with whom one has a personal relationship through a ritual, the essence of which is a caricature of the nurturer–nuturee relationship. This involves the ingestion of a powerful female symbol/substance that derives directly from the more traditional female symbol, the Earth Mother. By creating the metalevel, the earthly social structure "flips" as it were. The wives are on the descending generation relative to their husbands, whereas the males remain on the descending or "son" generation relative to peyote.

For a variety of reasons, this earthly social structure with a non-drinking, responsible male as head of household is more adaptive in the more inclusive (Western United States) context. But it comes about not through attempts to adopt the new, but by attempts to stay in or return to a traditional state. The Native American Church is a conservative attempt that results in a change, that is, on a superficial level, Navajos appearing or becoming more like Anglos.

Conclusion

Systemic family therapy is a part of and based on a theoretical orientation that has two essential conditions. It rests, first, on the notion of wholes. That is, the idea that the entity "family" is something more than just the sum of the individual members. Another way of putting this is that general systems theory is antireductionistic. The second essential feature of systemic family therapy is that it is process rather than content orientated. To state this in terms of the linguistic metaphor first suggested by information theorists, the level of analysis is syntactic and not semantic (i.e., the "structure" rather than the "meaning").

In the above discussion, I have endeavored to discuss culture in an analogous way, that is, processually and antireductionistically. As a first approximation, this has been a discussion of culture as a rather abstract, highly inclusive context.

These two contexts (family and culture) share another important characteristic. They are both open systems. That is, information passes bidirectionally between these entities and their contexts. The most common epistemological error that is made in analyzing family and culture is to ignore this characteristic and its implications. At a minimum it means that neither can be described in terms of a fixed set or list of fixed attributes. The essential characteristic of an open system is that by definition it is ever changing, but this change is ordered by, in the case of the one example, a cultural template. In addition, this change is always in a conservative direction. In the case of culture, this means that it is in the direction of something usually labeled "traditional." These traditional basic premises must be very abstract. If they are not, the particular way of life will, in the language of evolution, quickly become extinct. The details of a way of life are readily given up to maintain the general. Unfortunately most descriptions of culture have involved only lists of details.

The level of abstraction is also a key feature in therapy or in an intervention in general. The two examples of successful interventions on alcohol cited in this chapter (Alcoholics Anonymous and the Native American Church) are both more abstract than the symptom itself.

In Bateson's (1972) article on AA, he pointed out that previous attempts at intervention were unsuccessful because they always were aimed at the wrong level of abstraction. That is, they were not general enough. The first partially effective intervention struck at one of the most abstract premises of Western culture—the Cartesian mind–body duality.

The Native American Church is even more abstract than that. It is not just an intervention on individual drinkers, but it has the potential to intervene on and change a society. But the goal and the direction are traditional, maintaining some of the most abstract Navajo basic premises. This major change is based on an attempt to stay the same or, even more than that, to return to a more traditional existence. The more this is sought, the more Navajos become "appropriate" Anglos in the even more inclusive context.

ACKNOWLEDGMENTS

The research upon which this chapter is based was, in part, funded by a National Science Foundation Doctoral Dissertation Research Award and a National Institute of Mental Health Fellowship. The main field work was carried out by the author between August 1973 and September 1975 with fairly frequent visits subsequent to this.

Thanks to Vasilika Zafer for typing the manuscript, and to John Schwartzman and Linda Marrin for their comments and criticisms.

REFERENCES

Bateson, G. The cybernetics of "self": A theory of alcoholism. In *Steps to an ecology of mind*. New York: Ballantine Books, 1972.

Bateson, G., Jackson, D. D., Haley, J., & Weakland, J. H. Toward a theory of schizophrenia. *Behavioral Science*, 1956, *1*, 251–264.

Boszormenyi-Nagy, I., & Spark, G. *Invisible loyalties*. New York: Harper & Row, 1973.

Dyk, W. *Son of Old Man Hat*. New York: Harcourt, Brace & World, 1938.

Haley, J. *Strategies of psychotherapy*. New York: Grune & Stratton, 1963.

Jackson, D. D. The question of family homeostasis. *Psychiatric Quarterly Supplement.* 1957, *31*, 79–90. part 1

La Barre, W. *The peyote cult*. New York: Schocken Books, 1969.

Schwartzman, J. & Bokos, P. Methadone maintenance: The addict's family recreated. *International Journal of Family Therapy*, 1979, *4*, 338–355.

Watzlawick, P., Weakland, J., & Fisch, R. *Change: Principles of problem formation and problem resolution*. New York: W. W. Norton, 1974.

Witherspoon, G. *Navajo kinship and marriage*. Chicago: University of Chicago Press, 1975.

Author index

Subject index